Salvatore J. Parlato, Jr.

FILMS EX LIBRIS

Literature in 16mm and Video

McFarland & Company, Inc.,
Publishers
Jefferson, N.C., 1980

Other books by Salvatore Parlato:

Audio-Visual Advisor (1st and 2d editions)
Films – Too Good for Words
Superfilms

PN1997.85
P3

Library of Congress Cataloging in Publication Data

Parlato, Salvatore J
Films ex libris.

Includes indexes.
1. Film adaptations – Catalogs. I. Title.
PN1997.85.P3   016.79143   80-10181
ISBN 0-89950-006-4

An AmeriCanadian Publication

Manufactured in the United States of America

An Unauthorized Dedication

to Norman B. Moore

Norm is responsible for organizing the film collection at the Rochester, N.Y., Public Library in the late 1940's. He had the foresight to realize that the printed word was not the only way to store information and to provide diversion. The present media center, known as the Reynolds Audio-Visual Department, is one of the largest community resources of its type in the United States. In 1962 Norm moved back to Maine as head of the Waterville Public Library there. Still in his native state, he's now enjoying retirement in a town fittingly called Friendship.

Acknowledgments

Thanks to the following film companies for the photographs indicated, illustrating each new chapter beginning. **The Bible**: *The Flower of the Tales*, International Film Bureau; **Biographies**: *James Weldon Johnson*, Paramount Communications; **Children's Stories**: *Beep Beep*, Churchill Films; **Drama**: *Conscience in Conflict*, Learning Corporation of America; **Fables, etc.**: *Icarus Montgolfier Wright*, Pyramid Films; **Nonfiction**: *The Beginning of Life*, Benchmark Films; **Novels**: *Don Quixote de la Mancha*, Macmillan Films; **Poetry**: *The Strangest Voyage*, Mariner Productions; and **Short Stories**: *The Fall of the House of Usher*, Encyclopaedia Britannica.

Thanks to Fred H. Marcus for the quotation in the headnote to the Short Stories chapter—from the Preface to his book *Short Stories/Short Films* (Englewood Cliffs, N.J.: Prentice-Hall, 1977; 477p).

Part of the Introduction to *Films Ex Libris* appeared in the author's article, "Owl Creek—Bridging the Film Literature Gap," published in the December 1978 issue of *Media & Methods*.

Table of Contents

Introduction

Who was it that said, "To be able but unwilling to read is no better than being unable"? He (or she) was perfectly right. But today's alternatives to reading—specifically, films and television—should be treated not as competition to reading but rather as stimuli. These newer media can add to the appreciation of literary content. They provide inducements toward the written word. In other words, they can bridge the gap between the ability to read and the willingness to do so. Isn't that what *Occurrence at Owl Creek Bridge* has shown us? The filmization of Bierce's short story has brought about a renaissance of interest in that pre-movie-era author, creating readers for works of his that otherwise might have lain dormant indefinitely. So, if you're already familiar with the way *Owl Creek Bridge* has revolutionized the study of film and literature, then you're probably looking for more of the same. But, if you're not acquainted with that classic picture, you may not realize that so much good literature is available on acetate. In either circumstance, let *Films Ex Libris* help you catch up with the embarrassment of riches now at your disposal.

Whatever your personal V.Q. (Visuality Quotient), you've certainly known all along that there are plenty of full-length features in 16mm form, many of them based on such famous novels as *Andromeda Strain*, *Brian's Song* and *Slaughterhouse Five*. The existence of these classics and the pictures they inspired has, until recently, obscured the abundance of excellent short films generated by other forms of literature. Those genres are the very ones, along with the novel, that comprise this directory. Its more than 1400 entries include excerpts from novels-on-film but also encompass the other main forms of literary expression: poetry, short stories, fairy tales, fables, legends, drama, mythology, and non-fiction (Including biography, essays, and journalism).

Strangely enough, these same categories frequently show up in lists of filmstrips and audio tapes but, until now, have never been catalogued for the more persuasive and dynamic medium of motion-pictures. But *Films Ex Libris* does more than just identify such productions: it also non-judgmentally relates them to their print origins—a constant reminder of cinema's written "roots." And, in this era of behavorial objectives, this book seeks to help librarians and teachers to increase the reading of books as such, while expanding general access to the minds and imaginations that gave birth to the writings. Literary classics in their latterday film form are especially compatible with the needs and moods of contemporary libraries and classrooms. For that reason, short films—with their special flexibility and adaptability—are the media most likely to convert viewers of film into readers of books.

Another advantage behind these photographic resources is the subliminal one of exposing non-readers (whatever the reason for their limitation of letters) to the key concepts in the world of words. This fringe benefit, so to speak, is embraced by the shirtsleeves school of thought that claims that the importance of any classic is not so much the activity of reading as exposure to the author's thinking. Debatable as that point may be, who will deny that exposure to a good film can generate enthusiasm for the script that spawned it? If you doubt that argument, just try to borrow a bestseller when its box-office version is at its peak!

By the way, *Films Ex Libris* gives you a ready come-back the next time your patrons or students say they're "waiting for the movie to come out." Now you have an answer: "scriptogenic" movies, that is, films of the written word—proving again the symbiotic relationship between print and image. Now you can endorse them both, without fearing one or favoring the other.

There's another paradox in this business of going from books to films and then back to books. The apparent contradiction involves their comparative capacity to develop language skills. Some theorists subscribe to the belief that, just as "the proper study of mankind is man," the best way to learn to read is—to read! Unfortunately, this simplistic solution doesn't hold up under scrutiny. It's something like claiming that the best way to learn to ski is—to ski and never mind the physical conditioning, special clothing and required equipment. Or, to put it in more scholarly tones, the "plunge-in-head-first" logic is wrong because it confuses form with content, product with process. And—even more serious an error—it equates matter with motivation. In the epigram quoted a few lines above, Alexander Pope speaks of "mankind" as a subject, not as an activity or a process. And that's what reading is: a process. Print, as a communications device, naturally involves the process of reading. And, important as print is, it's only a vehicle. True, print is *our* vehicle right now; that is, it's the one that allows us to share ideas this very minute. But this particularly cozy code of ours is far from universally acceptable. Other seekers of information and diversion find them in non-print sources. Nowadays people who are unable or unwilling to read have options that didn't exist a few generations ago. And besides, even the most dedicated of readers enjoy the change of pace offered by cassettes and movies, media that allow them to reinterpret a subject in a different format or on another level of perception. The diversity of display can in itself give conceptual reinforcement that might otherwise be either impractical or impossible. In light of this, *Owl Creek Bridge* now becomes almost symbolic. It—and the other 1400 or so films within—can help *bridge* the gap between literature and visuality. Such "Owl Creek bridging" may well displease the print purists among us. But, then, think of the medieval scribes who resisted the use of Gutenberg's press!

Here are a few other things we can learn by "Owl Creek bridging": Literature and film are more alike than different. Good writing is as important on film as it is on paper. Novels aren't the only genre available on film. Most subjects can be appreciated on more than one level. Group reaction is the essence of the film experience. Ideas are at least as important as words.

Of course, we don't have to look very far for proof of those points. Both PBS and the commercial television networks give us good examples almost daily: *Civilisation, America, Roots, The Ascent of Man*, and many other fine programs are now available on film or videocassette. Here are more film titles that are becoming almost as popular as the writings that came before them: *Arrow to the Sun* (Texture Films), *Boarded Window* (Perspective Films), *Hailstones and Halibut Bones* (Sterling Educ.), *"J.T."* (Carousel Films), *No Man Is an Island* (Dana Productions), *Paddington Bear* (Film Fair), *Selfish Giant* (Pyramid Films), and *Velveteen Rabbit* (LSB Productions).

Not to be overlooked in this trend is the Britannica Humanities Film Program. Although now taken in stride, this interpretive series was a daring departure from precedent, bringing to a merciful end the era of the pedantic film. Encyclopaedia Britannica's successful gamble proved that weighty works (by Sophocles, Plato, Ibsen, et al.) were fit subjects for non-theatrical films and that great literature deserved high production standards.

By the way, in any debate about whether film or literature should come first, don't impale yourself on either horn of that dilemma. The dichotomy itself is an illegitimate one, totally overlooking such practical factors as accessibility of media, personal preferences or mood and the nature of the subject. A more crucial consideration than media primacy or sequence is the matter of proper introduction, correlation and follow-up. By giving attention to context, you can help your readers/viewers to recognize themes or principles shared by print and picture. The only unforgivable sin of bi-media programming is to offer neither the intellectual comfort of a preliminary tie-in nor the interpersonal pleasures of follow-up discussion. That's why it's up to you, whether librarian or teacher, to program more than just films. You've got to show *relationships*, too—among books, images, concepts and authors, whichever you use as your starting point. All these elements are related.

If film can help you achieve the same objectives as literature shouldn't it become part of your repertoire? Then use film. Use film, not as a compromise but as a complement. Use it as a "mirror image," to introduce literature or to review it. Use film for its own merits, too, especially with audiences that are already predisposed toward visuals. And that *doesn't* mean people of low language skills. As mentioned earlier, many literate viewers are as sophisticated about images as they are about words. They realize, for example, that Shakespeare—like all great dramatists—wrote his plays *to be seen*. In fact, you often hear that were he alive today, he'd be writing for Hollywood or for television, so strong was his passion for *showing* the excitement of ideas, the development of characters in action, and the unfolding of a story. Shakespeare was a good pyschologist, too. To attract his audience, Shakespeare used *showmanship*. Should we do less?

Salvatore J. Parlato, Jr.

Using This Book

Films Ex Libris offers you several starting places. If you are genre-oriented, for instance, you can begin at any of the nine chapters that represent the major classes of literature. The annotations themselves are the basic units of the book. They provide practically all the raw data (except prices) you need when selecting or using these materials. Although some films may belong to more than one category, no entries are repeated within the body of this volume—a decision based on economy and in recognition of the fact that many such generic decisions will seem arbitrary anyway. Most classification systems are to some extent subjective. So to satisfy yourself on that score, browse. Browse to your heart's content.

If you are personality-oriented, another good jumping-off point is the Authors-on-Film Index. To use it, just look up the writers of your choice. There, under their names, you will find the titles of the films that relate to them or their works. The number following each film title will lead you to the numbered, annotated entry within the body of the book. For obvious reasons, anonymous authors aren't listed in the Authors-on-Film Index. Similarly omitted are Scriptural sources, legends, myths, and folktales, all of which are easier to locate in their own separate sections. Because of space limitations, film titles in the Author Index are shortened. They usually leave out the articles (a, an, the) and when possible the subtitles.

A Title Index completes the volume; here are listed all the literary works given film treatment, making it easy to locate a work whose title was changed or not used as the film title.

This publication could hardly be more current. Even upon reaching the magic "thousand entries" mark after nearly four years of research, new materials kept being added right up to completion in the summer of 1979. As a matter of possible interest, the oldest film entered is the silent classic, *Uncle Tom's Cabin*, directed by D.W. Griffith in 1903. The most recent is *Strictly Speaking*, based on Edwin Newman's current bestseller. Most of these films "ex libris" were released in the last ten to twelve years. Because copyright disclosure is a random thing with film companies, some production dates are not given. Still, you will find the year of release accompanying nearly four out of five annotations.

For those who enjoy figures, there are 1410 entries in *Films Ex Libris*. They encompass 1012 literary works by 645 authors (not counting Mr. and Ms. Anon.).

Even though some out-of-print films often stay in circulation and remain useful to certain viewers, none have knowingly been retained in this compilation.

Unless noted to the contrary, the title of any original piece of literature is the same as the film that adapted it.

Entries and indexes are listed in letter-by-letter alphabetical order. For the greatest utility to the greatest number of users, foreign-language titles that begin with articles (for example, "La" or "Les") are alphabetized under those articles. Titles of essays, articles and poems are within quotation marks to differentiate them from books, plays, stories and films.

The materials itemized in *Films Ex Libris* are not to be construed as endorsed or recommended. By the same token, items omitted should not be interpreted as unsuitable for any reason. This edition contains all the known short (Under 60-minute) films for which adequate information was available in the final stage of manuscript preparation. As a reference tool, this book is designed to provide factual information, not qualitative evaluations.

All entries in *Films Ex Libris* are carried on 16mm sound film unless specifically noted as silents and are available for purchase within the United States. For details on acquisition, consult the Producer/Distributor Directory in the back of the book.

Of course, with the variety of formats on the market today, the term "film" should be interpreted as possibly including video cassette or disc.

The Bible

Alphabetically, this segment belongs "up front." It belongs here for other reasons, too. The Bible is a distinct form and source of literature and, as literature, has stood the test of time. It is the most widely-quoted work in the Western world and has generated more new literature than any other Western source. Although spiritual in content, the Bible is ecumenically Judaeo-Christian.

Apparently, I'm not alone in these convictions, as judged by the 39 Bible-based titles described within. Although this is the smallest of the book's nine sections, the subject matter is the most familiar, its audience a well-known quantity, and its authors truly need no introduction.

1 Abraham and Isaac. Bible story in sign language and sound. Produced for the benefit of deaf viewers, this film also has a completely narrated soundtrack. Filmed along the Colorado River and among the cliffs of Red Rock Canyon in California. Manual communication is by Lou Fant, Jr. Cleared for TV.
Joyce Media 20 min Color 1974

2 The Apostles — Part I. Series of 5 films available separately. 1. The Apostles see Jesus on the seashore. 2. The Apostles feel the Holy Spirit and begin to preach. 3. Saul is instrumental in stoning the apostle himself, changing his name to Paul. 4. Paul has a narrow escape in Damascus. 5. Peter is mysteriously released from prison. Produced for television by the American Lutheran Church.
Mass Media 22½ min Color 1975

3 The Apostles — Part II. Each of these animations is available individually: 1. Paul and Barnabas are mistaken for gods in Lystra. 2. Paul and Silas are imprisoned in Philippi. 3. Some priests plot to kill Paul in a Jerusalem prison. Paul's nephew arranges an escape. 4. Paul appeals to governor Festus to be tried by Caesar. 5. Paul and Luke sail for Rome in a bad storm. Even after a shipwreck, Paul is ready to face Nero. He has "fought the good fight." Produced for television by the American Lutheran Church.
Mass Media 22½ min Color 1975

4 Ark. The hero of this latter-day parable is a biologist who, like Noah, tries to preserve specimen couples. He protects this community within a glass house that eventually proves itself vulnerable to pollution, rodents, even—or especially—mankind, destroying his "Walden-under-Glass." Produced by Rolf Forsberg.
Barr 20 min Color 1970

5 The Bible: A Literary Heritage. Starring actor Donald Pleasence, and photographed in Israel, this film illuminates the diversity of literary forms found in the Bible. It includes dramatized examples of the short story (Abraham and Isaac), poetry (Psalms and the Song of Solomon) and social criticism (Ecclesiastes). The Bible as drama is explored in the story of Job. The film concludes by showing the impact of the Bible on Western art and culture.
Learning Corp 27 min Color 1970

6 The Bible As Literature, Part One. Saga and sin in the Old Testament. Includes the stories of the Creation, the expulsion of Adam and Eve, Cain's murder of Abel, Noah's Ark, the Fall of Jericho, David versus Goliath, Moses and the Ten Commandments, and the Tale of Suzannah. Produced by John Barnes.
Encyc. Brit. 27 min Color 1974

7 The Bible As Literature, Part Two. Old Testament history, poetry, and drama. Examines the book of *Joshua, Samuel,* and *Kings* as historical documents; the *Book of Proverbs* as lyrical poetry; and the Prophetical Books as protest literature. Producer: John Barnes.
Encyc. Brit. 24 min Color 1974

8 Christ Is Born. Produced in the Holy Land, this film chronicles the birth of Jesus. Scenes depict the history of the Hebrews from Abraham to the era of subjugation to Rome. Presenting the Nativity as history, it is suitable for members of all faiths. Reading from the Bible: John Huston. Produced by John Secondari for ABC's *Saga of Western Man* Series.
Learning Corp. 54 min Color 1968

9 The Christmas Story. This is a sign language "narration" (with sound) of the Nativity. Manual communication is provided by Lou Fant, Jr., exponent and practitioner of *Ameslan*, American Sign Language. cleared for television.
Joyce Media 26½ min Color 1975

10 David. Each of these animated films is available individually, if desired: 1. David is anointed by the prophet Samuel to be the next King of Israel after Saul. 2. David kills Goliath and swears friendship with Saul's son, Jonathan. 3. King Saul becomes jealous of David's popularity. David escapes to the mountains. 4. Jonathan tries to intercede with Saul on David's behalf. 5. David spares Saul's life. Saul foresees David's future greatness. Produced for television by the American Lutheran Church.
Mass Media 22½ min Color 1975

11 David and Goliath. This story from the Old Testament is performed in sign language by Lou Fant, Jr. It includes "voice-over" narration and music, and was filmed in the same California site used for similar Hollywood productions. Cleared for television.
Joyce Media 18 min Color 1972

12 David and Goliath. Animated version of Biblical contest. An example of faith in action, this animated film captures not only the struggle between two human enemies, but illustrates the eternal contest of spirit versus matter. Released by ECRF Productions.
Pyramid 13 min Color 1964

13 Elijah. Each animation is available individually as follows: 1. The prophet Elijah tells King Ahab that there will be no rain as long as the people worship the false god Baal. 2. Elijah meets the widow of Zarephath. Drought comes, but God sends them flour and oil. 3. Elijah prays to revive the widow's dead son. 4. Elijah's altar to God is miraculously set afire on Mt. Carmel. The people turn from worshipping Baal to God. 5. God forgives His people and sends rain. Produced for television by the American Lutheran Church.
Mass Media 22½ min Color 1975

14 Esther. Each of these animated productions is available separately or as part of a unit: 1. Esther, beautiful young Jewess in exile, is chosen to be queen of Persia. 2. Prime Minister Haman plots the death of the Persian Jews. 3. Esther discovers the plot and decides to go to the King, even though it may mean her own death. 4. Haman builds a gallows for Esther's cousin. The King, unaware, orders Haman to conduct a recognition service in the cousin's honor. 5. Esther pleads for the Jews. Haman is sentenced to his own gallows. Produced for television by the American Lutheran Church.
Mass Media 22½ min Color 1975

15 Exodus – The Moses Trail Revisited. A narrator reads excerpts from the Old Testament account of the Exodus, an historic odyssey of flesh and soul. His voice is heard along with scenes of the mountains and valleys of the Middle East, and with the sounds and sights of Bedouin tribes in their present-day migration, not unlike that of the Israelites 3000 years ago.
Mass Media 28 min Color 1973

16 Gift of Life. Biblical explanation of the life-death cycle. A poetic but biblically-based view of the human life cycle from birth to death, emphasizing the Christian perspective as reflected in modern scriptural translations in Kenneth Taylor's *The Living Bible*. Produced by ECRF.
Pyramid 19 min Color 1972

17 The Holy Land. Traces the New Testament chronologically from Bethlehem to Calvary, with glimpses into the Church of the Nativity, Nazareth, Jordan, Judea, Jericho, Galilee, and Jerusalem. Produced by Boulton-Hawker, Ltd., in collaboration with D.C. Chipperfield.
Int. Film Bureau 19 min Color 1962

18 Impressio. The Old Testament parable of David and Goliath is told in the form of animated bottles in a dusty cellar. As characters, the bottles take on personalities of their own by changing shape and assuming humanoid mannerisms. Produced and animated by Seppo Suo-Anttila.
Film Wright 14 min Color

19 Jeremiah Five part series. Each of the following animations is available individually: 1. The prophet Jeremiah warns the Israelites against their return to worshipping Baal. 2. Jeremiah tells the people that an invasion of Israel by Babylon is God's punishment. He is arrested. 3. Weak King Zedekiah refuses to take action. 4. Jeremiah is thrown into a well and is rescued. 5. Jeremiah follows his people into exile. Produced for television by the American Lutheran Church.
Mass Media 22½ min Color 1975

20 Jesus B.C. Viewers see God in an unconventional setting, as He

observes the progress of the world. Within a few minutes, thousands of years of history pass by: the Creation, the Flood, Sodom and Gomorrah, Babel, and the period preceding the Nativity. From this vantage point, the Trinity decides on a course of action for redeeming mankind. The role of God is played humanly but respectfully by actor William Windom. A Paulist Production.
Media Guild   27 min   Color   1978

21 Jesus: Birth and Youth. Each of the following five animations is available individually, if so desired: 1. Caesar demands a census. Mary and Joseph travel to Bethlehem where Jesus is born. 2. Nearby shepherds follow a star to Bethlehem. 3. Herod tells the Wisemen to return to him with report of Jesus. They are warned against Herod in a dream. 4. Herod orders the killing of all male babies in Bethlehem. Mary and Joseph escape to Egypt. 5. Jesus grows up, becomes a carpenter, and is baptized by John. Produced for television by the American Lutheran Church.
Mass Media   22½ min   Color   1975

22 Jesus: Healer and Miracle Worker. Each of these five animations is individually available, as identified: 1. Jesus heals a sick man who is lowered to him through a roof. 2. Some of the people plot against Jesus. He heals a man with a withered hand. 3. Jesus calms a storm at sea. 4. With five buns and two small fish, Jesus feeds thousands. 5. Jesus brings Lazarus back to life. Produced for television by the American Lutheran Church.
Mass Media   22½ min   Color   1975

23 Jesus: Struggling With Enemies. Each of these four animations is available individually or as a unit, identified here: 1. An unsuccessful attempt is made to arrest Jesus at the Feast of the Tabernacles. 2. Jesus rides into Jerusalem. The High Priests plot against him. 3. Jesus and his followers celebrate Passover in an upper room. 4. In the Garden of Gethsemane, Jesus is arrested. Produced for television by the American Lutheran Church.
Mass Media   18 min   Color   1975

24 Jesus: Suffering, Death and Resurrection. Each of these five animated films is available individually as identified here: 1. Jesus is tried by the Sanhedrin. Peter denies knowing him. 2. Pilate sends Jesus to Herod. Judas hangs himself. 3. Herod returns Jesus to Pilate. The people call for his crucifixion. 4. Jesus is crucified. 5. The empty tomb is discovered, and Mary Magdalene sees Jesus. Produced for television by the American Lutheran Church.
Mass Media   22½ min   Color   1975

25 Jesus: Teaching and Calling Disciples. Each of the following animations is available individually: 1. Peter and Andrew meet Jesus. He

turns water into wine. 2. Jesus calls for Peter, Andrew, James and John to become "fishers of men." 3. The people of Nazareth reject Jesus. 4. Jesus tells the story of the Prodigal Son. 5. Zacchaeus comes down from his hiding place in a tree to hear the parable of the Two Sons. 6. Jesus tells the story of the Good Samaritan. Produced for television by the American Lutheran Church.
Mass Media   27 min   Color   1975

26 Joseph. Five-part series. Each of the following animated films is individually available: 1. Joseph's brothers sell him into slavery in Egypt. 2. Joseph becomes a ruler in his new land. 3. Joseph's brothers travel to Egypt for food. Not recognizing him, they bow before his throne. 4. Joseph tests his brothers to see if they have changed. 5. Joseph reveals his identity. The family of Jacob is reunited to live in the land of Egypt. Produced for television by the American Lutheran Church.
Mass Media   22½ min   Color   1975

27 Joseph – Part I. This is the first half of the Old Testament story, performed in sign language (with sound) by Lou Fant, Jr., son of deaf parents and a professsor at California State University in Northridge. Cleared for television.
Joyce Media   30 min   Color   1975

28 Joseph – Part II. This segment concludes the Bible story, performed by Lou Fant in sign language and in sound. It was filmed in the Egyptian section of the Los Angeles County Museum of Art. Cleared for television.
Joyce Media   30 min   Color   1975

29 The Law and the Prophets. This over-view of the Old Testament uses the King James translation plus still/action pictures of artworks from major museums and private collections. These elements re-create conventional (but not conservative) images of God and the Biblical history of mankind. Narrator: Alexander Scourby. Producer: NBC-TV.
McGraw-Hill   51 min   Color   1968

30 Moses. Here, in sign language and sound, is the life of the prophet from his river rescue by Pharaoh's daughter to the entry into the promised land. Manual communication is by Lou Fant, Jr., exponent and practitioner of *Ameslan*, American Sign Language. Cleared for television.
Joyce Media   45 min   Color   1974.

31 Moses. Each of these five animated films is available individually or as a unit: 1. Pharaoh of Egypt orders the destruction of all Israelite babies. Moses is sent down the Nile in a basket. 2. Moses grows to manhood in the Egyptian court. God calls him to save his people. 3. Plagues descend on Pharaoh's court. 4. The Israelites escape across the Red Sea. 5. God

gives His people the Ten Commandments. Produced for television by the American Lutheran Church.
Mass Media   22½ min   Color   1975

32   Multiply and Subdue. A three-part visualization of Biblical segments of Genesis. Paralleled by the beauties of nature, the Old Testament messages remind us of our role as stewards of the earth, with the responsibility of preserving it from ecological pollution. Background consists of Bach organ music. Produced by Eric Hutchinson.
Pyramid   8 min   Color   1970

33   Noah. This is the Biblical story of the Ark, performed in sign language by Lou Fant, Jr., the noted author, actor, and teacher of the deaf. Photographed along the Pacific Coast of California. Cleared for television.
Joyce Media   20 min   Color   1973

34 Noah's Animals. This is the story of the Biblical flood, as told from the animals' point of view. Produced in animation by Video Program Services.
Lucerne Films   25 min   Color

35   Noah's Ark. Cartoon of Bible story with Mr. Magoo. In the early days of creation, as told in Genesis, Mr. Magoo as Noah is beset by the wickedness around him. The voice of the Lord is heard commanding him to build an ark to survive the flood. The gathering of the animals, the 40-day ride, the return of the dove, and the rainbow pledging God's eternal promise of mercy to man are dramatized in this cartoon-style animation.
Macmillan   26 min   Color   1965

36   No Arks. Noah's ark unexpectedly meets another! Noah, floating securely in his Ark, spends his days gazing at the empty horizon. Then in the distance he sees a speck...it is another Ark. Gun shots are exchanged and events take an unexpected turn. Narrated by Vanessa Redgrave. A British Film Institute production.
Films Inc.   11 min   Color   1970

37 Song of Songs. In this modification of "The Song of Solomon," the camera becomes the eye of the young lover as she dreams of and searches for her mate, finds him, and marries. Can be interpreted either romantically or allegorically. From the Old Testament.
Burt Martin   10 min   Color   1974

38 The Story of Christmas. In this non-verbal animation, cameo-like cutouts resemble illustrations from a medieval manuscript. Reinforcing this context is original music written in 16th/17th-century style on authentic Renaissance instruments. Produced by Evelyn Lambart for the

National Film Board of Canada.
Films Inc.   8 min   Color   1976

39 The Walls of Time. A documentary on the tumultuous history of the English-language Bible. It compares the translations of John Wycliffe, William Tyndale, and Kenneth Taylor, author of the recently published *Living Bible*. Produced by ECRF.
Pyramid   25 min   Color   1972

Biography

This category includes 153 films that didn't necessarily originate in literature. They are, however, so closely linked with writers and writings that, to isolate them arbitrarily would cause more of a conceptual wrench than doggedly sticking to book-based products. Take, for example, A *Dylan Thomas Memoir*. The content of that film belongs, at least partly, under poetry. But its emphasis on the person favors Biography. The same reasoning applies to *James Weldon Johnson* and *Yevtushenko*. Other authors in this category are those too versatile to confine to a single genre. You know the type: Poe (short stories and poetry), Carl Sandburg (poetry and biography), Twain (novels and essays), and Shakespeare (dramas and sonnets). But, in general, interpret Biography here to mean materials that put the stress on writers as people, while showing the relationship between personality and performance—an intertwining that only the mind can divide anyway.

40 The Adams Chronicles (series of 13). These television programs are based on Jack Shepherd's history of the American dynasty that lasted from 1750 to 1900. Funding for the series was provided by Atlantic-Richfield, the Mellon Foundation, and the National Endowment for the Humanities. Produced for the Public Broadcasting Service by WNET-TV (Channel 13), New York. Also available in videocassettes from Films Inc.
Indiana U. 741 min Color 1976

41 The Adams Chronicles — #1 John Adams: Lawyer (1758-1770). Living under British occupation intrudes upon the love of John Adams and Abigail Smith. During the growth of their family, Adams finds himself increasingly involved in the liberty movement — despite his former loyalty to England. After the Boston Massacre, Adams agrees to defend the troops, but his action leads many in Boston to question his loyalty to the colonies. Script: Sherman Yellan; directed by Paul Bogart.
Indiana U. 57 min Color 1976

42 The Adams Chronicles — #2 John Adams: Revolutionary (1770-1776). Adams' reputation grows during America's struggle for independence. Because of his commitment to liberty, pressures increase on all his family. He and Abigail must endure the first of many long separations. She is left alone with the children to tend to the farm in Massachusetts, while Adams serves as a delegate to Philadelphia's Continental Congress, which leads to the Declaration of Independence. Script: Sherman Yellan; directed by Paul Bogart.
Indiana U. . 57 min Color 1976

43 The Adams Chronciles — #3 John Adams: Diplomat (1776-1783). To represent America abroad, Adams leaves for France with his son, John Quincy, age eleven. Adams grows frustrated with Benjamin Franklin's machinations within the French court. He travels to Holland where he secures a large loan and political support from the Dutch. Quincy, by then fourteen, travels as secretary to the first American Minister to Russia. Between 1782-1783, peace treaties that Adams helped negotiate are signed with Great Britain. His perspective of America as a growing power determines much of his conduct in the new nation's service. Script: Sherman Yellan; directed by James Cellan-Jones.
Indiana U. 57 min Color 1976

44 The Adams Chronicles — #4 John Adams: Minister to Great Britain (1784-1787). Abigail, with daughter Nabby, joins John and Quincy in Europe. After Adams renews his friendship with Jefferson, Nabby marries Col. William Stephens Smith, secretary to the American delegation in London. The successful outcome of the Revolution is weakened by dissension in the United States and by the European view that the new nation is a pawn to be manipulated. Script: Millard Lampbell; directed by James Cellan-Jones.
Indiana U. 57 Color 1976

45 The Adams Chronicles—#5 John Adams: Vice President (1788-1796). Adams becomes the first Vice President under Washington, and suffers eight years of frustration. Caught between the ideologies of Jefferson and Hamilton, he is frequently at odds about what form of government the country should have. Script: Anne Howard Bailey; directed by Barry Davis.
Indiana U. 57 min Color 1976

46 The Adams Chronicles—#6 John Adams: President (1797-1801). Adams disagrees with Hamilton, Jefferson, and most of his cabinet about the country's government. England and France are at war. Adams keeps America away from war at the expense of his Presidency, for he loses his bid for re-election to Jefferson. One of the Adams' sons dies at thirty, which leads Adams to reassess the values of public life. Script: Corinne Jacker; directed by Barry Davis.
Indiana U. 57 min Color 1976

47 The Adams Chronicles—#7 John Quincy Adams: Diplomat (1809-1815). Quincy and his wife live in St. Petersburg where he is Minister to Russia. He later heads the peace commission in Ghent, ending the War of 1812. Their two eldest sons remain in the States with John and Abigail, while the youngest son accompanies them. They endure a profound, personal loss when a daughter born to them in St. Petersburg dies. Quincy becomes the second Adams to serve as the Minister to Great Britain. Script: Philip Reisman, Jr., directed by Anthony Page.
Indiana U. 57 min Color 1976

48 The Adams Chronicles—#8 John Quincy Adams: Secretary of State (1817-1825). The family is recalled from Europe when Adams is appointed Monroe's Secretary of State, and drafts the Transcontinental Treaty with Spain and the Monroe Doctrine. Although he becomes President, Adams and his family suffer through party politics. His European experience drives Adams to work for a nation able to stand against European pressures. The script is by Ian Hunter and is directed by Bill Glenn.
Indiana U. 57 min Color 1976

49 The Adams Chronicles—#9 John Quincy Adams: President (1825-1829). Adams' term as President is marked by frustrations. His wife, suffering in the Washington political scene, blames political preoccupations for the death of their eldest son. Adams, moving for a powerful central government, alienates support for his reelection. By historical coincidence, John Adams and Thomas Jefferson die on July 4, 1826—the fiftieth anniversary of the Declaration of Independence. The script is written by Tad Mosel and is directed by Fred Coe.
Indiana U. 57 min Color 1976

50   The Adams Chronicles — #10 John Quincy Adams: Congressman (1830-1848). Adams wins a seat in the House despite objections from his wife and son, Charles Francis. Another son dies from the overwork of trying to pay off an enormous family debt. Adams considers himself free, in his position as a U.S. Respresentative, to operate above politics and act as the "conscience of Congress." He wins public attention for his anti-slavery legislation. After seventeen years of service, he suffers a heart seizure and dies in office. Script: Tad Mosel; directed by Fred Coe.
Indiana U.   57 min   Color   1976

51   The Adams Chronicles — #11 Charles Francis Adams: Minister to Great Britain (1861-1863). As the Civil War rages, Charles Francis, son of Quincy, is appointed Minister to Britain. He travels to England with his wife, their daughter, and their sons Brooks and Henry, the latter serving as his father's secretary. Two other sons remain behind in the Union Army. Charles Francis, now the third Adams Minister to Britain, insures the achievements of his father and grandfather, his particular triumph being that he keeps the British from recognizing the Confederacy. Script: Roger Hirson; directed by James Cellan-Jones.
Indiana U.   57 min   Color   1976

52   The Adams Chronicles — #12 Henry Adams: Historian (1870-1885). Henry and Charles Francis II pursue different careers to fulfill their wartime vision of a reunited America. After careers as journalist and professor, Henry becomes an historian to explain the present. His wife, despondent over the death of her father, commits suicide. Charles Francis II turns to railroad reform and management. Henry and Charles Francis II examine the difficulties of being related to national figures and study the dilemma of adapting old standards in the late 19th century. Script: Sam Hall; directed by Fred Coe.
Indiana U.   57 min   Color   1976

53   The Adams Chronicles — #13 Charles Francis Adams II: Industrialist (1886-1893). Charles Francis II loses control of the Union Pacific Railroad to Jay Gould. Now both Henry and he turn to the past to understand what the country and the world have become. The Adamses consciously withdraw from public life and from the leadership of a nation that has rejected values inherent in the Adams philosophy. Script: Roger Hirson; directed by Fred Coe.
Indiana U.   57 min   Color   1976

54   Albert Camus: A Self Portrait. Beginning with a portrayal of the accident that killed Camus in 1960, this study of the Nobel prizewinner reveals him through his works. Camus discusses his philosophy in a rare on-camera appearance. Symbolically, the camera views his activities away from his native land in black and white — returning to brilliant color

to linger on the sun-drenched landscapes of Algeria. Directed by Georges Regnier; produced by Fred Orgain.
Learning Corp. 20 min Color with BW 1972

55 Alex Haley: The Search for Roots. In this autobiographical insight, the author of the novel, *Roots*, explains how and why he wrote it. Also available on videocassette. With study-guide for discussion and follow-up. Produced by Harold Mantell.
Films/Human 18 min Color 1977

56 The American Parade; Song of Myself. This dramatization of Walt Whitman's life employs his reminiscences as a connecting device. Includes parts of "Song of Myself" within the story-line context. Featured actor: Rip Torn. Produced by CBS News.
BFA Educ. Media 27½ min Color 1976

57 A.M. Klein: The Poet as Landscape. As a portrait of a major Anglo-Jewish writer living between 1909-72, the film describes the social forces behind his poetry. Narration, readings of Klein's works, and interviews with friends reveal the personality of this Canadian who was not only a poet but a lawyer, journalist, and community leader. His activities are described by Pulitzer-prize-winning critic Leon Edel, poet Irving Layton, and Klein's son Colman. Produced by David Kaufman (Toronto).
Carousel 58 min Color 1979

58 Anton Chekhov: A Writer's Life. Probing the "silence" between people, Chekhov introduced a new psychological reality in his plays *The Seagull, The Three Sisters, The Cherry Orchard,* and *Uncle Vanya*. Included in this film are excerpts performed by actors of the Moscow Art Theatre. This film also offers excerpts from Chekhov short stories transferred to the screen by Russia's leading actor. Narrated by Eli Wallach. Produced by Mosfilm. Adapted by Harold Mantell.
Films/Human. 37 min B&W

59 Being Abraham Maslow. The founder of the theory of "self actualization" describes his ideas but provides a psychological study of himself as a person. Dr. Maslow reviews his boyhood as the son of immigrants, his education, family life, and his view of society and the "good life." Produced by Leonard Zweig and Warren Bennis.
Filmakers 30 min BW

60 The Best Educated Man In the World. This self-description of George Bernard Shaw gives credit, not to the formal structure of instruction that he hated, but to his own appetite for reading. This film is a re-creation of his adolescence and early adulthood in 19th-century Dublin. Producer: Ontario Educational Communications Authority (Canada).
Films Inc. 30 min Color 1973

61 Blaise Pascal. Scientist, mathematician, inventor—Pascal was a 17th-century combination of Bertrand Russell, Einstein, and Edison. He came to see the emptiness of science for its own sake, considering God the only pursuit worthy of man's efforts. His ideas are summed up in his *Pensées* and defended in his *Lettres Provinciales*, the subject—along with Pascal himself—of *A Third Testament* by Malcolm Muggeridge who narrates this film. Produced for PBS television.
Time-Life 57 min Color 1977

62 Brendan Behan's Dublin. Varying views of this turbulent writer emerge from his parents, wife, daughter, and especially from himself. Also shown are the people and locales of his extended night life in Dublin. Behan's own words are narrated by Irish actor Ray McAnally. A Norcom Film.
Int. Film Bureau 29 min Color 1968

63 The Brontë Sisters. The actor Eric Portman, himself a native of Yorkshire, the Brontë family home, describes the lives and careers of Charlotte, Anne and Emily. In the places that inspired *Jane Eyre* and *Wuthering Heights*, he recites from their novels, letters, and poems. Written and directed by Terrence Ladlow in association with the Brontë Society.
Int. Film Bureau 19 min Color 1970

64 The Changing World of Charles Dickens. Against a background of 19th-century England, with its child labor and social inequities, English actors recreate moments from *David Copperfield, Oliver Twist, Dombey and Son, Great Expectations,* and *Hard Times.*
Learning Corp. 27 min Color 1970

65 Charles Dickens: An Introduction to His Life and Work. A Victorian audience gathers in a tent for a magic lantern show on the life and work of Charles Dickens. Includes dramatized scenes from *Oliver Twist, David Copperfield, Martin Chuzzlewit* and *A Christmas Carol*. This film is a shortened version of *The Charles Dickens Show,* also available from IFB. Producer: Seabourne Enterprises (England) with the assistance of the Charles Dickens Fellowship (London).
Int. Film Bureau 27 min Color 1978

66 Chisholm: Pursuing the Dream. This documentary traces Congressperson Shirley Chisholm's 1972 campaign for the presidential nomination. It parallels her autobiography, *Unbought and Unbossed*. As a political realist, Ms. Chisholm knew she could not win but entered the race for the sake of America's unrepresented minorities, i.e., women, blacks, the poor and the young. Produced by Bob Denby and Tom Werner for Fredonia Films.
New Line Cinema 42 min Color 1973

67 City of James Joyce. Views of Dublin, the city whose contrasts haunted Joyce's imagination and his writing. The bird market in Bride Street, the five lamps, and the strand at Sandymount are photographed, and a critical narrative points out counterparts in *Ulysses* and other Joyce works. Directed and produced by Bill St. Leger. Script by Irene French Eagor. Narrated by Andy O'Mahony.
Macmillan   9 min   B&W   1966

68 Coleridge: The Fountain and the Cave. This visualization of the life and poetry of Samuel Taylor Coleridge includes readings and interpretations of his *Rime of the Ancient Mariner, Kubla Khan,* and *Cristobel*. There are also excerpts from his letters and diary, along with those of Wordsworth and his sister. Poetry readings are by Paul Scofield. Produced by Bayley Silleck. (Also available in a 32-minute version.)
Pyramid   50 min   Color   1974

69 Courage to Succeed. This is the film version of Diana Nyad's autobiography, *Other Shores,* in which the 25-year-old athlete describes her achievements—and failures—as a marathon swimmer. She articulates, with conviction and clarity, her feeling that stamina and courage are both essential to championship performance. Produced by Saxon Communications Group, Ltd.
Texture Films   28 min   Color   1977

70 Creating a Children's Book. "Jolly Roger" Bradfield, author and illustrator of storybooks, discusses   his work with the neighborhood children. Some titles referred to, with animated excerpts, are *Giants Come in Different Sizes, A Good Knight for Dragons* and *Pickle Chiffon Pie*. Produced by Rex Fleming. Originally distributed by ACI Media.
Paramount   12 min   Color   1972

71   The Days of Dylan Thomas. Music, photographs and narration—including selections spoken by Thomas himself—present the life and works of the Welsh poet who becomes a legend in his own lifetime. Producer: Rollie McKenna for Contemporary Films.
McGraw-Hill   21 min   B&W   1965

72 D.H. Lawrence in Taos This biographical sidelight is a record of the British novelist's visit to New Mexico in 1922. It recalls the three-way competition there for the affection of the author of *Sons and Lovers,* who was to die only eight years later. Produced by Peter Davis.
McGraw-Hill   41 min   Color   1969

73   Dialogue. A   collection of personal memories and photos of publisher Alfred Knopf. It contains references to some of this century's greatest writers, including Albert Camus and John Updike. Narrated by Mr. and Mrs. Knopf. Directed by Jules Schwerin.
Phoenix   20 min   B&W   1974

74 Dietrich Bonhoeffer. All the circumstances prior to his imprisonment by Nazis were conducive to a useful life. A teacher, preacher, and scholar of renown, Bonhoeffer would have been an honorable product of a cultivated German home. The time spent in his cell was the most fertile of his life. There the theologian became a mystic, the pastor became a martyr, and the scholar produced *Letters and Papers from Prison*, one of the classics of Christian literature. The man, his mind, and these writings are the subject of narrator Malcolm Muggeridge, author of the book about Bonhoeffer, *A Third Testament*. Produced for PBS television.
Time-Life   57 min   Color   1977

75 Dostoyevsky: 1821-1881. Written and narrated by Malcolm Muggeridge, this film traces the relationship between the Russian author's personal life and his novels. Muggeridge visits places that provided the settings for *Crime and Punishment, The Brothers Karamazov*, and other major works by Dostoyevsky.
Learning Corp.   54 min   Color   1976

76 A Dylan Thomas Memoir. The voice of the Welsh poet, recorded at various readings before his death in 1953, recites while the camera visualizes the people and places he wrote about. Included are parts or all of seven poems plus two prose pieces: *Reminiscences from Childhood* and *A Visit to America*. Produced by Bayley Silleck.
Pyramid   28 min   Color   1972

77 Edgar Allan Poe: Background For His Works. Paintings in the style of Poe's writings suggest scenes from his work, along with information on his troubled personal life. Excerpts include: "To Helen", *Fall of the House of Usher, Murders in the Rue Morgue* and "The Raven."
Coronet   13 min   Color   1958

78 Edward Ardizzone. A visit with the contemporary author-illustrator at his art studio in Kent, England. His popular picture-book, *Little Tim and the Brave Sea Captain*, seems to reflect the sea-side home, maritime British lineage, and grandfatherly disposition of this creator of 160 works for children. Produced and directed by John Phillips.
Weston Woods   13 min   Color   1978

79 e. e. cummings: Making of a Poet. Poet's career in own voice and drawings. An insight into the life and philosophy of this controversial artist—expressed by e. e. cummings in his own voice, words, and illustrations. This documentary was produced by Harold Mantell.
Films/Human.   24 min   Color   1971

80 Elizabeth Swados: The Girl With the Incredible Feeling. Part of this film is an animation of the subject's juvenile book, *The Girl with the Incredible Feeling*. It's about a young person who realizes—just in

time—that her talents are being exploited. The rest of the film celebrates the multiple talents of the author, only in her twenties, who's also a composer and performer. Produced and directed by Linda Feferman.
Phoenix   39 min   Color   1976

81 Emily Dickinson. We meet Emily Dickinson in the garden than which she ventured no farther for the last twenty years of her life. As she recalls those years, viewers can begin to understand the essence of her life, her spirit, and her poems. The daughter of a tyrannical father, the recluse characteristically asked that her poems be burned upon her death. Fortunately for us, her request was not followed. One of five films from *The Authors* series. Produced by Gil Altschul.
Journal Films   22 min   Color   1978

82 Emily Dickinson: A Certain Slant of Light. Julie Harris, as "The Belle of Amherst," conducts a tour of the home and countryside that inspired this American poet. In the process, she recites representative works of her subject, including "A Certain Slant of Light," "The Brain Is Wider Than the Sea," "To My Small Hearth," and "Safe in Their Alabaster Chambers." Produced by Jean Mudge and Bayley Silleck.
Pyramid Films   27 min   Color   1977

83 The England of Elizabeth. Along with an overview of this 16th-century period, the film shows Shakespeare's home at Stratford-on-Avon, and provides reminders of the bard's boyhood and youth, his hasty marriage, and departure for London. Lines from a sonnet enhance the views of the Cotswolds, over which young Shakespeare journeyed one spring. The pervasive personality and influence of Elizabeth, the songs and sonnets of Shakespeare—all help to convey the power and spirit of the era. Produced by British Transport Films. Director: John Taylor. Music composed by Ralph **Vaughn Williams.**
Int. Film Bureau   26 min   Color   1959

84 Ernest Hemingway — Rough Diamond. Using the technique of an interview plus flashbacks, this film suggests Hemingway's life-style and philosophy. It includes reminiscences of his books and his life, revealing how they were related: conversations with Gertrude Stein; service in World War I; fishing with his father; scenes from *The Old Man and the Sea*; his father's suicide; and his Nobel prize in 1951. Elaine Stritch plays Gertrude Stein. From the *Prizewinners* series. Produced by Chatsworth Film Distributors, Ltd. (England).
Centron Films   29½ min   Color   1977

85 Essay on William Blake. Portrays the life (1757-1827) of the painter and poet who in his day was regarded variously as heretic, idealist, madman, and saint. He is today considered a valid social critic who was able to visualize and warn against the evils of an over-industrialized

society. Includes many of Blake's poems about war, regimentation, repression, poverty and—in spite of it all—idealism. Produced by National Educational Television.
Indiana U. 52 min   Color   1970

86   Eudora Welty. This is one of eight units from the *Writer in America* series in which native authors discuss the process of their craft. In this case, the subject singles out her novel, *The Optimist's Daughter*. Produced by Richard O. Moore, with the help of a grant from the National Foundation for the Arts.
Perspective   29 min   Color   1978

87 Ezra Jack Keats. Mr. Keats grew up in New York, where he lives and works. In this film, the writer-artist shares with us the city he knows, and shows how he paints his world into his books for children. Produced by Morton Schindel.
Weston Woods   17 min   Color   1970

88 Ezra Pound: Poet's Poet. Incorporates the voice of the poet himself, reading from *Hugh Selwyn Mauberley* and from *The Cantos*. The latter piece is especially representative of the diversity of moods of his work. Produced by Harold Mantell.
Films/Human   28½ min   B&W   1970

89 Far Away and Long Ago. This is the autobiographical version of the book of the same name by American author William Hudson, who also wrote *Green Mansions*. This film won a Golden Eagle award from CINE, the Council on International Nontheatrical Events.
Sterling Educ.   20 min   Color   1975

90   Federico García Lorca y Su Granada. This Spanish-language production introduces the poetry of Lorca along with the natural beauty of Granada, the ancient Andalusian city he celebrated in verse. Also useful as background for studies in Spanish culture and history. Language level: advanced. Produced by BSF.
Extension Media   24 min   Color   1974

91 The Fever Called Living. Edgar Allan Poe was one of America's greatest poets and short-story writers. He was also of the ablest literary critics and editors of his time (1809-1849). This film traces his life as a series of disappointments and tragedies, starting with his boyhood in Richmond, Virginia, and ending with his premature death at age 40. Produced by Leo A. Handel.
Handel Film   26 min   Color   1978

92 Frederick Douglass. Enacts the life of one of the first black men to speak out against slavery and for black education. Details his escape from

slavery in 1838, his involvement with the abolitionist movement, his service as U.S. minister to Haiti, his speaking tours, and editorship of the antislavery paper, *The Northern Star*. Based on a chapter in John F. Kennedy's book, *Profiles in Courage*. Produced for television by Robert Saudek.
IQ Films   50 min   B&W   1966

93 Genevieve Foster's World. This author-artist, known for her vivid and unusual approach to history for young people, talks informally about how she researches, organizes, and writes one of her books. Produced by William D. Stoneback.
Conn. Films   13 min   Color   1970

94 Georgia O'Keeffe. A biographical portrait of one of the great American artists of our time. Features her individualistic lifestyle, as well as her art. Incorporates comments by O'Keeffe herself. Based on the book coauthored by Georgia O'Keeffe and Juan Hamilton. Directed by Perry Miller Adato. Produced by WNET/13, New York City.
Films, Inc.   60 min   Color   1977

95 Gerard Manley Hopkins. Born an Anglican, Hopkins converted to Catholicism and became a Jesuit priest. His creative spirit expressed itself in his late 19th-century poetry, which is here read as background to his biography against the Welsh and Irish landscapes that inspired him. Available on special order only; no preview or rental.
Time-Life   30 min   Color   1974

96 Guilty or Not Guilty. Within a mock-trial format, George Bernard Shaw defends his unconventional attitudes toward pacifism, women's rights, formal education, and socialism. Directed by William B. Hill for Ontario (Canada) Educational Communications Authority.
s Inc.   28 min   Color   1976

Gwendolyn Brooks. This interview offers an introduction to the rks and personality of the Pulitzer Prize-winning poet. She explains ow her view of Chicago provides the source for most of her material, much of it black-oriented but nonetheless universal. She describes her work habits, her attitude toward poetry, and the things she enjoys most. From the *Creative Person* series.
Indiana University   30 min   B/W   1967

98 Hallelujah Darwin!. A light-hearted but factual biography of the famous evolutionist. A humorous ditty sets the tone for this treatment of *Origin of Species*, containing the key points of Darwin's theory of natural selection. Purchase or rental includes a five-page lesson guide. Produced in clay animation by Robert Vale.
Beacon   11 min   Color   1977

99   Hemingway. This documentary consists of one of the largest collections of still photographs and rare footage ever assembled on the late author. Major literary and artistic personalities of the 20th century are shown in this NBC television production.
McGraw-Hill   54 min   B&W   1962

100   Henry David Thoreau: A Mile From Any Neighbor. Reconstructs the inspiration and writing of *Walden*, including a flashback biography of the American philosopher credited with inspiring Gandhi to his successful applications of civil disobedience.
Jack Friend   28 min   Color   1973

101   Henry James. James is portrayed recalling his literary and personal life. He experimented unsuccessfully in many literary forms, most notably as a playwright and poet. His well-known works *Daisy Miller, Turn of the Screw, The Ambassadors,* and *The Golden Bowl* brought him some measure of fame. However, he describes his career as that of a "lost" author. One of five films from *The Authors* series. Produced by Gil Altschul.
Journal Films   22½ min   Color   1978

102   Henry Wadsworth Longfellow. Portrays representative events in the life of this American poet. Describes his early love for poetry and his career as teacher, scholar, and poet. Interposes selections from his poems, and depicts incidents that inspired him to write his best-known works.
Encyc. Brit.   20 min   B&W   1950

103   Herman Melville. Melville is portrayed retelling the story of his life and his earliest books of the sea, *Omoo* and *Typee*. Rhythm and force of epic proportions remain as he recalls the motivation for *Moby D*. Slowly his mood alters as he reviews the rejections for his greatest n His rediscovery, thirty years after his death, led to his current positi the author of perhaps the greatest American novel. One of five films *The Authors* series. Directed by Lee Gluckman.
Journal Films   22 min   Color   1978

104   Herman Melville: November in my Soul. The title and theme this film originate from the first chapter of *Moby Dick*, a masterpiece the novelist was never able to repeat. To outline Melville's bleak career, the script relies on a blend of interviews, source materials, and related locales. Produced by CBS News.
BFA Educ. Media   27 min   Color   1977

105   The House That Mark Built. Another view of Twain, seen as Samuel Clemens—husband, father, and entrepreneur—at his unusual home in Hartford, Connecticut. In his twenty years there (1871-1891),

Clemens became the most important writer of his period. Music by Gershon Kingsley. Director: Philip Mikan. A Raphel Associates Production.
Fenwick   26 min   Color   1971

106 I Am Pablo Neruda. Often referred to as the Walt Whitman of Latin America, this Chilean won the Nobel Prize for literature in 1971. His everyday life is examined in this film, and his poetry (translated by Professor Ben Belitt) is voiced by the English actor, Anthony Quayle. Produced by Harold Mantell.
Films/Human.   28½ min   B&W   1967

107 The Inner World of Jorge Luis Borges. Not since the English-speaking world discovered Kafka in the 1930's has any writer stirred the imagination of his readers in quite the same way as the Argentinian whose erudition and mystery are making his works required reading in more and more American schools. The film shuttles between suggestions of the life around Borges (readers in the library, crowds at a lecture, modern Argentine architecture) and the mind of Borges (quotations from books he read long ago, memories of Buenos Aires as it was in his childhood). Narrated by Jorge Luis Borges and Joseph Wiseman. Produced by Harold Mantell.
Films/Human.   28½ min   Color   1972

108 I Seem to be a Verb. Expresses the many facets of the philosophy of Buckminster Fuller, contemporary "Renaissance Man" whose expertise ranges from literature to the design of the original geodesic dome at Expo 67 in Canada. Produced by Lester Berman and Arden Rynew.
Texture   25 min   Color   1975

109 James Daugherty. A visit to the home and studio of the author-illustrator-historian. Mr. Daugherty's comments contribute to an understanding of the relationship between the artist and the Americans he portrays: Lincoln, Thoreau, and Daniel Boone, to mention a few. Producer: Morton Schindel.
Weston Woods   19 min   Color   1972

110 James Dickey: Poet – Lord Let Me Die But Not Die Out. Records the words of this contemporary Southern poet as the camera follows him on a three-week barnstorming tour. He is depicted as a man trying "to break through this glass wall we all live behind." From the EBE *Humanities Series.*
Encyc. Brit.   37 min   Color   1970

111 James Fenimore Cooper. In the film, Cooper recounts his almost accidental transition from gentleman farmer to author of *Leatherstocking Tales*. He describes his youth and the energy and high romance that produced *The Pioneers, The Pilot,* and *The Last of the Mohicans*. His later

years find him a constant litigant as he attacks the press for what he considers libelous reviews of his *History of the Navy* and *Letter to His Countrymen*. One of five films from *The Authors* series. Produced by Gil Altschul.
Journal Films   22 min   Color   1978

112   James Weldon Johnson. Among this black poet's diverse activities were teaching, music, and international diplomacy. This biographical sketch includes references to "Lift Every Voice and Sing" by J. Rosamond Johnson, which has become the black national anthem. Also includes a dramatic reading of "The Creation," recited by actor Raymond St. Jacques. Produced by Art Evans.
Paramount   12 min   Color   1972

113   Janet Flanner (Genét). Under the pen-name of Genét, this American foreign correspondent has chronicled life in Paris since 1926, a period and place that embraces the larger-than-life figures of Hemingway, Stein, Lindbergh, and Picasso. Part of the *Writer in America* series, funded by the National Foundation for the Arts. Producer: Richard O. Moore.
Perspective   29 min   Color   1978

114   John Baker's Last Race. The real-life story, "John Baker's Last Race," in the August 1975 issue of the *Reader's Digest*, is about a man who came from utter obscurity to become a premier miler of Olympic calibre. Yet his early death did not come before he had transformed Aspen Elementary School in Albuquerque into a school where kids succeeded. Author of the original profile is William J. Buchanan.
Brigham Young   34 min   Color   1976

115   John Gardner. In the comfort of his Illinois farm, this novelist describes the character and objective of the "moral fiction" behind his *Jason and Medea, Grendel*, and *October Light* — stories that explore the world and try to explain it, too. Part of the *Writer in America* series, funded by the National Foundation for the Arts. Produced by Richard O. Moore.
Perspective   29 min   Color   1978

116   John Keats: His Life and Death. This is an extended version of the 31-minute film *John Keats: Poet*. It explores in depth the poet's love affair with Fanny Brawne, along with the events surrounding his premature death in Rome at the age of 26. Written by Archibald MacLeish for the EBE *Humanities Series*.
Encyc. Brit.   55 min   Color   1974

117   John Keats: Poet. Written by Archibald MacLeish, this dramatization covers the life of Keats up to his early death in Rome at the age of 26. Excerpts from his letters and poetry reveal both his genius as a

poet and his integrity as a person. Photographed in London and Rome. From the *Humanities Series.*
Encyc. Brit.   31 min   Color   1974

118   Kurt Vonnegut, Jr.: A Self Portrait. This biographical film, narrated by the novelist himself, was photographed in places pivotal to his writings and life: New York, Indianapolis, Schenectady, Cape Cod, and Dresden. He comments on his most famous novels, including *Cat's Cradle, Slaughterhouse Five,* and *Breakfast of Champions.* **Produced by Harold Mantell.**
Films/Human.   29 min   Color   1975

119 Lansgton Hughes. Black performer Dallie and her troupe present selections from the following poems by Langston Hughes: "The Negro Mother," "The Best of Simple," "The Big Sea," and "I Wonder as I Wander." These poetic performances are interwoven with biographical background on Harlem's poet laureate. Produced by WCAU-TV, Philadelphia.
Carousel   24 min   Color   1970

120   The Legacy of Anne Frank. This treatment of the modern-day heroine correlates with her *Diary.* It traces her all   too   brief life, but, more important, her gift of love and letters. Uses documentary material and new on-location footage. Produced in Holland by NBC Television News.
McGraw-Hill   29 min   Color   1969

121   The Legend of Mark Twain. This biography of the well-known American author includes dramatizations from two of his works, *The Celebrated Jumping Frog of Calaveras County* and *The Adventures of Huckleberry Finn.* Produced by Myron Solin.
Benchmark   32 min   Color   1967

122 Leo Tolstoy. This portrait of the life and work of Tolstoy is presented in photographs, engravings, newsreel scenes, and contemporary paintings. The narration alludes to the writer's social thought and the relationship of his life to his novels, plays, short stories, and fame. The stage-scenes from the dramatic productions of *Anna Karenina, Resurrection,* and *Morning of a Landowner,* are in Russian. Produced by the Central Documentary Film Studio, Moscow.
Macmillan   48 min   B&W

123   Leo Tolstoy. Pacifism, vegetarianism, opposition to capital punishment, communal living—these are some of the legacies of this man of peace who left his aristocratic standing to become a shoemaker and to make all men his brothers. He would have nothing to do with earth-

ly authority, yet a mighty establishment turned out at his funeral. The novelist's life and thought are the subject of this film based on *A Third Testament* by Malcolm Muggeridge who is the narrator. Produced for Public Broadcast Service.
Time-Life   57 min   Color   1976

124 Lorraine Hansberry: The Black Experience in the Creation of Drama. The late Ms. Hansberry, in her own words and voice, tells of the self-discovery and development of her talents. Includes scenes from her plays *Raisin in the Sun* and *The Sign in Sidney Brustein's Window*, with performances by Sidney Poitier, Ruby Dee, and Claudia McNeil. Scripted by her husband, Robert Nemiroff.
Films/Human.   35 min   Color   1975

125   Louisa May Alcott. Reveals overlooked facts in the life of this writer of stories for young people who was also a nurse and reformer. She displayed untiring ambition, humor and practicality, as enacted in this period dramatization.
Encyc. Brit.   17 min   B&W   1950

126   A Lover's Quarrel with the World. Using only the words of Robert Frost, this documentary examines the man as a poet and a teacher. The locale, rural New England, suggests his kinship with nature, as well as its influence on his writing style and content. Originally distributed by Pyramid Films.
BFA Educ. Media   40 min   B&W   1962

127 Mark Twain: Background for His Works. This elementary study of Twain's work employs actual locales, quotations, and re-enactments. His boyhood on the Mississippi is shown as a source of inspiration. His other works were influenced by his life as a journalist, story-teller, and humorist. Revised version of the original 1957 production.
Coronet   13½ min   Color   1978

128 Mark Twain Gives an Interview. The actor Hal Holbrook impersonates Twain, using the documented language of his subject. This abbreviated version of Holbrook's stage and television characterization takes advantage of his well-researched acting and the writer's original wit.
Coronet   14 min   Color   1961

129   Mark Twain's Hartford Home. In 1873, America's most successful writer commissioned the construction of a villa of varicolored brick, sweeping wood cornices, gables, and balconies. Film-host E.G. Marshall tours the premises, revealing that it now is near restoration to its original prime condition. Produced for ACI Media by Comco.
Paramount   23 min   Color   1976

130 Mark Twain: When I was a Boy. It was along the mighty Mississippi that the novelist grew up, and this recreation of the era shows why the river was such an influence on Twain's writing. Quotations from *Life on the Mississippi* and *Huckleberry Finn* reveal the events of his youth and how he felt about them. Includes scenes of Hartford, Connecticut. Script supervised by Justin Kaplan, author of *Mr. Clemens & Mark Twain*. *National Geographic*   25 min   Color   1977

130a Maurice Sendak. During an informal visit with Mr. Sendak in his New York studio apartment, the author-artist chronicles the development of his books. He also discusses music and art, and reveals their influence on his own productivity. Producer: Mort Schindel. *Weston Woods*   14 min   Color   1964

131 Mayakovsky: The Poetry of Action. In the 1920s, Mayakovsky's verses thrilled his countrymen. Millions continue to read him today. This documentary recalls the giant who cast a spell over the artistic life of Russia in the twenties. It is a film for all who seek a better understanding of the relationship of poetry to power. Narration by John Cullum. English version (with Mayakovsky heard in Russian) produced by Harold Mantell. *Films/Human.*   22 min   Color   1972

132 Millay at Steepletop. Edna St. Vincent Millay lived and wrote at her farm, "Steepletop," in upstate New York between 1925 and 1950, the year she died. Her younger sister, Norma Millay Ellis, tours the estate on film. Edna's readings are intermingled with family pictures of the poet. Directed by Kevin Brownlow. Script by Sloane Shelton. *Films/Human.*   25 min   Color   1976

133 A Miserable Merry Christmas. This true story, based on a chapter from *The Autobiography of Lincoln Steffens*, is about a boy whose Christmas pony arrived a little late in the day. As such, it shows how his emotions on that holiday ran the full gamut between disappointment and glee. Produced by Educational Channel 13, WNET-TV, New York. *Encyc. Brit.*   15 min   Color   1973

134 Mr. Shepard and Mr. Milne. This film, about the collaboration of Ernest Shepard and A.A. Milne, tells the story behind their children's books. It includes visits to the locales that were the scenes of the "Pooh" stories and poems. Produced by Mort Schindel. *Weston Woods*   29 min   Color   1972

135 Muriel Rukeyser. "People think it's easy to make a poem"—a fallacy that this politically-minded artist tries to correct in this filmed profile. Her personality fits in perfectly with her New York studio overlooking Manhattan and the Hudson River—a site in itself indicative

of the contrasts of her writing style. Produced as part of the *Writer in America* series by Richard O. Moore. Funded by the National Foundation for the Arts.
Perspective   28 min   Color   1978

136   My Childhood: James Baldwin's Harlem. The novelist describes, on camera, the poverty and humiliations that marked his growing up in a black urban ghetto in New York. Produced for network television in tandem with a study of Hubert Humphrey's boyhood in a small South Dakota town. Recommended by the National Council of Teachers of English.
Benchmark   25½ min   B&W   1964

137   The Mystery That Heals. This study of Carl Jung in his old age shows his attitude toward death and Christianity. It includes interviews with Aniela Jaffe, editor of his autobiography, *Memories, Dreams, Reflections,* and with Dr. C.A. Meier, a colleague from his early years. Discussion guide available. Produced for BBC-TV.
Time-Life   30 min   Color   1972

138   Pablo Neruda: Poet. This documentary is an in-depth profile of the Chilean poet, with many examples of his works. Neruda won the Nobel Peace Prize in 1971. Film available with English or Spanish soundtrack. Produced by Douglas Harris and Dr. Eugenia Neves.
Tricontinental   30 min   B&W   1972

139   Paul Laurence Dunbar: America's First Black Poet. Produced on the hundredth anniversary of his birth, this tribute to the first American black to be recognized as a poet is a collage of still pictures, paintings, African art, dramatizations, poetry, story readings, and biography. The poetry readings are "We Wear the Mask," "Banjo Song," "The Real Question," "Theology," "Love Pictures," and "Ode to Ethiopia." The story, *The Lynching of Jube Benson*, is visualized through tintype-like stills. Produced by Carlton Moss and Fisk University.
Pyramid   23 min   Color   1972

140   Pictures Out of my Life. Consists of the drawings and recollections of Canadian Eskimo artist Pitseolak, from the book of that name by Dorothy Eber. Now in her seventies, Pitseolak's drawings illustrate her memories of Arctic life with its unique birds, animals, and spirit belief. Coproduced by the National Film Board of Canada and the Canadian Department of Indian and Northern Affairs.
Nat'l Film Board   13 min   Color

141   Poe: A Visit with the Author. This biographical material on Edgar Allan Poe includes dramatic readings of his poems "The Raven," and "Alone," and the story *The Tell-Tale Heart*. Produced by Dr. Henk

Newenhouse.
Perennial Educ. 30 min Color 1968

142 Poet of His People. This profile of Pablo Neruda consists of a mixture of live-action footage, still photographs, computer graphics, dance, and poetry—his own, naturally. Featured is his "Barcarola" as representative of his work and his life. Produced by Lillian Schwartz.
Lilyan Productions 13 min Color 1978

143 A Publisher Is Known by the Company He Keeps. This documentary gives an insight into the commercial and personal relationship between Alfred Knopf and his "stable" of great writers during the 1920's and 1930's. Includes references to Thomas Mann and Willa Cather. Narrated by Mr.Knopf. Directed by Jules Schwerin. Produced by Louis deRochemont.
Phoenix 25 min B&W 1962

144 R.D. Laing on R.D. Laing. In this interview, conducted by a fellow psychiatrist from London, Dr. Laing reviews his childhood, his work at Glasgow University, and his book, *The Divided Self*. Interviewed by Dr. Desmond Kelly at St. George's Hospital (England).
Harper & Row 15 min Color

145 Robert Browning—His Life and Poetry. Surveys the life and works of the Victorian poet; includes readings by costumed actors who dramatize the complete "My Last Duchess" and some of the monologues. Emphasizes the psychological insight of his work. Detailed study-guide is available.
Int. Film Bureau 21 min Color 1971

146 Robert Duncan. Surrounded by the books and paintings of his San Francisco house, this poet reads from and interprets some of his works, including "The Proposition." He also explains his early interest in language, his homosexual life-style, and the "business" of poetry. From the *Writer in America* series, filmed under a grant from the National Foundation for the Arts. Produced by Richard O. Moore.
Perspective 28½ min Color 1978

147 Robert Frost. The late poet discusses his life and work at his farm home in New England. A life-long critic of regimentation in schools, Frost recalls the wide range of personal experiences—as a mill worker, country-school teacher, cobbler, small-town editor, and farmer—that furnished the background for his poetry. He reads "Stopping by Woods on a Snowy Evening" and "The Drumlin Woodchuck." National Broadcasting Company, producer.
Films, Inc. 30 min B&W 1958

148   Robert Frost: A First Acquaintance. Presents the art and memories of the poet, in the words of Frost and his daughter Lesley. Filmed mostly "on location" at the family farm in Derry, New Hampshire. Some poems included are: "Mending Wall," "Stopping by Woods on a Snowy Evening," The Last Word of a Bluebird," and "The Road not Taken." Produced by Harold Mantell.
Films/Human. 16 min   Color   1974

149   Robert McCloskey. Robert McCloskey, who creates picture-books, tells how he works, showing not only his craftsmanship, but also how he gets his ideas. Produced by Mort Schindel.
Weston Woods 18 min   Color   1965

150 Rose Kennedy Remembers. This is a biography of the Kennedy matriarch and an insight into the rest of that unusual family. Includes references to their political vocation and the tragedies associated with it. Based on *Times to Remember*, her memoirs. Film previously distributed by Doubleday Multi-Media Company.
Phoenix 24 min   Color   1975

151 Ross MacDonald. He even looks the part, just like his fictional detective, Lew Archer. One of America's foremost mystery writers talks about his genre and about early influences on his decision to reach the popular market for serious purposes. The Southern California locale seems to match the author's easy but earnest demeanor. From the *Writer in America* series, funded by the National Foundation for the Arts. Producer: Richard O. Moore.
Perspective 29 min   Color   1978

152 Rudyard Kipling — The Road from Mandalay. Photographed at Kipling's original home in Sussex, this motion picture recreates a special time in his life — the day he was awarded the 1907 Nobel prize for literature. Through flashbacks, actor Ian Holm portrays highlights in Kipling's life, including his birth in India and his residence in Vermont where he wrote most of his *Jungle Books*. From *The Prizewinners* series. Produced by Chatsworth Film Distributors, Ltd. (England).
Centron Films 30 min   Color   1977

153   Seamus Heaney: Poet in Limboland. Northern Ireland's foremost young poet seeks to lead his people out of the bog of their bitter history. Written amidst the terror and tension of civil war, Heaney's poetry inversely parallels Wordsworth's tranquil recollection of the French Revolution. This film shows Heaney in the battle-scarred cities and in the peaceful farmlands of Ulster. Reciting his poetry against the background from which it sprang, he provides insight into contemporary Anglo-Irish literature and the nature of life in the midst of revolution. Narrated by Seamus Heaney and Denys Hawthorne.
Films/Human. 28½ min   Color

154 Shakespeare of Stratford and London. This documentary treatment of the subject concentrates on the Bard's personal life and on the era that shaped him as boy and man. It was produced in cooperation with the Shakespeare Birthplace Trust of Stratford-on-Avon (England).
National Geographic 40 min Color 1977

155 Shakespeare: Soul of an Age. This made-for-TV production is an attempt to recreate the spirit of Elizabethan England. Filmed in the countryside and in older parts of London, it includes dramatic Shakespearean readings by Sir Michael Redgrave.
McGraw-Hill 54 min Color 1963

156 Sheridan's World of Society. Both a biography of playwright Richard Brinsley Sheridan and a look at the 18th-century society in which the dramatist-statesman lived. Uses paintings, cartoons and portraits by artists of the era.
Int. Film Bureau 17 min Color 1971

157 Sigmund Freud: His Offices and Home. This biographical study focuses on the great psychoanalyst's surroundings in Vienna 1938, just before Freud left for England to escape Nazi harassment. It is based on photographs taken by Edmund Engelman, highlighting Freud's collection of antiques and the parallel drawn between his interest in archeology. Narrated by actor Eli Wallach. Producer: Gene Friedman.
Filmakers 17 min BW

158 Soren Kierkegaard. Malcolm Muggeridge narrates this study of the philosopher he includes in *A Third Testament*. Kierkegaard's outlook on life was affected by his physical state: he was ugly with a poor physique and raised in a gloomy home by elderly parents. Yet it was these very circumstances that led him to an intropsective life concerned with the lot of man and his destiny. He deplored the press and the politics that turned man into an animal, part of a herd. To quote Kierkegaard: "Everyone in whom the animal disposition is preponderant believes that millions are more than one; whereas spirit is just the opposite—that one is more than millions and everyone can be that one." Produced for PBS.
Time-Life 57 min Color 1977

159 Stephen Crane. Crane is portrayed retelling the story of his life and his masterpiece, *The Red Badge of Courage*, as well as *The Open Boat* and *Maggie: A Girl of the Streets*. This personal view of Crane stresses his role as a pioneer in literature who expanded realism with an impressionistic, symbolistic, and romantic style. One of five films from *The Authors* series. Produced by Gil Altschul.
Journal Films 21 min Color 1978

160 The Story of a Writer. The working habits of a professional author are revealed as Ray Bradbury, American science-fiction writer, talks with students about how he conceives, tests, and structures his unusual plots. Organization and attitude are two important considerations when beginning a manuscript, according to Bradbury.
Sterling Educ.   25 min   B&W   1965

161   The Story of My   Life: Hans Christian Andersen. This biography of Andersen, told in words from his diary, shows his life in the world of 1805-1875. Reconstructed are original documents including drawings, paintings, photos, and his belongings. Silver Reel Award Winner. A Danish Culture film. Written and directed by Jorgen Roos.
Macmillan   27 min   B/W   1955

162   This is Edward Steichen. Focuses on the philosophy of this master photographer, as demonstrated in his selection of pictures for the *Family of Man* exhibit commissioned by the Museum of Modern Art. This same collection inspired the picture-book of that name, one of the most successful ever. Film produced by WCBS-TV, New York. Originally distributed by Association Films.
Macmillan   27 min   B&W   1965

163   Thornton Wilder. This documentary ranges from Grover's Corners, New Hampshire to Peru; from Germany to Broadway to Hamden, Conn., the author's home. Included are sequences of Wilder with German director Max Reinhardt and writer Gertrude Stein. To illustrate commentary by Wilder from his Pulitzer Prize-winning novel, *The Bridge of San Luis Rey*, the cameras visit a monastery in the Andes to show the locale and the people of that book. Readings from *Our Town* and *The Bridge of San Luis Rey* are by Thornton Wilder. Narrated by David Wayne with members of the Wilder Family. Produced by Harold Mantell.
Films/Human.   24 min   B&W

164   Toni Morrison. In this profile of a contemporary American author, she describes her own novels: *The Bluest Eye, Sula,* and *Song of Solomon*. Ms. Morrison also explains the pride she took in editing the biographies of Muhammed Ali and Angela Davis, and in writing full time while caring for two young sons. From the *Writer in America* series, produced by Richard O. Moore under a grant from the National Foundation for the Arts.
Perspective   28 min   Color   1978

165   The Trials of Franz Kafka. This early 20th-century writer foretold with vision and artistry the anxiety and alienation of modern man. Photographed in Kafka's native Prague, this film explores "the trials" of childhood, youth, and adulthood that he transformed into novels and stories central to our understanding of life today. Narrated by Kurt Von-

negut, Jr. A production of Kratky Film (Czechoslovakia) and Harold Mantell.
Films/Human.   15 min   B&W

166 A Tribute to Dylan Thomas. This film provides a biographical insight into the poet, along with a literary sampling of his output. Narration is by fellow Welshman Richard Burton. (Prints available on special order only.)
Pyramid   30 min   B&W   1962

167 Tribute to Malcolm X. The influence of Malcolm X upon the black liberation movement is reported in this interview with his widow, Betty Shabazz. Malcolm X, whose father was killed and whose mother was committed to a mental institution when he was a child, became a minister of Islam and a leader of the black struggle until his assassination. One of a series of National Educational Television programs produced by black film-makers. Alex Haley wrote *The Autobiography of Malcolm X*.
Indiana U.   15 min   B&W   1969

168   Understanding Shakespeare: His Sources. Introduces the English rural life against which young Shakespeare grew up. Strolling players are seen visiting one of the great houses and performing in the market place. The film follows Will to London where he worked as an actor and mixed with the rougher elements in the taverns. Later scenes show him searching in private libraries for new subjects for plays, such as Plutarch's *The Noble Grecians and Romans* and Holinshed's *Chronicles*. He is also seen watching the plays of rival authors. Educational collaborator: Dr. Levi Fox.
Coronet   18½ min   Color   1971

169 Virginia Woolf: The Moment Whole. Combining family-album stills with motion-visuals, and scripted exclusively from the subject's own works, this treatment strives for simulating a visit to the author herself. Major quotations are from *A Room of One's Own* and *The Waves*. Produced by Janet Sternburg for NET. Originally distributed by ACI Media.
Paramount   10 min   Color   1972

170 A Visit with J. I. Rodale. A prolific playwright, Rodale 30 years ago foresaw our current environmental crisis and pioneered the organic movement in America. Treated for many years as a crank and a faddist, his theories have recently received full vindication. Completed shortly before his death in 1971, this is the only documentary ever made of this farsighted individual. Produced by Rodale Press.
Bullfrog Films   15 min   Color   1972

171 Walt Whitman: Background for his Works. This treatment

shows the poet's works as being strongly influenced by social factors of changeable 19th-century America. Presents scenes of his personal environment and of the stormy period of history he experienced.
Coronet   12½ min   Color   1957

172 Walt Whitman: Poet for a New Age. Key incidents from Whitman's life, along with segments of his poetry, reveal his belief in democracy, in the unity and sanctity of all life, his hatred of war, and his belief in the primacy of love. Produced by Professor Lou Stomen, UCLA Theatre Department. Part of the *Humanities Series*.
Encyc. Brit.   29 min   Color   1971.

173 Walt Whitman's Civil War. Whitman's poems and eyewitness prose accounts of the war suggest the power of his style and his despair at the tragedy of war. Archive photographs and live reenactment provide the basic visual content.
Churchill   15 min   Color   1972

174   Walt Whitman's World. The poet's humanity and social philosophy are reflected in his diaries and Civil War notes made in the hospital where he served as a conscientious objector. Atmosphere of the period is reflected in original manuscripts and authentic illustrations. Produced by Walter P. Lewisohn.
Coronet   16 min   Color   1966

175   Washington Irving's World. Period paintings and prints represent the life and literature of this early American writer. The narrative is based on quotations from his works and his private letters. Includes scenes of his beloved homestead "Sunnyside." Produced by Walter P. Lewisohn.
Coronet   12 min   Color   1966

176 W.B. Yeats: A Tribute. The poet's own works reflect the life of this great Irish poet, dramatist, and patriot. Commentary is spoken by Cyril Cusak; poetry recited by Siobhan McKenna and Michael MacLiammor. Produced by the National Film Institute of Ireland. Director: George Fleischmann.
Macmillan   22 min   BW   1950

177 The Weapons of Gordon Parks. This is the true story of the former *Life* photographer and war correspondent, told in his own words and voice. In his autobiography, *A Choice of Weapons*, and in this production, Parks shares his insights as one of 15 black children of poor parents in Kansas. He shares, too, his good fortune of having the "weapons" of love, talent, and will. Produced by Warren Forma.
McGraw-Hill   28 min   Color   1968

178 William Blake. While concentrating on his paintings, this film points out the symbols and ideas that show up in his poetry, too. Works covered are: "Songs of Innocence," "Songs of Experience," "Book of Thel," "Marriage of Heaven and Hell," "Book of Urizen," and "Europe." Narrated by Lord Kenneth Clark. From the Romantic vs. Classic Art Series, produced by the *Reader's Digest*.
Pyramid 26 min Color 1974

179 William Blake. One of the most inspired of all English poets saw the Heavenly City in his imagination, painted it, described it, and to a great extent lived in it. Looking at his paintings, reading his poetry, and coming to know the bizarre lifestyle he led, we would today perhaps label him insane. But Malcolm Muggeridge would disagree — as he does in this film and in his book on which it is based, *A Third Testament*. Though Blake's visionary life prevented him from enjoying success or recognition, it filled his days with delight, and enabled him to die in old age in the full confidence of salvation. Produced for PBS television.
Time-Life 57 min Color 1977

180 William Faulkner's Mississippi. Probes the inner conflicts that Faulkner felt due to the discrepancy between his love of Mississippi and his hatred of the injustices committed in the name of Southern tradition. Includes reading from *Absalom Absalom, Intruder in the Dust*, and *The Sound and the Fury*. Produced by Robert Quennette.
Benchmark 49 min B&W 1967

181 William Mayne. The contemporary British author of stories for children talks of his books, his childhood, and the English village where he lives. Produced by Joanna Foster and William D. Stoneback.
Conn. Films 16 min Color

182 William Shakespeare. Recounts the life of Shakespeare from his boyhood through his productive years as a playwright and actor in London. Collaborator: Levi Fox, M.A., Director, Shakespeare's Birthplace Trust. Produced by John Barnes who conceived and directed the EB Humanities Series.
Encyc. Brit. 24 min Color 1955

183 William Shakespeare: Background for His Works. Provides introductory information about the Bard, including his personality, marriage, the settings for his plays, and his historical era. Includes brief scenes from his more familiar plays, and explains the basic design and structure of the Globe Theatre.
Coronet 14 min Color 1951

184 Women. George Bernard Shaw, in his life and in his plays, was an early champion of equal rights without regard to gender. This

dramatic portrayal provides insights into how he formed these "revolutionary" attitudes. Produced by the Ontario (Canada) Educational Communications Authority.
Films Inc.   30 min   Color   1973

185 The World of Carl Sandburg. In this biographical dramatization, a black woman contemplates her life, a father talks to his son, and a married couple grow to hate each other. Uta Hagen and Fritz Weaver bring Sandburg's world to life in this film about one of the modern era's giants of literature and poetry. Based on Norman Corwin's stage presentation. Produced for NET (National Educational Television) by Nathan Kroll. Directed by Kirk Browning.
Phoenix   59 min   BW   1959

186 The World of Piri Thomas. Piri Thomas, author of *Down These Mean Streets*, is not only a writer, but a painter...and a former junkie. Besides reading excerpts from his novel and his poetry, he points out the source of much of his subject matter: the daily desperation of life in Spanish Harlem, home of two-thirds of America's 900,000 Puerto Rican citizens. He pleads for understanding – and correction – of their plight.
Indiana U.   60 min   B&W   1962

187 The Worlds of Rudyard Kipling. Narrated by Anthony Quayle, this first- and third-person account offers documentary insights into the man and his environments. The camera takes us from his study in England, to India where he worked as a journalist, and to Vermont where he wrote many of his poems and stories. We then return to the English village where he finally settled down. Filmed by Limbridge Productions ltd. and Edward Patterson Associates.
Best Films   25 min   Color   1977

188 Wright Morris. This author of 18 novels discusses his most recent, *The Fork River Space Project*. Although his works are set in metropolitan regions, he credits his childhood years on the plains as his chief literary influence. From the *Writer in America* series, funded by the National Foundation for the Arts. Produced by Richard O. Moore.
Perspective   29 min   Color   1978

189 Writing: An Interview with Irving Stone. In an informal interview at his home-studio, author Irving Stone traces his writing career, reveals his motivations, methodolgy, and tips to novice writers. Stone and his wife Jean, who does most of his research, discuss several of his biographical novels such as *The Agony and the Ecstasy* (Michelangelo) and *Passions of the Mind* (Freud). Produced by Doron Kauper and Mario Machado.
Coronet   18½ min   Color   1978

190 Yeats Country. The commentary of the film identifies the places shown and the things William Butler Yeats wrote of: his youth in Sligo; his association with Lady Gregory and the literary movement; the Norman tower in Galway; the questioning of his middle age; and Ireland's struggle for independence. Producers: Joe Mendoza and Patrick Carey.
Int. Film Bureau 18 min Color 1965

191 Yevgeny Yevtushenko: A Poet's Journey. Examines the poetry and the personality behind it that has made Yevgeny Yevtushenko an idol of contemporary youth in the Soviet Union and the Western world. Yevtushenko is seen at work and at play in his Moscow apartment and in characteristic encounters with audiences and friends during his travels abroad. English translations of his poetry are voiced by Kenneth Haigh. Production by Harold Mantell.
Films/Human. 28½ min B&W 1970

Children's Stories

In the Poetry section of this book, you'll see a suggestion about exposing younsters, early in life, to good verse. The same recommendation applies to prose, a resource rich and varied enough to justify a separate category for the younger set. This chapter consists of stories that "fall between the cracks" of other child-oriented categories such as Fables and Novels. By contrast, most of these entries are fantasies originally conceived by contemporary authors for readers younger than ten or twelve years of age. Others are mood pieces or awareness films adapted from books that are just as open-ended. In all, you'll find 177 film annotations within, every single one of them delineating a separate story. There is no duplication of titles from the other sections of this directory, so check elsewhere for other program possibilities for hard-to-predict but easy-to-please audiences of youngsters.

192 Alligators All Around. From "Alligators all around" to "zippity zound," a family of alligators clowns its way through a variety of experiences in this version of Maurice Sendak's alphabet book. Animated. Music composed by Carole King. Produced by Sheldon Riss.
Weston Woods   2 min   Color   1975

193 The Amazing Cosmic Awareness of Duffy Moon. Duffy is "The Shrimp" of his class, a kid so little and different he's a sitting duck for the taunts of every bully in the neighborhood. In a surprise ending, Duffy finds the inner strength to meet the challenge and turn adversity into advantage. Duffy's adventures can be an inspiration for any young person who has been slighted for apparent shortcomings. Based on the book, *The Strange but Wonderful Cosmic Awareness of Duffy Moon* by Jean Robinson. Produced by Daniel Wilson. Director: Larry Elikann.
Time-Life   32 min   Color   1975

194 Anatole and the Piano. This animated version of the children's book by Eve Titus tells the story of a mouse who searched for a toy piano that didn't have a tinny sound. When he finally found one, it was taken away and given to a famous pianist. But because Anatole helped the pianist, he gave Anatole the piano, and even wrote a special concerto for him that Anatole later played in the Mouse Concert Hall.
McGraw-Hill   12 min   Color   1960

195 Andy and the Lion. This iconographic motion picture derived from the picture book of the same title by James Daugherty tells the story of a boy who befriends a circus lion. Loosely based on Aesop's fable. Producer: Mort Schindel.
Weston Woods   10 min   Color   1955

196 Annie and the Old One. The Old One, beloved grandmother of a Navajo girl named Annie passes much of her wisdom on to her granddaughter. They spend a great deal of time together tending sheep, fixing meals, laughing, and enjoying the beauty of the land. But one day the Old One reveals a sad truth: when the rug on the loom is finished, she will go to Mother Earth. Annie cannot imagine life without her grandmother and plots to keep the rug from completion. The Old One discovers Annie's distress and helps her to understand the cycle of life. Adapted from a book by Miska Miles. A Greenhouse Films production, directed by Ted Abenheim.
BFA Educ. Media   14½ min   Color   1976

197 Apt. 3. The sound of rain outside Sam's apartment building is paralleled by wistful harmonica music from an unknown neighbor. Sam and his little brother begin a search for its origin. Their discovery of a blind man playing the harmonica gives them an insight beyond vision and a sense of beauty in the midst of gloom. From the children's

storybook written and illustrated by Ezra Jack Keats. Iconographic animation.
Weston Woods   8 min   Color   1976

198 Arthur's World. From the picture book by Mischa Richter, this story tells of a boy's yearning to see the unknown world beyond his backyard fence. In the process of imagining his views of the world and its surprises, Arthur learns to appreciate the wonders within his own home.
Sterling Educ.   11 min   Color   1971

199 Attic of the Wind. This blend of pictures and poetry speaks to the need of children to hold on to small beloved things, those fragile and precious moments that melt like the snowflake. Art and music create a fantasy world where the past is always as fresh as the magic of childhood. Written by Doris Herold Lund. Illustrated by Ati Forberg. Iconographic animation. Photographed and edited by Alexander Cochran.
Weston Woods   6 min   Color   1974

200   A Bear Called Paddington (Film #1). Consists of three animations of chapters from *A Bear Called Paddington* by Michael Bond. Film-chapter titles are: "Please Look After This Bear," "A Bear in Hot Water," and "Paddington Goes Underground." Each title is available separately. Produced by Film Fair of London.
Film Fair   16½ min   Color   1977

201   A Bear Called Paddington (Film #2). Composed of three animated versions of chapters from *A Bear Called Paddington* by Michael Bond. Individual chapter-film titles are: "A Shopping Expedition," "Paddington and the Old Master," and "A Disappearing Trick." Each film is available separately, if desired. Produced by Film Fair of London.
Film Fair   16½ min   Color   1977

202 The Beast of Monsieur Racine. Fantasy, in animation, of a French squire who befriends a beast that not even the Academy of Science can classify—throwing all of Paris into an uproar. Adapted by Gene Deitch from the children's book by Tomi Ungerer.
Weston Woods   9 min   Color   1974

203 Ben and Me. Story of Amos, a poor church mouse, who becomes the worthy mentor of Benjamin Franklin. Instrumental in developing many of Franklin's inventions, Amos also helped him perform his most famous experiments. Their relationship even became part of the Declaration of Indpendence! Based on Robert Lawson's classic story. Animated. Director: Hamilton Luske.
Disney   21 min   Color   1953

204 Big Henry and the Polka Dot Kid. Based on a story by Canadian

writer Morley Callaghan, this film follows an orphan boy, who is adopted by his aunt and uncle. In saving the life of a blind old dog, he teaches his uncle that "being practical" is not the only thing in life. Produced by Linda Gottlieb and directed by Richard Marquand. The stars are Ned Beatty, Estelle Parsons, and Chris Barnes. Original title: *Luke Baldwin's Vow*.
Learning Corp. 33 min Color 1976

205 Blueberries for Sal. Uses pictures from Robert McCloskey's book to portray a story about the common needs of man and beast as symbolized in the winsome characters of a girl and a bear. Producer: Morton Schindel.
Weston Woods 9 min Color 1967

206 The Camel who Took a Walk. In the jungle lies a tiger, his presence concealed by the rich colors of the growth. But his plans to pounce upon the proud camel go awry when she suddenly changes her mind. Mysterious organ music lends suspense to this animated tale about a simple twist of fate. Written by Jack Tworkov. Illustrated by Roger Duvoisin.
Weston Woods 6 min Color 1957

207 The Case of the Cosmic Comic. The youthful character from Robert McCloskey's *Homer Price* story meets Super-duper, and reverses the usual idol/worshipper script by coming to the rescue of his hero. Adapted and directed in live-action photography by Mary Templeton.
Weston Woods 28 min Color 1976

208 The Case of the Elevator Duck. An imaginative young black boy, who lives in an urban housing project, decides to play detective. He gets his first "case" when he discovers a duck in the elevator and resolves to find the owner, which leads him into a series of unexpected exploits. Written and directed by Joan Silver; produced by Linda Gottlieb. Based on the children's book by Polly Berrien Berrends.
Learning Corp. 17 min Color 1974

209 The Cat and the Collector. An old man befriends a stray cat but their relationship is almost ruined when his pet instinctively kills a bird. Iconographically filmed and edited by Kristine Holm. Based on the picture-book by Linda Glovach. Producer: Morton Schindel.
Weston Woods 6 min Color 1975

210 The Cat in the Hat. This early Dr. Seuss classic comes to life in a freely adapted television version. Impulsive and imaginative, the cat romps through the house, dispelling boredom for a brother and sister on a rainy day—naturally only while mom is away. A DePatie-Freleng/CBS Production. Animated.
BFA Educ. Media 24½ min Color 1972

211 Caterpillar. This animated tale is about a boy and the caterpillar that dances to the tune he plays on his harmonica. Soon the boy and his pet are off on concert tours. Acclaim skyrockets them to fame and fortune. At Christmas the boy fills the house with gifts for his caterpillar but his pet has disappeared. He searches everywhere, to no avail. But one spring day, as he plays his harmonica, remembering the happy times, he sees a beautiful butterfly dancing to his music. Created by Zdenek Miler (Prague). From a story by Norman Corwin.
Learning Corp. 16 min Color 1971

212 Changes, Changes. This story about wooden blocks and dolls illustrates the meaning of change. As the events and situations change, so do the forms. The wood motif is extended to the musical score performed only on wooden instruments. From the picture-book written and illustrated by Pat Hutchins. Animated by Gene Deitch.
Weston Woods 6 min Color 1972

213 Charlie Needs a Cloak. Charlie is a shepherd who, in the springtime, decides to make himself a new cloak. He shears his sheep and fashions his garment from the wool. This animated film, paralleled by an Italian tarantella, follows the process of making wool into cloth. From the storybook written and illustrated by Tomie dePaola. Adapted and animated by Gene Deitch.
Weston Woods 8 min Color 1977

214 The Cow Who Fell in the Canal. The escapades of an adventurous cow are told in animated illustrations by Peter Spier, along with the music and sounds of Holland. Narrated by Owen Jordan. Produced by Cynthia Freitag for Morton Schindel. Based on the story by Phyllis Kasilovsky.
Weston Woods 8 min Color 1970

215 A Crack in the Pavement. Based on the book by Ruth Howell and Arline Strong, this animated story is about a city boy who took his environment for granted. Then a caterpillar showed him the value of the "life forces" around him. No narration. A Dan Bessie production.
Film Fair 8 min Color 9172

216 The Cricket in Times Square. This animated story is about a Connecticut insect whose violin-like music brings success to a failing newsstand in a New York subway station. The cricket and his friends—a mouse, a cat, and the newsboy—are based on the characters in George Selden's book. Produced by Chuck Jones Enterprises.
Xerox Films 26 min Color 1973

217 Crow Boy. After years of keeping to himself, a Japanese boy learns he has the gift of imitating bird sounds, and earns a new nickname.

Animation is based on author Taro Yashima's illustrations. Music composed by Frantisch Belfin. Direction by Cynthia Freitag. Producer: Cordelia Head.
Weston Woods 13 min Color 1971

218 Curious George Rides a Bike. And what mischief that bike and his curiosity get him into! In a dizzy series of adventures, the little monkey builds a navy of paper boats, lands in a traveling show as a performer, gets an ostrich into trouble, and rescues a runaway bear. Through it all, a musical score varies with the mood of each scene. Book written and illustrated by H.A. Rey. Produced in iconographic animation by Morton Schindel.
Weston Woods 10 min Color 1958

219 Curl up Small. An animated film from the book by Sandol Stoddard Warburg, this story is intended to help children to think about their place in the world. They hear the poetic instructions of all the mothers to their babies. The mother fish defines the physical world as water; the mother bird, as all air and wind and sky; and to the baby bear, the world is described as bigger and wider than he needs to know while he is little. They are told that the thing for babies to do is "curl up small" in the safe warm lap of mother. Produced by John Korty.
Sterling Educ. 7 min Color 1967

220 Delicious Inventions. This musical lesson in good manners has five children tour a very unusual production plant. It is an extract from the movie *Willy Wonka and the Chocolate Factory*, based on Roald Dahl's *Charlie and the Chocolate Fantasy Factory*. The cast includes Gene Wilder and Jack Albertson, who are directed by Mel Stuart. Produced for the Quaker Oats Company.
Films Inc. 15 min Color 1976

221 The Doughnuts. When the doughnut machine goes berserk and fills Uncle Ulysses' luncheonette with hundreds of doughnuts, Homer Price comes up with an ingenious solution. From the Robert McCloskey Book, *Homer Price*. Live-action production. Directed by Beth Sanford and Edward English.
Weston Woods 26 min Color 1963

222 Dragon in a Wagon. The narration of this film consists of rhymes full of nonsensical fun such as a whale in a jail and a dragon in a wagon. From a book by Janette Rainwater, illustrated by John M. Gilbert. Part of the *Imaginative Play* series.
Screenscope 5½ min Color 1971

223 The Dragon's Tears. This film tells the story of a dragon that lives in a mountain cave and terrifies the village below, except for one boy who invites him to his birthday party. Based on a story by the contem-

porary Japanese writer. Hirosuke Hamada. A Contemporary Films release. Animated by John Korty in cooperation with the National Broadcasting Company. Narrated by Robert Morse. Music by Teiji Ito.
McGraw-Hill 6 min Color 1962

224 Dragon Stew. King Chubby, Klaus the Cook, and a fire-breathing dragon are the main characters in this animated fantasy about a recipe contest. The surprise ending may motivate young readers. Based on the book by Tom McGowen. Illustrated by Tina S. Hyman.
BFA Educ. Media 13¼ min Color 1972

225 Drummer Hoff. In verse and music, this animation describes the building and firing of a magical cannon. Into a field come uniformed soldiers, each carrying part of the remarkable machine. Corporal Farrell brings the barrel, Sergeant Chowder brings the powder, but Drummer Hoff fires it off. As the story closes, the soldiers have gone, and the cannon again lies battered and silent in the field filled with flowers and birds. Story by Barbara Emberley. Figures are paper puppets patterned after Ed Emberley's woodcuts. Directed by Gene Deitch of Czechoslovakia.
Weston Woods 6 min Color 1969

226 Elisabeth and the Marsh Mystery. Based on Felice Holman's children's book, this is the story of a bright, inquisitive girl and her discovery of a mysterious bird in a marsh near her home. With the help of her father, best friend, and the curator of the local Natural History Museum, Elisabeth learns much about this exotic creature and experiences a greater appreciation for the beauty of wildlife. An Evergreen production by Daniel Smith and Gary Templeton.
Phoenix 21 min Color 1977

227 Emily — The Story of a Mouse. This children's story is about the one-year life span of a field rodent and her surviving children. Emily's story does not end with her death, for it is the return of all living things to the earth that enriches it so that new life can be provided for — including Emily's own children. Animation based on the artwork from Leo Lionni's storybook.
Benchmark 5 min Color 1975

228 The Erie Canal. Illustrations by author, Peter Spier, form the basis for a song-and-story study of this frontier waterway, the first cheap and fast route to the American frontier of 1825. Iconographically filmed and edited by John B. Schindel.
Weston Woods 7 min Color 1976

229 Evan's Corner. This animation tells the story of a young black who finds privacy in the ghetto by claiming a certain place for himself.

Developments lea.. ..m to realize, though, that people aren't meant to live in their own corners, but to step out and to help others. Based on the book by Elizabet. Starr Hill. Animated by Stephen Bosustow.
BFA Educ. Media 23 min Color 1969

230 Faces. "What you see depends on how you look at it," declares Max, the freckle-faced young star of this film. His questions, comments, and contortions demonstrate the importance of communication with others and sensitivity to the things all around. Originally distributed by Warren Schloat and Guidance Associates. Produced by coauthor George Ancona, from the picture book by him and Barbara Brenner.
Xerox Films 5¼ min Color 1973

231 Fawn Baby. Fawn-Baby learns from Doe-Mother how to live in the woods. From a story by Gladys B. Bond, illustrated by Robert J. Lee. From the *About Real Animals* series. Animated.
Screenscope 5½ min Color 1971

232 A Firefly Named Torchy. Is it easy to be different? Torchy dosen't think so because, instead of just twinkling, he flashes—much to the displeasure of his fellow fireflies and other forest friends. Try as he might, he just can't seem to tone down...until his trip to the big city persuades him not to change. Original story by Bernard Waber. Animated by Stephen Bosustow.
Xerox Films 7½ min Color 1972

233 The Five Chinese Brothers. Five identical-looking brothers outwit the townspeople and save themselves from a tragic demise. Story written by Claire Bishop; illustrated by Kurt Wiese. Animated in iconographic (i.e. artbased) style by Mort Schindel.
Weston Woods 10 min Color 1958

234 Flurina. Flurina, while on a visit to the Alps, saves a bird from an eagle. She tries to make the bird a pet, but finally realizes she must let it go to join its flock. Lonely, Flurina climbs up to a cave where she finds a valuable gem. Then her bird friend swoops down in a farewell salute, as she and her family leave for home. Based on a book by Selina Chonz and illustrated by Alois Cariget. Animated by filmmaker John Halas of Halas and Batchelor (England) for ACI Media.
Paramount 14 min Color 1969

235 The Fox Went out on a Chilly Night. A traditional folk song about a fox chase through the New England countryside in the autumn. Based on the children's book by illustrator Peter Spier, whose artwork provides the iconographic animation. Producer: Morton Schindel. Director: Cynthia Freitag.
Weston Woods 8 min Color 1969

236 Frederick. While other mice collect grain for winter, Frederick savors the summer and fall seasons in order to share them with his brothers during the winter. This picture book, as a film, won five animation awards for author Leo Lionni and coproducer Giulio Gianini. Originally released by Connecticut Films.
Distribution 16 6 min Color 1971

237 Gabrielle and Selena. This film recreates the story of two 8-year-olds. Selena, a black girl, and her best friend, Gabrielle, a white girl, are tired of being themselves. Thinking that life might be more interesting if each lived in the other's house, they decide to change places one day. A Stephen Bosustow Production based on the book by Peter Desbarats.
BFA Educ. Media 13 min Color 1972

238 George, the Gentle Giant. Lonely George, neither fierce nor frightening (even though he is a giant), looks for playmates. From a story by Adelaide Holl, illustrated by Frank Daniel. From the *Friends and Neighbors* series.
Screenscope 5½ min Color 1971

239 Georgie. Tells the story of Georgie, a friendly ghost who is forced to leave home and haunt a barn. Based on the picture-book by Robert Bright. Produced in iconographic (art-based) animation by Morton Schindel.
Weston Woods 6 min Color 1956

240 Georgie to the Rescue. An animated version of the book by Robert Bright. Georgie is a friendly ghost who lives in a house in the country inhabited by Herman the cat and Miss Olive the owl. One day they decide to visit the city. But there Miss Olive is captured and delivered to the zoo. Georgie and Herman go to the rescue. Georgie scares the nightwatchman while Herman steals the keys. Back at the hotel, Miss Olive perches on the flagstaff, while Georgie clanks the elevator up and down. Next day they all go home and take up their normal routine. Animated. Producer: Israel Berman.
Sterling Educ. 10 min Color 1971

241 Giants Come in Different Sizes. "Jolly Roger" Bradfield, writer and illustrator of children's books, leads a group of children to a cove where he reads one of his stories to them. In animations that reproduce the book's illustrations, he tells the story of the kingdom of Dingleburg whose inhabitants cultivate hamburger trees. Trouble starts when a vindictive magician sends a cloud to blot out the sun. The king's barber sends for giants, and the largest one sneezes the cloud away. An original song, sung by children, provides the musical background. Produced by Bradfield-Fleming for ACI Media.
Paramount 13 min Color 1970

242 The Giving Tree. A tree unselfishly offers itself to a boy for climb-ing, for shade, and for pleasure. As the boy grows up, he wants different things from the tree—money from its apples and lumber from its trunk and limbs. The boy's life takes him farther and farther from the tree—but old age brings their relationship full circle. Based on the book by Shel Silverstein. Produced by Nick Bosustow and Shel Silverstein. Directed and animated by Charlie O. Hayward. Music and narration by Shel Silverstein.
Bosustow 10 min Color 1973

243 Goggles. Peter finds a pair of motorcycle goggles without lenses. He and Archie set off with their treasure when they run into some big boys who demand the goggles. With the help of Peter's loyal dachshund, they all outwit the bullies. Written and illustrated by Ezra Jack Keats. Directed by Isa Wickenhagen. Iconographic.
Weston Woods 6 min Color 1974

244 Green Eggs and Ham. "Things are not always what they appear to be," or "Try it—you just might like it," is the message in this **animated** tale by Dr. Seuss. The story unfolds in cumulative rhyme as "Sam I Am" tries to share his "Green Eggs and Ham" with an unwilling acquaintance. Produced by DePatie-Freleng for CBS Television.
BFA Educ. Media 9 min Color 1974

245 Green Eyes. An appealing little kitten grows up in the country, seeing its changes season by season. From a story by A. Birnbaum, illustrated by the author. From the *About Real Animals* series. Animated.
Screenscope 5½ min Color 1971

246 The Happy Lion. The hero of this story lives in a quiet and friendly French village. But when its keeper leaves the cage open, the lion decides to take a walk. The townspeople panic ... all except young Fran-çois, who saves the day, the town, and the animal! Based on the story by Louis Fatio, with illustrations by Roger Duvoisin. Produced by Rembrandt Films.
Macmillan 7 min Color

247 The Happy Owls. In an old stone ruin live two owls that are happy all year long. One day, some quarreling barnyard birds send a peacock to ask the secret of the owls' happiness. The owls explain that observing the change of seasons makes them rejoice and brings them peace. But the fowls, not ready for such wisdom, only turn their backs and go on squab-bling. Animated from the artwork of author Celestino Piatti. Produced by Morton Schindel and William L. Snyder.
Weston Woods 7 min Color 1969

248 Harold and the Purple Crayon. One evening, a boy decides to

go for a walk in the moonlight. But there isn't any moon, so he takes his purple crayon and draws one. So begins another adventure of the diminutive wielder of the magic crayon. Written and illustrated by Crockett Johnson. Directed by David Piel. Animated.
Weston Woods 8 min Color 1970

249 Harold's Fairy Tale. Harold draws an enchanted garden, only to discover that nothing can grow there because of a giant witch. With the aid of his purple caryon, he defeats the witch and makes the garden bloom, but not before he encounters a variety of strange experiences. Written and illustrated by Crockett Johnson. Animated by Gene Deitch.
Weston Woods 8 min Color 1974

250 Hercules. Tells the story of a humanoid horse-drawn fire engine that became obsolete, only to become a hero and be enshrined in a museum. Iconographic (picture-based) animation is based on the illustrated storybook by Hardie Gramathy. Produced by Mort Schindel.
Weston Woods 11 min Color 1956

251 A Home Run for Love. Set in the 1940's, the story is about a fatherless white boy who learns about friendship and love by sharing his passion for baseball with an elderly black chef who works in his mother's inn. Adapted by Arthur Heinemann from Barbara Cohen's book *Thank You, Jackie Robinson*. Includes vintage footage of the Dodgers at Ebbets Field. Produced by Martin Tahse.
Time-Life 47 min Color and BW 1979

252 The Hound That Thought He Was a Raccoon. Rutherford Montgomery's light-hearted account of the friendship developed under unusual circumstances between a hound and a raccoon that grew up like brothers. Live-action photography. Comes in two parts on separate reels.
Disney 48 min Color 1962

253 Hush, Little Baby. Family life in 18th-century America is the environment of this folk lullaby, illustrated on wood in colonial nursery style. Based on the picture-book by Aliki, creator of the wood-cut artwork. Photographed and edited by Alexander Cochran. Producer: Morton Schindel.
Weston Woods 5 min Color 1976

254 I Am Freedom's Child. Based on the premise that good feelings about self are essential to social participation, the context of this film is concerned with the relations between social and personal objectives. It concludes with the statement, "As I learn to like the differences in me, I learn to like the differences in you." From the children's book by Bill Martin, Jr. Produced by Ben Norman.
Film Fair 5¼ min Color 1971

255 I Can Fly. A girl creates a make-believe world as she tries to fly like a bird and squirm like a worm. Based on a book by Ruth Krauss. From the "About Boys and Girls" series.
Screenscope 5½ min Color 1971

256 Icarus Montgolfier Wright. In this story written in 1962, author Ray Bradbury projected the year to be 1970. The occasion is the eve of a boy astronaut's blast-off to the moon. As he sleeps, the boy dreams of the pioneers of flight: Icarus, who could not resist flying too close to the sun; the Montgolfiers, two French brothers who built the first hot-air balloon; and the Wrights, whose experiments ushered in the era of flight. When morning comes, the boy astronaut gives himself a new name and a new goal. Illustrations by Joe Mugnaini. Produced by Format Films.
Pyramid 23 min Color 1963

257 If I Were... A boy imagines how it might be if he became different species of animals. From a story by Barbara Hazen. Illustrated by Lee Ames. From the *Imaginative Play* series.
Screenscope 5½ min Color 1971

258 In the Jungle There is Lots to Do. This animated film is based on a well-known children's book by Mauricio Gatti, published in Uruguay. It not only presents amusing characters, music, and lyrics but also encourages cooperation rather than competition as an educational experience for young viewers. Music composed and arranged by David de Launay.
Tricontinental 17 min Color 1978

259 Ira Sleeps Over. A boy is happy about being invited to stay overnight at a friend's house...until his sister brings up the question about bringing along his teddy bear. Should he brave it alone for the first time ever? Ira gets plenty of advice but eventually makes this important decision himself. Live-action. Produced by Andrew Sugerman. Adapted from Bernard Waber's book.
Phoenix 17 min Color 1977

260 Is That a Happy Hippopotamus? This reading by folk-singer John Davidson is intended to excite interest in the original children's picture-book by Sean Morrison. Art-work by Aliki. Produced by the Bank Street College of Education, New York.
McGraw-Hill 6 min Color 1967

261 I Wonder Why. Based on the book by Shirley Burden, this film is a photographic essay which visualizes the thoughts of a young black girl who likes the things other people like, but wonders why "people don't like me." A Robt. M. Rosenthal production.
McGraw-Hill 5 min B&W 1964

262 Jenny's Birthday Book. Tells the story of how a cat's friends help her celebrate her birthday. Based on the storybook of the same name by Esther Averill. The animation is iconographic, that is, based on the original picture-book illustrations. Produced by Mort Schindel.
Weston Woods   6 min   Color   1956

263 Joanjo: A Portuguese Tale. The story of a Portuguese boy whose male relatives are all fishermen. He longs to get away from a life centered on fish, and dreams of becoming a storekeeper, then Mayor, Governor, and finally King. But his ambitions lead to disaster, and he is glad to wake up and find himself safe and at home by the sea. The dream sequence is done in collage animation. The rest of the story is in live-action photography actually shot in Nazare, the village in the book by Jan Balet. Originally distributed by ACI Media.
Paramount   12 min   Color   1970

264 Jonathan and the Dragon. A boy manages to oust an unwanted dragon after the wisest men in the town fail to do so. From a story by Irwin Shapiro, illustrated by Tom Vroman. From the *Friends and Neighbors* series.
Screenscope   5½ min   Color   1971

265 "J.T.". This is Jane Wagner's television story about a Harlem boy who befriends a wounded cat. J.T. shelters the animal in a deserted building, feeds it, and nurses it back to health. When it later dies in a street accident, J.T. realizes that he's lost a friend but found himself. Produced in live-action for the CBS *Children's Hour* series.
Carousel   51 min   Color   1969

266 The Judge. The animation for this story uses the original artwork of the Caldecott Award book by Harve and Margot Zemach. It's about a skeptical judge who disregards—and is annihilated by—the catastrophe warnings of five people brought before him. From the *Famous Author/Illustrator Films* series.
Miller-Brody   7 min   Color   1976

267 Just Awful. Relates a tale of an incident common to nearly all children—a tumble in the school yard and a visit to the school nurse. This film, based on a book by Alma Marshak Whitney, also may be used to show how everyday experiences can be translated into interesting stories. Produced by Moreland-Latchford, Ltd. (Canada).
Paramount   8 min   Color   1973

268 Kangaroo and Kangaroo. A tale of two thrifty marsupials that saved all manner of things "just in case." Based on the story book by Kathy Braun.
Sterling Educ.   10 min   Color   1973

269 The King who Never Really Lived. Ferenc Mora's story is brought to life by the pioneer of Hungarian animated films, Istvan Imre. The king is disturbed by an impertinent fly. Upon his orders, the whole court chases the intruder: the majordomo with a ladder, the master of the hunt with a sling. At last the court jester teaches the angry king a lesson from an old proverb: "Brain is stronger than brawn."
Macmillan 12½ min Color 1961

270 Lafcadio, The Lion who Shot Back. This is the story of the cub that failed to make friends with hunters, then becomes the world's greatest marksman—only to realize he has lost his true identity. Black-and-white line animation is based on the drawings of storybook author Shel Silverstein.
Learning Corp. 22 min B&W 1978

271 The Large and Growly Bear. This is the children's story of the lovable beast that, try as he might, was incapable of frightening anyone else but himself. Animation is based on picture-book art by author Gertrude Crampton.
Screenscope 5½ min Color 1971

272 Lentil. Tells the story of a boy who couldn't whistle but who saved the day with his harmonica. Picture-book by Robert McCloskey. Produced by Mort Schindel in iconographic (camera-movement) animation.
Weston Woods 9 min Color 1957

273 Leopold, The See-Through Crumbpicker. This children's story, based on the picture book by James Flora, is about an invisible character and how he finally makes himself seen with the help of his friend Minerva. Produced by Mort Schindel in iconographic (simulated movement) animation.
Weston Woods 9 min Color 1971

274 A Letter to Amy. An iconographic (animated stills) treatment of the story of young Peter's special letter to Amy, climaxed by his joy as the last birthday guest arrives. Story by Ezra Jack Keats. Directed by Cynthia Freitag. Produced by Morton Schindel.
Weston Woods 7 min Color 1970

275 The Little Black Puppy. A boy's puppy is disliked by his family until it wins their approval and love as it grows up. From a story by Charlotte Zolotow, illustrated by Susan Perl. From the *About Boys and Girls* series.
Screenscope 5½ min Color 1971

276 Little Blue and Little Yellow. The award-winning children's book, fashioned into an animated film, has as main characters splotches of pure

color. When Little Blue and Little Yellow hug each other, they both become green and their parents don't know them. This makes them so sad, they cry blue and yellow tears, sort themselves out, and are reunited with their parents. For children, the story teaches a lesson on the basic laws of color. Produced by Leo Lionni, author of the picture-book.
McGraw Hill   10 min   Color   1961

277 Little Dog Lost. As Tim helps Jody look for his puppy, they visit many neighborhood stores. From a story by Adelaide Holl, illustrated by Harry Carter. From the *Friends and Neighbors* series.
Screenscope   5½ min   Color   1971

278 The Little Drummer Boy. Story of a young musician's gift on the occasion of the first Christmas. Based on the same story as the seasonal song of that name. Illustrations by author Ezra Jack Keats. Animated. Producer is Mort Schindel.
Weston Woods   7 min   Color   1971

279 The Little Engine that Could. This animated film is based on Watty Piper's children's classic that tells of the machine that pulled a trainload of toys to the children on the other side of the mountain. Useful for language arts activities, the film also teaches the values of positive thought.
Coronet   10 min   Color   1963

280 A Little Girl and a Gunny Wolf. This story, narrated by black children in their own idiom, is illustrated by their drawings which have been animated. The Little Girl is warned by her mother not to go into the forest, but she goes anyway. The Gunny Wolf, an unreal animal, captures her, but she soothes him to sleep with a nonsense song, then runs safely home where she promises never to go into the forest again. Story based on the book, *The Gunniwolf,* by Wilhelmina Harper. Produced by Steve and Marion Klein for ACI Media.
Paramount   6 min   Color   1971

281 Little Pig. Upon her mother's death, a Chinese girl is left to care for her infant brother. Set in the city of Hong Kong, this film shows how they travel to an unknown aunt, only to discover that her family is struggling to make ends meet. The girl is driven to theft but, through the efforts of an understanding Confucian scribe, she is saved from disgrace and learns a valuable lesson. Original story by Sylvia Sherry. Coproduction with the BBC.
Learning Corp.   27 min   Color   1976

282 The Little Red Lighthouse. Tells the story of a lighthouse that learns it is still useful even if a more powerful light has been installed on the great bridge. From the story by Hildegarde Swift. Illustrations by Lynd

Ward. Photographed in iconographic (artwork-based) animation. Produced by Morton Schindel.
Weston Woods 9 min Color 1955

283 The Littlest Angel. In adapting Charles Tazewell's Christmas story for the screen, words were omitted in some sentences where the picture made the meaning clear. Otherwise, this film is a straightforward translation of the story into motion-picture. The cartoon character of the Littlest Angel was conceived and executed by Hugh Harmon. The original score for the film was composed and conducted by Seymour Saxon.
Coronet 13½ min Color 1950

284 Little Tim and the Brave Sea Captain. Tim, a stowaway boy, becomes the ocean steamer's mascot. During a storm, the ship strikes a rock, and Tim—along with his skipper—bravely awaits the end but they are rescued just in time. Iconographically filmed and edited by Dan Smith. From the picture-book by Edward Ardizzone. Producer: Morton Schindel.
Weston Woods 11 min Color 1976

285 The Lorax. The witty and wise words of "Dr. Seuss" spin a fanciful tale of unusual characters with a serious message: Clean up the environment—before it's too late! Animated for CBS Television by DePatie-Freleng Productions.
BFA Educ. Media 24¾ min Color 1972

286 Luke was There. A boy runs away from his disillusioning experiences with the adult world, until he learns the meaning of trust from a perceptive black counselor. Based on the award-winning book by Eleanor Clymer. From the *Learning to Be Human* series.
Learning Corp. 32 min Color 1976

287 Madeline. Humorist-illustrator, Ludwig Bemelmans, created the character of Madeline, a French schoolgirl. Here is an animated version of one of his stories in verse. The film follows Madeline while at a Parisian girls' school, and culminates in her trip to the hospital to have her appendix removed—an experience that arouses the envy of her classmates. Animator: Stephen Bosustow. Previously distributed by Learning Corp. of America.
Bosustow 7 min Color 1952

288 Madeline and the Bad Hat. Madeline, the picture-book character, calls her friend Pepito a "Bad Hat" because he traps frogs, birds, bats, and even cats. He learns his lesson, though, and delights Madeline by liberating his menagerie. Animated. Based on the book by Ludwig Bemelmans.
Macmillan 8 min Color 1966

289 Madeline and the Gypsy. When our cartoon heroine is stranded, with her friend Pepito, among carnival gypsies, they make the most of it, visiting some of the most exciting places in France. In spite of the maneuvers of the Gypsy Mamma, the school principal finally "rescues" her students. Based on Ludwig Bemelmans' picture-book.
Macmillan   7 min   Color   1966

290 Madeline's Rescue. The animation character goes too far in her teasing and falls in the river. Genevieve the dog rescues Madeline and is adopted by her classmates. The school's trustees disapprove, Genevieve is banished, but somehow all ends happily. Based on the book by Ludwig Bemelmans.
Macmillan   7 min   Color   1966

291 Make Way for Ducklings. The hazards of city living—for a family of ducks, that is—are chronicled in the illustrations of author Robert McCloskey. Iconographic animation of the storybook artwork shows how the busy Mallard family took up residence in Boston's Public Garden. Produced by Morton Schindel.
Weston Woods   11 min   Color   1955

292 Mandy's Grandmother. When girl meets grandma from England, they don't hit it off right away. But, after a series of misunderstandings and unintended hurt feelings, they both learn to accept and love one another for what they are. Based on the children's book by Liesel Moak Skorpen. Producer-Director: Andrew Sugerman.
Phoenix   30 min   Color   1978

293   The Marvelous March of Jean François. A chronicle, in animation, of a drummer boy in Napoleon's "Grande Armée." The lad's ingenuity and steadfastness take him around the world, through the perils of war and the weather, and then back to his homeland of France again. Animated from the picture-book of John Raymond.
Sterling Educ.   18 min   Color   1970

294 Mike Mulligan and his Steam Shovel. Nearly a useless cast-off, Mike Mulligan's steam shovel finds an exciting job to do and endears itself again to the citizens of Popperville. From the story by Virginia Lee Burton. Produced in iconographic (still-picture) animation by Mort Schindel.
Weston Woods   11 min   Color   1958

295 Millions of Cats. This story, about an old man and old woman in search of a pet cat, deals with the issue of overpopulation as well as the quality of life. Based on the illustrated storybook by Wanda Gag. Produced in iconographic (still-picture) animation by Mort Schindel.
Weston Woods   10 min   B&W   1955

296 Milo's Journey. Fantasy of a boy's trip to the land of the Doldrums. There he meets creatures called Lethargians who tell him it's illegal to think or even to laugh. From the movie, *The Phantom Tollbooth*, based on the story by Norton Juster. Voices by Mel Blanc and Hans Conreid. Director: Chuck Jones. An MGM production.
Films Inc.   15 min   Color   1976

297 Miss Nelson is Missing. Miss Nelson is an excellent teacher but her class refuses to listen to her. One day she mysteriously fails to appear and the poisonous "Miss Swamp" takes over. The kids realize how much they like Miss Nelson and begin a search for her. Having taught her students an important lesson Miss Nelson (Alias Miss Swamp) reappears as herself to a suddenly appreciative class. Based on the book by Harry Allard. Produced in animation.
Learning Corp.   15 min   Color   1979

298 Miss Twiggley's Tree. The story concerns a woman who lives in a house in a tall oak tree. Although she is friendly, the townfolk are upset by her unusual lifestyle, and try to get rid of her. However, in the end, an important lesson is learned: it's a mistake to judge people because they are different. From the book written and illustrated by Dorothea Warren Fox.
Sterling Educ.   14 min   Color   1972

299 More About Paddington (Film #1). Includes three animations of chapters from *More About Paddington* by Michael Bond. Individual chapter-film titles are: "A Family Group," "A Spot of Decorating," and "Paddington Turns Detective." Films are available separately, upon request. Produced by Film Fair of London.
Film Fair   16½ min   Color   1977

300 More About Paddington (Film #2). Incorporates three animated films, each correlating with a separate chapter from *More About Paddington* by Michael Bond. The chapter-movie titles are: "Trouble at Number Thirty-Two," "Paddington and the Christmas Shopping," and "Christmas." Films are available separately, or on one reel. Producer: Film Fair of London.
Film Fair   16½ min   Color   1977

301 Most Marvelous Cat. Johann, the German cat, finds out that his music-teacher owner, Herr Professor, hasn't enough money to pay the rent. In an all-out effort to help, Johann's money-hunting efforts result in a series of jobs as an actor, a duster, then a mouse catcher, and finally as a symphony orchestra conductor. Animated. Produced by Howard Beckerman. From the children's storybook by Gloria Wiener.
Xerox Films   10½ min   Color   1973

302 Mowgli's Brothers. This is Kipling's tale of an infant boy who is rescued and raised by wolves in the jungles of India. This animated film about love, justice, and loyalty features the voices of Roddy McDowall and June Foray as the main characters. **Produced by Chuck Jones.**
Xerox Films   26 min   Color   1976

303 Munro. A four-year old boy is drafted into the army but neither sergeant, colonel, psychiatrist, nor chaplain can accept the fact that a mistake has been made. (His predicament is all too familiar to us adults!) Animation is based on Jules Feiffer's cartoon art. Produced by William L. Snyder.
Macmillan   9 min   Color   1960

304 My Dog is Lost. This story rendition by singer Harry Belafonte is designed to encourage reading of the story of Juanito, a Puerto Rican boy in New York. Produced by the Communications Laboratory of the Bank Street College of Education (New York). Based on the picture book by Ezra Jack Keats.
McGraw-Hill   10 min   Color   1966

305 My Grandson Lew. It is late at night, but Lew is wide awake, thinking about his grandfather. He goes to his mother and tells her that he misses Grandpa. She listens as Lew describes Grandpa's beard...his blue eyes...a night by the fire...and a visit to the museum. When he finishes, his mother finally tells Lew that Grandpa will not come to visit again; "You never asked, so I never told you. Grandpa died." Dramatization directed by Donald MacDonald. It is based on the book by Charlotte Zolotow.
Barr Films   13 min   Color   1976

306 My Mother is the Most Beautiful Woman in the World: A Ukrainian Folktale.   It is harvest time, and villagers for miles around are bringing in the wheat. But Varya is lost. She cannot find her mother. People ask, "What does your mother look like?" She answers, "My mother is the most beautiful woman in the world." When mother is finally found, she proves to be the most beautiful woman in the world—if only, perhaps, in the eyes of her daughter. A Stephen Bousustow animation from the book by Becky Reyher and Ruth Gannett.
BFA Educ. Media   9 min   Color   1968

307 The Neatos and the Litterbugs. Porkey has won a prize but he can't find the ticket to claim it. The story involves the Neato family in cleaning up the littered community to find the ticket. The Neatos go home to tell Mother Porcupine of their failure to find the ticket, but Mother surprises them. Study-guide is available. Based on the Little Golden Book of the same name by Norah Smaridge. Produced by Sandler Films. Animated.
Screenscope   7 min   Color   1974

308 Night's Nice. Verse, image, and sound – all three combine here to describe a child's feelings about the discovery of the special world of afterdark: the stars, yellow-eyed cats, city lights, and – finally – sleep. Based on the picture-book by Barbara and Ed Emberley.
Sterling Educ. 10 min Color 1971

309 Nobi and the Slave Traders – An African Legend. Adapted from a book by Ludwig Renn, this is the story of young Nobi who plays happily with jungle animals until white slave traders attack his village. The sound track has no narration. Actions of the animated puppets are supplemented by audio effects and African rhythms. Produced by DEFA Studio for Animated Films.
Encyc. Brit. 30 min Color 1970

310 Norman the Doorman. Norman is a mouse with more talent than most other museum doormen. In his spare time, he creates a mobile sculpture out of mouse-traps, and wins a prize from the very museum where he works. Author Don Freeman's illustrations are animated by Cynthia Freitag. Music by Josef Ceremuga.
Weston Woods 15 min Color 1971

311 No Talking. Lester, unable to say a word, still manages to buy a birthday present for his mother. From a story by Louise M. Foley, illustrated by William Pappas. From the *About Boys and Girls* series.
Screenscope 5½ min Color 1971

312 The Odds and Ends Playground. Danny, his friends, and the people of the neighborhood create a playground from a littered vacant lot. From a story by Norah Smaridge, illustrated by Pat Porter. From the *About Boys and Girls* series.
Screenscope 5½ min Color 1971

313 Once There Were Bluebirds. Animated art and rhymed narration show how the natural beauty of nature can fall prey to the greed of business and industry. The closing scene consists of a spatial view of earth – and the distant sound of coughing. Produced by Dick Van Benthem. Based on the book by Bill Martin, Jr.
Film Fair 5 min Color 1972

314 One Kitten for Kim. Based on the book by Adelaide Holl, the film is about a boy who owns seven kittens but can only keep one and must give the other six away. Kim does what he is told except that people give him other animals in return for the kittens! Produced by Moreland-Latchford, Ltd. (Canada).
Paramount 10 min Color 1971

315 One Monday Morning. A boy imagines that the King, Queen, lit-

tle prince, a knight, a royal guard, cook, barber, jester, and dog come to visit him on Monday and throughout the week. But he isn't home to receive his important visitors! Animation based on the picture-book by Uri Shulevitz, the coproducer along with Tom Spain.
Weston Woods   10 min   Color   1972

316   Paddington at Large. The two films titles within this reel are based on *Paddington at Large* by Michael Bond: "Paddington Hits the Jackpot" and "A Sticky Time." Both are available individually for purchase or rental. Animated by Film Fair of London, England.
Film Fair   11 min   Color   1977

317   Paddington at Work. This is an animation of Chapter 13, "Too Much Off the Top," from Michael Bond's storybook, *Paddington at Work*. Produced by Film Fair of London, England.
Film Fair   5½ min   Color   1977

318   Paddington Bear. This is a reel based on Michael Bond's animal character. It consists of these two animated stories: "Mr. Curry Takes a Bath" and "Fortune Telling." Either film is available for separate rental or purchase. Producer: Film Fair, London (England).
Film Fair   11 min   Color   1977

319   Paddington Goes to Town. Consists of two animated chapters from *Paddington Goes to Town* by Michael Bond. The film titles are: "Paddington Hits Out" and "A Visit to the Hospital." Either film is available for individual rental or purchase. Producers: Film Fair, London.
Film Fair   11 min   Color   1977

320   Paddington Helps Out. This is one of the longer reels from the series based on Michael Bond's *Paddington Helps Out*. The following animations are all available separately, upon request: "Paddington Makes a Bid," "Do-It-Yourself," "Something Nasty in the Kitchen," and "Trouble in the Launderette." Produced in animation by Film Fair, London.
Film Fair   22 min   Color   1977

321   Paddington Marches On. The following four films are animated chapters from Michael Bond's *Paddington Marches On*: "Paddington and the Cold Snap," "Paddington Makes a Clean Sweep," "Mr. Gruber's Mystery Tour," and "An Unexpected Party." These titles are available separately, if so requested. Produced by Film Fair, London.
Film Fair   22 min   Color   1977

322   Paddington on Top. This animation parallels Chapter 2 from *Paddington on Top*, a children's book by Michael Bond. The title of Chapter 2, shown on this film, is "Paddington Cleans Up." Produced by Film

Fair of London, England.
Film Fair 5½ min Color 1977

323 Paddington Takes the Air. Consists of animated versions of two chapters from *Paddington Takes the Air* by Michael Bond. The film-chapter titles are: "A Visit to the Dentist" and "Paddington Recommended." Both titles are available separately for rental or purchase. Producer: Film Fair, London.
Film Fair 11 min Color 1977

324 Paddle to the Sea. A Children's odyssey—the live-action journey of a hand-carved toy canoe from Canada's northern forest, down the length of the St. Lawrence river, all the way to the ocean. From a story of the same name by Holling C. Holling. Produced by William Mason. Originally distributed by McGraw-Hill.
Nat. Film Bd. 28 min Color 1966

325 Pancho. Story of a Mexican boy who manages to rope a bull that has been terrorizing his village. Based on the illustrated storybook by Berta and Elmer Hader. Animation is iconographic (based on the book's still pictures). Produced by Mort Schindel.
Weston Woods 6 min Color 1960

326 Patrick. Our main character sets out for the town marketplace, looking for a fiddle. He buys one from a junkman and, with his new-found sound, fills the countryside with color and movement. This non-verbal animated treatment of Quentin Blake's story symbolizes the vitalizing effect of music on the human spirit. Produced by Mort Schindel.
Weston Woods 7 min Color 1973

327 Pear-Shaped Hill. Bill and Jill see many things as each climbs an opposite side of the hill, and then meet at the top. From a story by Irving A. Leitner, illustrated by Bernice Myers. From the *Friends and Neighbors* series.
Screenscope 5½ min Color 1971

328 The Peasant's Pea Patch. A Russian farmer plants a patch of peas that grow wondrously well until hungry cranes devastate the crop. The farmer, to capture the birds, plans to lure them with vodka and honey. The cranes strike back, abduct the farmer, and dump him into a freezing pond. Then our hero meets a bear that drags him to the upper reaches of a tree. The folk tale ends in a state of serio-comic disaster. From the story by Guy Daniels. Animator: Steve Bosustow.
Xerox Films 7½ min Color 1973

329 Peter's Chair. Peter, fed up with boyhood's trials, decides to run

away, taking along his dog and his favorite chair. When he realizes he can no longer fit in the old seat, he learns something about growing up. Animated (from still pictures) by Cynthia Freitag. Producer: Morton Schindel. From the story book by Ezra Jack Keats.
Weston Woods 6 min Color 1967

330 Petunia. Petunia the goose finds something strange: a book! She remembers that Mr. Pumpkin once said, "Who owns books, and loves them, is wise." So, carrying the book under her wing, Petunia goes around dispensing advice. When she tells friends that a box labeled FIRECRACKERS is full of candy, the explosion that follows injures her friends and demolishes her pride. The book is blown open and, for the first time, Petunia sees the pages — pages she can't read. So she sets about learning to read, knowing that only then can she gain wisdom. Animated by Kathleen Houston. Produced by A-V Aids, New Zealand. Original story by Roger Duvoisin.
Weston Woods 19 min Color 1971

331 A Pickle for a Nickel. A man who likes quiet owns a parrot that a little boy teaches to talk. From a story by Lilian Moore, illustrated by Susan Perl. From the *About Real Animals* series. Animated.
Screenscope 5½ min Color 1971

332 A Picture for Harold's Room. Harold needs a picture for his room, so he decides to draw one. Stepping inside, he becomes a giant, towering over village and mountains. Then, as he walks beside the railroad tracks he placed along the way, he sees that he is smaller than the daisy he has just drawn. How will he get back to his normal size? The solution will make sense to Harold fans. Written and illustrated by Crockett Johnson. Animated by Gene Deitch.
Weston Woods 6 min Color 1971

333 The Poky Little Puppy. The story of a tardy canine whose lateness used to assure him extra dessert...until Mother Dog got wise and surprised him in two different ways. A study-guide is available. Based on the Little Golden Book by Janette Lowery. Animated. Produced by Sandler Films.
Screenscope 7 min Color 1974

334 Pushmi-Pullyu. This is an excerpt from the 20th Century-Fox musical, *Dr. Dolittle,* based on the story by Hugh Lofting. In this segment, the lead character (played by Rex Harrison) makes friends with that rare

two-headed animal, the "pushmi-pullyu." Directed by Richard Fleischer.
Films Inc. 11 min. Color 1976

335 Rabbit Hill. Based on Robert Lawson's book, this is a story about a group of different animals living together at the Hill. Since the old owners left, Rabbit Hill has been run down. When the animals hear that a new family is moving in, they wonder what it will mean to their lives. Produced with real animals from the Stamford, Conn. Zoo. Narrated by Burl Ives. From the Children's Theatre by NBC-TV.
McGraw-Hill 53 min Color 1968

336 Reach Out. The book by Bill Martin, Jr., that inspired this children's film explores the importance of opening our minds to new sights, new sounds, and new people as a way of counteracting the tendency to settle for the routine and the familiar. A Ben Norman production.
Film Fair 5¼ min Color 1971

337 The Red Carpet. Tells the story of a carpet that ran away to greet the Duke of Sultana. Story by Rex Parkin. Produced by Morton Schindel in iconographic (still-picture) animation.
Weston Woods 9 min Color 1955

338 Rikki-Tikki-Tavi. For us Westerners, a mongoose is not a typical household pet. But, for a British famliy in Edwardian India, it is because it's the natural enemy of the deadly cobra. Rikki saves the family from that villain snake and becomes more than a pet—a hero! Narrated by Orson Welles. Animation by Chuck Jones Productions.
Xerox Films 26 min Color 1976

339 Rosie's Walk. What Rosie doesn't know (and the illustrations reveal) is that a fox stalks close behind the proud little hen. To the tune of "Turkey in the Straw," Rosie struts across the barnyard, keeping her country cool, unwittingly leading the fox into one disaster after another. Animated. Based on the story written and illustrated by Pat Hutchins. Animation directed by Gene Deitch for Kratky Film (Prague).
Weston Woods 5 min Color 1970

340 Runt of the Litter. This is the story of a girl, a piglet, and a spider. It's an excerpt from the Paramount picture based on *Charlotte's Web* by E.B. White. Animation by Hanna-Barbera. Voices: Debbie Reynolds, Paul Lynde, and Agnes Moorehead. Directed for Paramount Pictures by Charles Nichol and Iwao Takamoto.
Films Inc. 12 minutes Color 1976

341 Sam, Bangs & Moonshine. This adaptation of Evaline Ness's story

is about a young fisherman's daughter Samantha (Sam for short) and her habit of pretending – her father calls it "moonshine." Sam is forever going off to secret worlds and talking to her faithful cat, Bangs. Sam has a devoted friend, Thomas, who believes every word she tells him. One day Thomas and Bangs are caught in a storm, all because of Sam's make-believe stories. Luckily, Sam's father rescues Thomas, and Bangs returns home unharmed. In the end, Sam learns the difference between bad moonshine and good moonshine. Producer: Robert Johnson.
BFA Educ. Media   15 min   Color   1977

342 The Seven Wishes of Joanna Peabody. Butterfly McQueen, who acted her way to immortality as Prissy in *Gone with the Wind*, stars in this adaptation of Genevieve Gray's book. It's about an urban black family and some strange vibrations emanating from their television set. Butterfly plays a video-age fairy godmother who tunes into young Joanna Peabody's home right in the middle of "Let's Make a Deal" and makes an offer of her own: Joanna has been chosen the lucky recipient of seven wishes. It takes a few choices before Joanna realizes the trouble a person can get into when she only thinks of herself.
Learn. Corp.   29 min   Color   1978

343 The Smallest Elephant in the World. Implying that the world has a place for anyone or anything regardless of size, this children's story is about an elephant no bigger than a cat. Animated. From the story by Alvin Tresselt. Produced by the National Broadcasting Company.
Sterling Educ.   6 min   Color   1966

344 Smile for Auntie . The storybook character, created and illustrated by Diane Peterson, represents the universally familiar relative who's forever trying to force a smile from children. Adapted for animation by Gene Deitch. Produced by Morton Schindel.
Weston Woods   5 min   Color   1979

345 The Sneetches. Star-Belly Sneetches are no better or worse than Plain-Belly Sneetches, and Sylvester McMonkey McBean's mechanical machine helps to prove this point, after he's turned a tidy profit at the expense of all of the Sneetches. In true Dr. Seuss style, this cartoon subtly informs children that differences are only relative and, in essence, really don't matter. A DePatie-Freleng Production for the CBS Television network.
BFA Educ. Media   13¼ min   Color   1974

346 The Snowy Day. Based on the 1963 Caldecott Award picture-book by Ezra Jack Keats, this animation is an interpretation of a city boy's discovery of the delights of winter weather. Narrated by Jane Harvey. Produced by Morton Schindel and Mal Wittman.
Weston Woods   6 min   Color   1964

347 Soup and Me. Adapted from the children's stories by Robert Newton Peck, this is a day in the life of young Rob and his year-older friend Soup, who gets them in lots of trouble. From the ABC "Weekend Special" series.
ABC Media 24 min Color 1978

348 Squares Are Not Bad. By getting all mixed up unintentionally, geometric shapes learn that differences in appearances make no difference at all. From a story by Violet Salazar, illustrated by Harlow Rockwell. From the *Imaginative Play* series.
Screenscope 5½ min Color 1971

349 The Stolen Necklace. A traditional story from India, retold in animation. A princess owns a necklace of pearls. While she is bathing in a pool in her garden, one of the monkeys in the trees there steals the necklace. Which monkey is the thief? The gardener thinks up a way to trick the thief. All ends happily, with the necklace restored, the gardener rewarded, and the monkey unrepentant. A William Clairborne film for ACI Media. Based on the book by Anne Rockwell.
Paramount 8 min Color 1971

350 Stone Soup. An old French folk tale reveals a trick used by three soldiers to gain food and lodging from selfish peasants. Drawings present a panorama of village life during Napoleon's time. Iconographic animation based on Marcia Brown's picture-book of the same name. Produced by Mort Schindel.
Weston Woods 11 min Color 1955

351 The Story About Ping. The story of a poor little Chinese duck that's afraid of being spanked, his narrow escapes, and his delight in his safe homecoming. Story by Marjorie Flack. Produced by Mort Schindel in iconographic (that is, camera-manipulated) animation.
Weston Woods 10 min Color 1955

352 Storymaker. Follows author-illustrator Don Freeman as he creates the children's picture book, *Inspector Peckit*. Shows how a new story and artwork are devised when the editor turns down the original manuscript.
Churchill 14 min Color 1972

353 Strega Nonna. In a town in Italy, the townspeople seek wise old Strega Nonna—"Grandmother Witch"—to cure headaches, secure husbands, and banish warts. Among her secrets is the trick of summoning pasta from her enchanted pot with merely a song. One who is enchanted is her helper, Big Anthony. After eavesdropping on her witchery, he spreads the news to others.But when they laugh at him, Big Anthony unleashes a torrent of pasta threatening to engulf the town. Strega Nonna's reaction? "The punishment must fit the crime!" Written and

illustrated by Tomie de Paola. Music by Francesco Belfino. Animated by Gene Deitch.
Weston Woods   9 min   Color   1978

354 Stuart Little. The subject of this fantasy by E.B. White is a five-inch-tall mouse that lives an otherwise "normal" human life in New York. Johnny Carson's narration explains the problem of being the smallest "person" in the nation's biggest city. Produced by the NBC Children's Theatre.
McGraw-Hill   52 min   Color   1968

355   Sunshine. This is the tale of a landlord who won't rent to people with babies, pets, or noisy hobbies. He thinks he's found the perfect tenant in Miss Moore, a kindly old lady. Instead he meets his match, but all ends on a happy note. From the story and illustrations by Ludwig Bemelmans. Produced by Rembrandt Films.
Macmillan   10 min   Color

356 The Superlative Horse. Based on Jean Merrill's children's story, this tale from ancient China is about a powerful ruler who loved horses. When the position of chief groom must be filled, he gives the aspirant for the job, Han Kan, an important task: he must find a "superlative horse" as a test of his ability. Han Kan's choice is an unusual one and astonishes everyone by being exactly right. Moral: we should not judge things, animals, or even people by their appearances, but by their inner qualities. Directed by Michael Sheppard. Produced by Urs Furrer.
Phoenix   36 min   Color   1975

357 Swimmy. This animated film is Leo Lionni's interpretation of his original story about the small fish, Swimmy, that outwits a hungry tuna and leads the other fish in exploring the underwater world. A fable about cooperation and ecology. Produced by Leo Lionni and Giulio Gianini. Previously distributed by Connecticut Films.
Distribution 16   6 min   *Color*   *1969*

358 Talk to the Animals. In this musical excerpt from the 20th Century-Fox film, a doctor realizes he feels more comfortable around animals than people. Based on the book *The Story of Dr. Dolittle* by Hugh Lofting. Cast includes Rex Harrison and Anthony Newley. Directed for 20th Century-Fox by Richard Fleischer.
Films Inc.   10 min   Color   1976

359 The Tawny Scrawny Lion. There was once a lion that, because it was always hungry, chased animals every day so that it could get enough to eat. The animals chose a little rabbit to talk with the lion. The clever rabbit found a special way to treat the lion, thus saving itself and the other animals as well. And, best of all, the lion was satisfied and happy.

Animated. Study guide available. Based on the storybook by Kathryn Jackson. Produced by Sandler Films.
Screenscope 7 min Color 1974

360 The Thinking Box. Sidney Poitier reads the story of a child who prefers to think about "important" things like dust, colors, and fruit instead of such mundane activities as waking up early, washing, and brushing teeth. Original picture-book by Sandol Stoddard Warburg. Film produced by the Bank Street College of Education in New York.
McGraw-Hill 10 min Color 1968

361 The Three Robbers. Once upon a time there were three robbers. They went around under large black capes and tall black hats. With a blunderbuss, pepper-blower, and a huge red axe, they terrified the countryside until they met a girl named Tiffany. Under her golden charm the robbers decide to turn their stolen gold to good use, and all ends happily. From the storybook by Tomi Ungerer. Artwork animated by Gene Deitch.
Weston Woods 6 min Color 1972

362 Too Many Bozos. A boy tries many different pets before he finds just the right one. From a story by Lilian Moore, illustrated by Susan Perl. From the *About Real Animals* series. Animated.
Screenscope 5½ min Color 1971

363 The Velveteen Rabbit. This novella, by Margery Williams, is intended for youngsters between kindergarten and fourth grade. It's the live-action story of a boy who, because of possible scarlet-fever contagion, has to get rid of his stuffed pet. The ending is happy, though, when his discarded doll-bunny returns as a real live one. Produced by Leonard S. Berman.
LSB Productions 19 min Color 1974

364 Walter the Lazy Mouse. An animated version of Marjorie Flack's book. Walter is a member of a large family. He oversleeps and is late for everything. He gets the wrong answers in class because he arrives too late to understand the lesson. One day he comes home to find that his family has moved, so used to his absence that they forgot him. He learns to look after himself and to play with others. In the fall, with the help of a turtle, he finds his family, attends to his schoolwork, and wins a prize. Produced by Viking Films.
Sterling Educ. 10 min Color 1972

365 What If? Droll, impossible situations are resolved in surprisingly plausible ways. From a story by Robert Pierce, illustrated by the author. From the *Imaginative Play* series.
Screenscope 5½ min Color 1971

366 What Kind of Feet Does a Bear Have? This reading by actor James Garner is designed to introduce young viewers to examples of homonyms, idioms, and similes. From the *Reading Incentive Film Series*, produced by the Bank Street College of Education in New York. Based on the story by Judith Rossner.
McGraw-Hill   5 min   Color   1967

367 Where the Wild Things Are. This animated fantasy, based on the Caldecott Award Winner by Maurice Sendak, takes place in a child's imaginary world where, in an ordinary bedroom, forests sprout, a ship floats by, and mysterious creatures caper about. Images are matched by equally bizarre sounds. Adapted by Gene Deitch. Producer: Morton Schindel.
Weston Woods   8 min   Color   1973

368 Whistle for Willie. When a boy wants to be able to whistle for his dog, he tries very hard to learn. The story of his trying is told in such simple words and pictures that learning to whistle seems to be the happiest thing any boy could do. Animation based on the book by Ezra Jack Keats.
Weston Woods   6 min   Color   1965

369 Wilbur's Story. Pig's friends—girl, spider, and rat—help save him from the sausage-maker. From the Paramount picture of *Charlotte's Web* by E.B. White. Voices are Paul Lynde, Debbie Reynolds, and Agnes Moorehead. Animation by the Hanna-Barbera Studios for release by Paramount.
Films Inc.   15 min.   Color   1976

370 The Winter of the Witch. Nicki and his mother get acquainted with the not-so-wicked witch, and learn her recipe for "happiness pancakes." The film offers human observations on the world we live in and about basic values. Based on *The Old Black Witch* by Harry and Wendy Devlin. Live-action. Produced by *Parents Magazine*.
Learning Corp.   22 min   Color   1960

371 The World's Greatest Freak Show. Alastair Phlug wants to be rich and famous. But, alas, he's just an incompetent magician. One day, Phlug offers to bring his amazing feats to a country called Tizuvthee. Back comes the reply, "Bring your amazing performing freaks." He scouts up three impoverished persons who suit his definition of "freaks." Off they sail to Tizuvthee where Alastair Phlug himself turns out to be the biggest, unhappiest freak of all. Narrated by Hans Conried. From the story by Ellen Raskin. Animator: Steve Bosustow.
Xerox Films   11 min   Color   1973

372 Yankee Doodle. This picture-book story by Steven Kellogg is about a colonial boy who wanders into British territory but is rescued by American soldiers—to the tune and verse of the Yankee Doodle song. Iconographically filmed and edited by Alexander Cochran. Produced by Isa Wickenhagen.
Weston Woods 10 min Color 1976

373 Zachary Zween. This is the Americanized version of Mabel Watts' British book, *The Story of Zachary Zween*, about a boy whose initials keep him last in line of a field-trip to Manhattan. He becomes lost in the process and, to the envy of his school-mates, gets a personalized police-car tour of the city's sights. Live-action photography; minimal dialogue.
Sterling Educ. 12 min Color 1972

374 The Zax. A North-Going Zax and a South-Going Zax meet midway on their journey across a wasteland. Neither is willing to step aside for the other. While the rest of the world ignores them, their stubbornness is reduced to its most absurd conclusion. Story by Dr. Seuss. A DePatie-Freleng Production for CBS. Cartoon animation.
BFA Educ. Media 5 min Color 1974

375 Zlateh the Goat. This live-action version of a folktale by the great Yiddish author, Isaac Beshevis Singer, is about village life in pre-war Poland. The adventures that befall Aaron and his pet on their way to the butcher's portray the interdependence of man and nature. This reliance on one another ultimately saves their lives. Film adaptation by Gene Deitch. Produced by Morton Schindel.
Weston Woods 20 min Color 1973

Drama

Of all the writings converted to film, drama is the most natural. Proof: the large number of films listed here. Theatre, by its very nature, demands actualization. Ironically, though, because of the beauty or strength of theatrical language, we often become content with words alone. Then, after prolonged exposure to such verbal riches, we tend to overlook the characters and events the playwright was trying to stage in the first place. Luckily for latter-day audiences, filmmakers themselves are theatrically minded and treat their borrowed plays dramaturgically. And, just as fortunately, there is a wealth of thespian material for them to draw from. Result: the 134 dramatic productions now available.

376 An Actor Works (A Scene from the Trojan Women). How does a 20th-century actress select from her own background the elements needed to project a portrait of a long-dead queen? Viveca Lindfors shows how she taps resources of memory, imagination, and skill in order to identify with Queen Hecuba in *The Trojan Women*, Euripides' masterpiece. Originally distributed by Doubleday. Producers: Bert Rashby and J. Leon Weinstock.
Phoenix 20½ min Color 1970

377 Act Without Words ("Acte Sans Paroles"). This animated interpretation of Samuel Beckett's bitter little one-act mime examines the darker implications of man's existential condition: a world where nothing happens, nobody comes, nobody goes, and where "they give birth astride of the grave. The light gleams for an instant, then it's night once more." A Janus New Cinema Film by Guido Bettiol.
Pyramid 10 min Color 1965

378 Antony and Cleopatra. Act II, Scene II (excerpt): Enobarbus describes his stay with Antony in Egypt, including Cleopatra's first appearance on her barge in the Nile. He predicts Antony will never be able to leave Cleopatra. Act V, Scene II (excerpt): Cleopatra, captured, speaks with the Clown who brought her a basket of figs, then kills herself with the asps hidden there. From the *William Shakespeare* series. Produced by Realist Film Unit. Directed by Peter Seabourne.
Int. Film Bureau 11 min Color 1973

379 Antony and Cleopatra—The World Well Lost. A study of the conflict between Antony's roles: his duty as a statesman and his obligation as Cleopatra's lover. Can performance of duty be reconciled with personal dignity and love? That question is one that this film can raise for group discussion. Produced in Canada by the Ontario Educational Communications Authority. From the *Exploring Shakespeare* series. Formerly released by NBC.
Films Inc. 23 min Color 1969

380 Arthur Miller's The Reason Why. This film is based on the playwright's one-act allegory. In its objective of showing the senselessness of war, it examines humanity's practice of killing helpless animals, but leaves open the question of whether man is intrinsically violent. Featured actors are Robert Ryan and Eli Wallach.
BFA Educ. Media 13½ min Color 1970

381 As You Like It: An Introduction. Narration provides the transitional information needed between the performance of scenes by British actors. This format is designed to summarize Shakespeare's plot, while retaining the most dramatic parts. Produced by BHE Education, Ltd. and Seabourne Enterprises (United Kingdom).
BFA Educ. Media   24 min   Color   1969

382 As You Like It – Doing Your Own Thing. The basic themes of this film are the superficiality of some relationships and the romanticism of "dropping out" of society. The film begins with a montage of changing seasons and the voice of a woman reading a love poem. Jacques points to the Forest of Arden where Orlando is feverishly writing love sonnets to Rosalind and pinning them on trees. Subsequent excerpts cover Rosalind's discovery of the poems and the admirer's identity. Is their love merely infatuation? Are they evading reality? Are couples today trying to break down the barriers of deception? From the series *Exploration in Shakespeare*, produced by the Ontario Educational Communications Authority. Originally distributed by NBC.
Films Inc.   23 min   Color   1969

383 Birth of Modern Theatre. Scenes from Chekhov's *Uncle Vanya* reflect the evolution of Western theatre. Features the acting of Laurence Olivier, Michael Redgrave and Sybil Thorndike. Directed by Olivier. Narrator: John Dexter. Produced by Harold Mantell.
Films/Human.   47 min   BW   1975

384 Books Alive: A Raisin in the Sun. An introduction to America's racial problem is detailed in this Lorraine Hansberry play. *Raisin* is the story of a son who assumes responsibility as the head of the family. Walter Lee Younger, portrayed by Greg Morris, tries to better himself and his family in the face of prejudice and poverty. Produced by Turnley Walker.
BFA Educ. Media   6 min   Color   1969

385 Breaking Out of the Doll's House. In this scene from the full-length production of *A Doll's House*, Jane Fonda plays the part of the 19th-century prototype of a liberated woman who had been conditioned to being sheltered almost to the point of social suffocation. She leaves her husband in order to become a human being again. Filmed in Norway, the home of author Henrick Ibsen. Directed by Joseph Losey.
Learning Corp.   32 min   Color   1975

386 The Cherry Orchard, Part I – Chekhov: Innovator of Modern Drama. Through examples from the play, Norris Houghton (the

narrator) shows why Chekhov's characters cannot be pigeonholed and why his plays have little external plot action. His questions help show that it is often the internal qualities that produce the sharp cutting edge of truth. From the EBE Humanities Series.
Encyc. Brit. 21 min Color 1968

387 The Cherry Orchard, Part II – Comedy or Tragedy? With actress Maureen Stapleton as Chekhov's heroine, narrator Houghton examines the playwright's technique of characterization, and suggests that words are often used to disguise, rather than reveal, true feelings. From the *Humanities Series*.
Encyc. Brit. 22 min Color 1968

388 Classical Comedy. Scenes from Aristophanes' *Ecclesiazusae* (Women in Command) and Plautus' *Miles Gloriosus* (The Braggart Soldier) reflect the origins of Western theatre. Like the other units of the *History of Drama* series, supplementary media are available for purchase. Produced by Harold Mantell.
Films/Human. 58 min Color 1975

389 The Comedy of Manners. Scenes from Molière's *The Misanthrope* relect the evolution of Western theatre. This costumed production uses the translation of Richard Wilbur. Narrated by Cyril Ritchard. Like the other films in the *History of Drama* series, supplementary media are available for purchase. Produced by Harold Mantell.
Films/Human. 52 min Color 1975

390 Conscience in Conflict. Probes a recurring theme of literature: to what extent should a person hold fast to principles? Thomas More, as Chancellor and friend of Henry VIII, must decide whether to follow his conscience or give in to the pressures of his King. Orson Welles explains the dilemma that has intrigued writers from Shakespeare to Camus. Specially edited from the Columbia Pictures' feature, *A Man for All Seasons.* Acting by Paul Scofield and Wendy Hiller; direction by Fred Zinneman; screenplay by Robert Bolt, author of the Broadway play.
Learning Corp. 33 min Color 1973

391 Coriolanus – The People's Choice. The dilemma of Coriolanus, Shakespeare's autocratic soldier-politician, who is unable to simulate gratitude in order to win the votes of the common people. The background illustrates modern political campaigns and rallies. Produced in Canada by the Ontario Educational Communications Authority. Part of the *Exploring Shakespeare* series, originally distributed by NBC Educational Enterprises.
Films Inc. 23 min Color 1969

392 Cyrano. In this light treatment of Rostand's poetic drama, *Cyrano de Bergerac*, Mr. Magoo plays the gallant poet-soldier with the gigantic nose and the equally big heart. His friend Christian wins the heart of fair Roxanne with Cyrano's love poems, but is lost in battle. For fifteen years Cyrano visits her daily. Wounded by his enemies, he dies happy for he realizes that Roxanne has learned of his love for her. Cartoon animation by UPA.
Macmillan   26 min   Color   1965

393 The Devil's Disciple. This is an excerpt from the United Artists film based on George Bernard Shaw's satire on the American Revolution. It presents the court-martial scene from Act III, and features Laurence Olivier and Kirk Douglas. Originally distributed by Teaching Film Custodians.
Indiana U.   9 min   B&W   1959

394 A Doctor in Spite of Himself (Un Médecin Malgré Lui). This is an adaptation of Molière's stylized comedy about a pair of young lovers, a doting father, and a charlatan who practices dubious medicine to smooth the path of true love. From the *On Stage* series with actor Monty Wooley. Produced by Dynamic Films.
Macmillan   15 min   B&W   1954

395 The Doctor's Dilemma. Consists of the entire second act of George Bernard Shaw's play. In it, a physician must decide whether to save the life of a worthy but ordinary colleague or that of an amoral and artistic genius. From the Metro-Goldwyn-Mayer production. Originally distributed by Teaching Film Custodians.
Indiana U.   12 min   Color   1958

396 Doll's House, Part I – The Destruction of Illusion. Instead of Ibsen's Norway, the locale is a typical American suburb, and the characters are a typical American family. This introduction analyzes what happens to Nora between the rapture of the opening scene and the final slam of the front door. From the *Humanities Series*.
Encyc. Brit.   33 min   Color   1968

397 Doll's House, Part II – Ibsen's Themes. Here the Ibsen characters reassemble to speak frankly for themselves. As each set of circumstances is revealed, the narrator identifies the themes that recur in other Ibsen plays. From the *Humanities Series*.
Encyc. Brit.   28 min   Color   1968

398 A Doll's House: The Oppression and Emancipation of Women. This is a specially-edited abbreviation of the international release featuring Claire Bloom, directed by Hillard Elkin. Its fidelity to the period retains Henrick Ibsen's original dramatic context. Produced by

Paramount Pictures.
Paramount 39 min   Color   1977

399 Early English Drama. Scenes from the anonymously authored *The Second Shepherd's Play* reflect the evolution of Western theatre. Also includes *Quem Quaeritis* and part of Brome's *Abraham and Isaac*, both filmed within a few miles of Wakefield, England. Produced by Harold Mantell.
Films/Human. 52 min   Color   1975

400 Eh Joe. Featuring actor George Rose and the voice of Rosemary Harris, this is a film rendition of the Samuel Beckett playlet originally written for BBC television and first produced in this country in 1966. Film script by Beckett. Director: Alan Schneider.
Grove Press 34 min   B&W   1965

401 The Emperor Jones. Presents excerpts from the performance by the American Dance Festival Repertory at Connecticut College. Based on Eugene O'Neill's drama about a black ruler, who loses his Caribbean kingdom to whites. Choreography by José Limón. Produced by the American Dance Festival.
Univ. of Rochester 24 min   Color   1975

402 Enter Hamlet. Pop art finds expression in this fusillade of images in which each word of Hamlet's soliloquy ("To Be or Not To Be") is given its own picture. The result is a large number of visual puns in a short period of time. A New Cinema Film. Animated by Fred Mogubgub. Recitation by Shakespearean actor, Maurice Evans. Formerly distributed by Pyramid Films.
Janus Films 3 min   Color   1970

403 Fair is Foul, and Foul is Fair. This production is the companion piece to National Geographic's *Macbeth*, described elsewhere in this section. It provides additional material on the politics and mores of the era, showing how Shakespeare's interpretations of them became the substance of his theatrical skills. Both films were produced in cooperation with the Shakespeare Birthplace Trust of Stratford-on-Avon.
National Geographic 20 min   Color   1977

404 The Floodwatcher. This ecological skit, adapted from a play by J. I. Rodale, is meant for grades 3 through 9. The plot revolves around John, the floodwatcher, who laments the use of chemicals in agriculture because this leads to an increase in his work as a floodwatcher. John is further abused by a romantic clown named Doolittle, the only person to whom John can communicate his ecological passion. Produced by Rodale Press.
Bullfrog Films 13 min   Color   1972

405 The Forum Scene (Julius Caesar). Consists of Act III, Scene 2 of the Shakespearean tragedy, starring Charlton Heston from his pre-Hollywood days. This is the scene in which Caesar's ghost appears to Brutus before the Philippi and during the last seconds before his self-induced death by the sword. Enacted entirely by American performers. Made by Avon Productions.
Int. Film Bureau   17 min   B&W   1950

406 The Goad. Freely adapted from Samuel Beckett's philosophical comedy *Act Without Words II*, this film conveys the themes and effects that distinguish all of Beckett's drama. For a long while, director Paul Joyce was afraid to show the film to Beckett. But when the master playwright finally saw it, he said, "It's not exactly my play, but I like it."
Grove Press   17 min   B&W

407 The Greeks: In Search of Meaning. The collision between principle and authority is dramatized through Antigone's defiance of Creon in an excerpt from Sophocles' play, *Antigone*. We see the "War Establishment" mocked by early "women liberationists" in the comedy, *Lysistrata*, by Aristophanes. And the philosophical problem of how man faces doom is shown in the death of Socrates. Produced by John Secondari and Helen Jean Rogers.
Learning Corp.   25 min   Color   1971

408 Hamlet. Act I, Scene IV (excerpt): Hamlet goes with Horatio and Marcellus to the castle ramparts, where he sees his father's ghost. Act V, Scene I (excerpt): The gravedigger discovers the skull of Yorick, and Hamlet muses on death. Enacted by a British cast. Produced by Anvil Film and Recording Group, Ltd. Directed by Peter Seabourne.
Int. Film Bureau   10 min   Color   1973

409 Hamlet. The key scenes of this condensation are kept intact, and enactments are fully costumed amid authentic sets of the period. This dramatization is available with a companion documentary, *The Time is Out of Joint*, described elsewhere in this section. Both films were produced in cooperation with the Shakespeare Birthplace Trust of Stratford-on-Avon.
National Geographic   35 min   Color   1977

410 Hamlet. Picasso-like drawings visualize scenes from Shakespeare's play. A narrator summarizes the plot, and the chief speeches are recited: the ghost on the battlements; Hamlet's encounter with Ophelia; "To be or not to be"; the visiting players; Hamlet's reproach of his mother; Ophelia's death; the duel with Laertes; and Hamlet's death. Both an introduction to *Hamlet* and an artist's interpretation of it. Produced by ACI Media.
Paramount   14 min   Color   1974

411 Hamlet: Act III, Scene I. In this component of the *Great Scenes from Shakespeare* series, as in the other five films, British performers act out key passages, in costume, on an Elizabethan stage. **Produced** by Seabourne Enterprises, Ltd. (United Kingdom).
BFA Educ. Media 8 min Color 1971

412 Hamlet I – The Age of Elizabeth. Prof. Maynard Mack introduces the politics and customs of the Elizabethan Age, the theatre, its conventions and audience. Compares their similarities and differences to those of the modern theatre. Produced by the Massachusetts Council for a Television Course in the Humanities (the original *Humanities Series*).
Encyc. Brit. 28 min Color 1959

413 Hamlet II – What Happens in Hamlet. Hamlet is introduced as a play on three levels: a ghost story, a detective story, and a revenge story. The major characters and their interrelationships in the play are explained and demonstrated. Produced by the Council for a Television Course in the Humanities (Mass.). Directed by John Barnes.
Encyc. Brit. 28 min Color 1959

414 Hamlet III – The Poisoned Kingdom. Professor Mack observes that *Hamlet* is really the story of a ruined kingdom where the poisonings are both figurative and literal, affecting major characters in the play. Pertinent scenes are performed by the Stratford Festival Theatre of Canada. From the *Humanities Series*. Directed by John Barnes.
Encyc. Brit. 28 min Color 1959

415 Hamlet IV – The Readiness Is All. The literary and moralistic values of Shakespeare's classic are summarized by Professor Maynard Mack of Yale, with key dramatizations by costumed actors of the Stratford Theatre of Canada. Directed by John Barnes. Produced by the Masssachusetts Council for a Television Course in the Humanities.
Encyc. Brit. 28 min Color 1959

416 Hamlet – The Trouble with Hamlet. Hamlet's despair, his attitude toward others, and his environment are explored. The emphasis is on his confrontation with the classic existentialist dilemma. Produced by the Ontario Educational Communications Authority. Originally distributed by NBC Educational Enterprises.
Films Inc. 23 min Color 1969

417 Hedda Gabler. This abridgement of Henrick Ibsen's drama is part of a multi-media unit called *The Theatre of Social Problems*. In this play, written in 1890, the Norwegian dramatist seems to be asking whether his heroine is a destroyer of men or merely their victim. Produced in London by Harold Mantell.
Films/Human. 59 min Color 1976

418 Henry IV, Part I: Act II, Scene IV; Act V, Scene IV. This film is one of six in the *Great Scenes from Shakespeare* series. In it, English actors perform selected passages on an authentic Elizabethan stage. Produced by Seabourne Enterprises, Ltd. (England).
BFA Educ. Media 16¼ min Color 1971

419 Henry IV, Part II: Act V, Scene V. This film is from the *Great Scenes from Shakespeare* series. Authentically costumed players enact selected segments of this drama on an Elizabethan stage. Produced by Seabourne Enterprises, Ltd. (United Kingdom).
BFA Educ. Media 7½ min Color 1971

420 Henry IV – The Making of the Ideal King. Prince Hal's transformation from libertine to responsible leader. Passages from Henry IV are quoted, showing the development of the ideal king. The action moves from Boar's Head Tavern to Westminster Abbey. From the *Exploring Shakespeare* series, produced by the Ontario Educational Communications Authority (Canada). Originally distributed by NBC Educational Enterprises.
Films Inc. 23 min Color 1969

421 Henry IV (Part 2). Act II, Scene II (excerpt): Prince Hal reads a letter Falstaff has sent him; he and Poins plan to disguise themselves as waiters and spy on Falstaff. Available with or without a correlated audiotape cassette. From the *William Shakespeare* series. Produced by Anvil Film and Recording Group, Ltd. Directed by Peter Seabourne.
Int. Film Bureau 5½ min Color 1973 [*part 1 not available*]

422 The Italian in Algiers. The plot of Rossini's comic opera provides the story of this animated tale – though not a word is sung or spoken. The hilarious escapades of Isabel and Lindoro are introduced by a glorious music track, the overture to this musical play written by Angelo Anelli. Produced by Giulio Gianini and Emanuele Luzzati.
Texture Films 10 min Color 1971

423 The Jewish Wife. From the one-act play, *The Rise and Fall of the Master Race*, by the German playwright Brecht, this is the story of a goodbye. The place is Hitler's Germany, and the goodbye is that of a Jewish woman to her Aryan husband before she flees to safety. The film opens with the woman making phone calls to friends and relatives to tell them she is leaving. She tries to make light of the situation and yet, as each call comes to an end, her tears betray her. Actress: Viveca Lindfors. Directed by Jeff Young. Originally distributed by Doubleday.
Phoenix 29 min Color 1971

424 Jubilee. This satire is drawn from Chekhov's play, *The Anniversary*. Amid plans for a corporate celebration by bank officials, the president

and his bookkeeper, both rushing to balance their accounts, are interrupted continuously. Matters become more and more disorganized, finally reaching near-hysterical proportions. In the midst of the uproar, a delegation bearing a gift for the president arrives. Seeing the confusion, they decide to postpone everything, and the jubilee dissolves into chaos. Enacted by the Moscow Art Theatre, with Russian dialogue in English subtitles. Directed by Vladimir Petrov.
Macmillan 40 min B&W 1946

425 Julius Caesar. The following excerpts are enacted by a British cast: Act II, Scene II, in which Brutus persuades Caesar not to follow Calpurnia's premonition of danger in the Senate; and Act IV, Scene III where Brutus and Cassius quarrel but then renew their friendship. Produced by Realist Film Unit. Directed by Peter Seabourne.
Int. Film Bureau 14 min Color 1973

426 Julius Caesar: Act I, Scene II. Part of the *Great Scenes from Shakespeare* series, in which authentically costumed actors perform on an Elizabethan stage. Produced by Seabourne Enterprises, Ltd. (United Kingdom).
BFA Educ. Media 7 min Color 1971

427 Julius Caesar: An Introduction. Narration provides the transitions between selected scenes performed by a company of British players. This structure is designed to provide an over-view of the drama while including its best known passages. Produced by BHE Education and Seabourne Enterprises (UK).
BFA Educ. Media 27½ min Color 1969

428 King Lear. This is the scene from Shakespeare's great tragedy in which King Lear is rejected by his daughters and driven to the verge of madness. From the *On Stage* series, with actor Monty Wooley. Produced by Dynamic Films.
Macmillan 15 min B&W 1954

429 King Lear – An Introduction. Brief narrations link the performance of pivotal scenes. This format is designed to outline the play's structure, while highlighting its most dramatic passages. Produced by BHE Education, Ltd. and Seabourne Enterprises (England).
BFA Educ. Media 27½ min Color 1970

430 King Lear – Who Is it Can Tell Me Who I Am? Shown is the world of folly, madness, despair, and destruction that King Lear appears to unleash, and the growth of a man in selfknowledge and awareness. The film ends with the unresolved question of Lear's regeneration. From the *Exploring Shakespeare* series. Produced by the Ontario Educational Communications Authority. Originally distributed by NBC Educational

Enterprises.
Films Inc.　23 min　Color　1969

431　Last Straw. A bumbling young man seeks help from a doctor who turns out to be even more maladjusted. At first, their Laurel-and-Hardy encounter is funny, as the quack psychiatrist attempts to find a method of treatment for his first patient in months. In spite of his incompetence, the doctor succeeds in helping the man realize that he has a great deal to live for and should try to make the best of life. Based on a play by Charles Dizenzo. Produced by Drew Denbaum. Photography: Ernest Holzman.
Phoenix　20 min　BW　1976

432　Lincoln: Politician or Hero? Against the backdrop of events that led to civil war, the career that culminated in Lincoln's presidency is examined. Upon his election, Lincoln is disturbed by the campaign tactics he has witnessed and is in awe of the task before him. As he faces a divided nation, Lincoln must be politician as well as hero. Extract from the 1940 feature *Abe Lincoln in Illinois*, based on the play by Robert Sherwood. Introductory and closing statements by Henry Fonda.
Films Inc.　24 min　B&W　1975

433　The Long Christmas Dinner. In this version of Thornton Wilder's play, the dining room at the Bayard house at Christmas time is the setting. This short play covers 90 years in the life of this family, beginning in 1880 when a young man, his wife and mother sit down to eat their first Christmas dinner in that house. Their lives and the lives of their children and grandchildren are suggested through subsequent holiday dinners. Directed by Larry Yust.
Encyc. Brit.　37 min　Color　1975

434　The Lower Depths (Excerpts). Character acting is the outstanding feature of these two scenes from the Maxim Gorky play. The first excerpt sets the mood of the play—the story of a group of social outcasts living together. Features players of the Moscow Art Theatre under the direction of Vladimir Yurenev, with Kachalov as the Baron. Russian dialogue with English subtitles.
Macmillan　20 min　B&W　1947

435　Macbeth. Performing excerpts from Act I, Scenes I and III, and Act IV, Scene I, three witches weave their spells, and prepare to make their prophecies. In Act II, Scene I (excerpts), Macbeth sees a vision of a dagger and contemplates the murder he is about to commit.
Int. Film Bureau　11 min　Color　1973

436　Macbeth. The main segments of this condensation remain intact, while the enactments are performed in full costume amid authentic sets of the period. This dramatization is available with a companion piece,

Fair Is Foul, and Foul Is Fair, described elsewhere in this section. Both films were produced in cooperation with the Shakespeare Birthplace Trust of Stratford-on-Avon, England.
National Geographic 36 min Color 1977

437 Macbeth: Act I, Scene VII. This unit from the series *Great Scenes from Shakespeare* features costumed actors on an authentic Elizabethan stage. Produced by Seabourne Enterprises, Ltd. (Great Britain).
BFA Educ. Media 7¼ min Color 1971

438 Macbeth: An Introduction. Narrative summaries bridge the performance of key scenes by English actors, a format designed to maintain interest and impact. Produced by BHE Education, Ltd., and Seabourne Enterprises (Great Britain).
BFA Educ. Media 25½ min Color 1968

439 Macbeth — Nothing Is but What Is Not. This film suggests that Macbeth, living in a world of fantasy, has not yet found his identity. The hypothesis that he must "do a deed" forms the basis for an examination of murder, oppression, and repression. Produced by the Ontario Educational Communications Authority (Canada). Originally distributed by NBC Educational Enterprises.
Films Inc. 23 min Color 1969

440 Macbeth I: The Politics of Power. Douglas Campbell interprets the characters in the play. Are the witches goddesses of fate, wicked hags, or figments of Macbeth's imagination? How is it possible to portray Macbeth as a murderer who remains a tragic hero through the play? Is Duncan a corrupt senile man? From the *Humanities Series.*
Encyc. Brit. 28 min Color 1964

441 Macbeth II: The Themes of Macbeth. As on-screen narrator Campbell explains it, the entire play is built on a paradox: "Nothing is but what is not." A dramatized lesson from the *Humanities Series.* Directed by John Barnes.
Encyc. Brit. 28 min Color 1964

442 Macbeth III: The Secret'st Man. "Everyman," in Macbeth's words, "is the secret'st man of blood." According to Douglas Campbell, we cannot hate Macbeth, nor believe that his life signifies nothing. Perhaps this capacity for good and evil within the same human heart sums up Shakespeare's message. (This is the last of three dramatizations and interpretations from the *Humanities Series.*)
Encyc. Brit. 33 min Color 1964

443 Man and Woman. Filmed in Padua to give a sense of the age, Franco Zeffirelli's production features the battle between the sexes in

which Petruccio bets that he has the most faithful and "tamed" wife. In the end, of course, the shrew is tamed but, as Orson Welles points out, Kate in her own way has tamed Petrucchio, too. Welles' narration compares Shakespeare's comic treatment of man versus woman with the darker view held by Ibsen, Albee, Tennessee Williams, and others. Specially edited from the Columbia Pictures feature *The Taming of the Shrew* with Elizabeth Taylor and Richard Burton.
Learning Corp.   33 min   Color   1971

444   Marriage (Svabada). A satire on the hypocrisy and petty bargaining that precede a provincial wedding party. Directed by Isador Annensky. Based on Anton Chekhov's play, *The Wedding*. Acted by the Moscow Art Theatre. Russian dialogue with English subtitles.
Macmillan   44 min   B&W   1973

445 Medieval Theatre: The Play of Abraham and Isaac. Shows how a family of traveling players produced *The Play of Abraham and Isaac* at an English estate in 1482. Attitudes of actors and peasants are contrasted with those of the aristocracy and church. Speech, costumes, sets, and props are based on 15th-century records. Produced by The Movie Show Co. Collaborator: Lewis J. Owen, Ph.D., Professor of English, Occidental College. From the *Humanities Series*.
Encyc. Brit.   26 min   Color   1974

446 The Merchant of Venice: Act I, Scene III; Act IV, Scene I. Part of the *Great Scenes from Shakespeare* series, with costumed actors on an authentically constructed Elizabethan stage. Produced by Seabourne Enterprises, Ltd. (United Kingdom).
BFA Educ. Media   26 min   Color   1971

447   A Midsummer Night's Dream. Mr. Magoo, as Puck, romps through Shakespeare's five-act comedy of ancient Greece. The tone and atmosphere of the play suggest the fairyland in which a Queen is tricked and a King wears a donkey's head. Heroes of Greek mythology provide an introduction to this play. Cartoon animation.
Macmillan   26 min   Color   1965

448   A Midsummer Night's Dream: An Introduction. Narrative bridges connect the performances of key scenes by an English company of actors. This format is designed to preserve the continuity of the play and its dramatic impact. Produced by BHE Education, Ltd., and Seabourne Enterprises, Ltd. (Great Britain).
BFA Educ. Media   25½ min   Color   1970

449 Modern American Drama. This segment of the *History of Drama* series focuses on Eugene O'Neill's *Long Day's Journey into Night*. It features the acting of Jason Robards, Katherine Hepburn, Ralph Richard-

son, and Dean Stockwell. Narrated by José Quintero, stage director of many of O'Neill's works. Produced by Harold Mantell.
Films/Human. 54 min BW 1975

450 The Moor's Pavane (Variation on the Theme of Othello). The basic story of the Moor, Othello, is told within pavane dance form by José Limón and his group. Music arranged by Simon Sadoff from Henry Purcell. Lines from Shakespeare's *Othello* are spoken by Bram Nossen. A Brandon Films release, produced by Walter V. Strate.
Macmillan 16 min Color 1950

451 Much Ado About Nothing. Act IV, Scene I (excerpt): Benedick and Beatrice declare their love for each other, and Beatrice persuades Benedick to challenge his friend Claudio who had just wronged her cousin Hero. Act IV, Scene II (complete): Benedick attempts to write a love sonnet, but is interrupted by Beatrice. They resume their verbal sparring, when Ursula arrives with news that Hero has been exonerated. A Realist Production.
Int. Film Bureau 11½ min Color 1973

452 The New Tenant. This example of "theatre of the absurd" expresses Euguene Ionesco's sense of the incoherence of modern life. Almost a vaudeville act, the scene of a sixth-floor walkup soon fills up with furniture the occupant systematically stacks from wall to wall. Only when trapped by his own design does he realize the miseries brought by material possessions. From the *Short Play Showcase* series.
Encyc. Brit. 31 min Color 1976

453 Night Journey. The modern dance style of Martha Graham is the vehicle for this retelling of Sophocles' theatrical masterpiece *Oedipus Rex*. Settings by Isamu Noguchi, direction by Alexander Hammid.
Phoenix 29 min B&W 1961

454 Oedipus Rex I: The Age of Sophocles. Yale professor Bernard Knox introduces the Ancient Greeks, their way of life, and how they answered some of the basic questions of their world. He also discusses the origins and customs of Greek theatre and the story of Oedipus. Produced by the Massachusetts Council for a Television Course in the Humanities (the original *Humanities Series*). Directed by John Barnes.
Encyc. Brit. 28 min Color 1959

455 Oedipus Rex II: The Character of Oedipus. Important scenes from the play are presented. Oedipus' character and actions are described and analyzed in view of Aristotle's theory of the "fatal flaw" in all tragic characters. Second lesson in the series of four films. Enacted by the Stratford Players of Canada. Narrator: Bernard Knox. From the original *Humanities Series*.
Encyc. Brit. 28 min Color 1959

456 Oedipus Rex III: Man and God. Third in the series of four lessons. Not as theological as it sounds, dealing with the abstraction of divinity more as a concept than as a moral force. Scenes performed by the Stratford Players of Canada. Narrator and film-scholar is Bernard Knox. From the original *Humanities Series*.
Encyc. Brit. 28 min Color 1959

457 Oedipus Rex IV: The Recovery of Oedipus. Man's existence is seen as somewhere between God and beast, always searching for his rightful place. Knowledge of life through the painful search for truth is revealed in this lesson. Dramatized by the Stratford Festival actors of Canada. Last in the sequence of four films. Film-interpreter: Dr. Bernard Knox of Yale. From the original *Humanities Series*.
Encyc. Brit. 28 min Color 1959

458 Othello. Act II, Scene I (excerpt): Iago, in soliloquy, reveals the motivation and method of his revenge. Act V, Scene II (excerpt): Othello awakens Desdemona; she denies his accusations, but he kills her.
Int. Film Bureau 9½ min Color 1973

459 Othello — An Anatomy of a Marriage. Othello is a character of mighty opposites who is as extravagant in his love as in his hatred. A young man and woman discuss marriage and jealousy with regard both to Othello and Desdemona and to themselves. Produced by the Ontario (Canada) Educational Communications Authority for the *Exploring Shakespeare* series. Originally distributed by NBC Educational Enterprises.
Films Inc. 23 min Color 1969

460 Our Town and Ourselves. This is the second of two lessons on Thornton Wilder's classic in which Clifton Fadiman points out such theatrical devices as music, leitmotif, and condensation of line. Mr. Fadiman also explains the playwright's objective of helping the audience to reconcile itself to the joys and sorrows of everyday reality. From the original *Humanities Series*, directed by John Barnes.
Encyc. Brit. 28 min Color 1959

461 Our Town and Our Universe. In this first of two films on Thornton Wilder's play, Clifton Fadiman reveals some of the conventions of stage action. Then he analyzes *Our Town* as a commentary on the contrast between each moment of our lives and the vast stretches of time in which individuals live out their roles. Produced by the Massachusetts Council for a Television Course in the Humanities (the original *Humanities Series*). Director: John Barnes.
Encyc. Brit. 28 min Color 1959

462 Pinter People. This production blends an interview with Harold

Pinter and five of his short plays, all complete and all in animation. They are: *Trouble in the Works, Request Stop, Applicant, The Black and White,* and *Last to Go.* Created for NBC's *Experiment in Television,* with the voices of Pinter, Vivien Merchant, and Donald Pleasence. A Canadian film by **Gerald Potterton.**
Grove Press 58 min Color

463 Power and Corruption. Orson Welles, narrator, explores a theme that has always fascinated writers: why are people attracted to power? And what influence does power have upon their natures? Orson Welles compares Shakespeare's treatment of power and corruption to other writers' such as William Golding in *Lord of the Flies,* Christopher Marlowe in *Dr. Faustus,* and Robert Penn Warren in *All the King's Men.* Specially edited from the Columbia Pictures feature *Macbeth* directed by Roman Polanski.
Learning Corp. 34 min Color 1973

464 Rhinoceros. A condensed visual translation from Eugene Ionesco's play on the theme of conformity. Produced by Boris Borresholm. Animated by Jan Lenica. A Contemporary Films release.
McGraw-Hill 11 min Color 1964

465 Richard II. Act II, Scene I (excerpt): John of Gaunt speaks to his brother York of "this sceptered isle," and prays that Richard will heed the dangerous path he pursues. Act V, Scene V (excerpt): Richard, deposed and imprisoned, contemplates his fallen state and "this all-hating world." Produced in Great Britain.
Int. Film Bureau 12 min Color 1973

466 Richard II — How to Kill the King. Richard's fall from power and Bolingbroke's success are shown as a clash between the old world of Richard, based on the false security of divine sanction and the more realistic world of Bolingbroke, where personal merit and strength are the dominant factors. Contemporary parallels are drawn. Produced by the Ontario Educational Communications Authority. Originally distributed by NBC Educational Enterprises.
Films Inc. 23 min Color 1969

467 Richard III. Act I, Scene I (excerpts): Richard, in the "winter of our discontent" soliloquy, states his belief that his deformed body makes him fit only for villainy, then reveals his plot to gain the throne. Act I, Scene II (excerpt): Lady Anne scorns Richard, who has just declared his love for her. But he persuades her to believe him and, when alone, he wonders at his ability to win a lady whose husband and father-in-law he had just killed.
Int. Film Bureau 11½ min Color 1973

468 The Rise of Greek Tragedy. Scenes from Sophocles' *Oedipus the King* reflect the origins of Western theatre. Like the other films in the *History of Drama* series, supplementary media are available for purchase. Features character interpretations by James Mason, Claire Bloom, and Jan Richardson. Narrated by Anthony Quayle. Produced by Harold Mantell with the Athens Classical Theatre.
Films/Human.   45 min   Color   1975

469   Romeo and Juliet. This rendering of Shakespeare's love story is enacted by John Barrymore, Leslie Howard, Basil Rathbone and Norma Shearer amidst the splendor of Renaissance Italy. Selected sequences include the duel scene, the death scene, Friar Laurence's cell, and flashes of the Capulet-Montague family feud. Produced by Metro-Goldwyn-Mayer. Directed by George Cukor.
Films Inc.   40 min   BW   1936

470   Romeo and Juliet. Prologue: The chorus emerges from the inner stage and tells the audience what they are about to witness. Act V, Scene III (excerpt): Romeo, beside Juliet's body in the tomb, drinks poison and dies. Friar Laurence discovers the body just as Juliet awakens. He cannot persuade her to leave and, when he has gone, she kills herself.
Int. Film Bureau   8 min   Color   1973

471   Romeo and Juliet. The key scenes of this condensation are kept intact, and enactments are performed in full costume amid authentic sets and props. The dramatization is available with a specially made companion piece, *Star Crossed Love*, described elsewhere in this section. Both films were produced in cooperation with the Shakespeare Birthplace Trust of Stratford-on-Avon.
National Geographic   36 min   Color   1977

472   Romeo and Juliet. This production, at the Czechoslovakian National Theatre in Prague, was staged by Otto Krejca, whose technique of filming actors in rehearsal enabled him to experiment successfully with interpretation. Music by Jan Flusak. Photographed and edited by Short Film Studio.
Roland   45 min   B&W

473   Romeo and Juliet: Act II, Scene II. Part of the *Great Scenes from Shakespeare* series, with costumed actors on a stage patterned after Elizabethan theatres. Produced by Seabourne Enterprises, Ltd. (Great Britain).
BFA Educ. Media   9¼ min   Color   1971

474   Romeo and Juliet in Kansas City. In Kansas City's "rock palace," the Cowtown Ballroom, conductor Jorge Mester and the Kansas City Philharmonic play Tchaikovsky's *Romeo and Juliet Overture* for an

audience of young adults. With references that parallel Shakespeare's play and their own age, youths can understand new relationships between music and literature. Produced by Allan Miller.
Pyramid 28 min Color 1975

475 Romeo and Juliet: Passions of Love and Hate. This adaptation of Franco Zeffirelli's production is an on-location (Verona) interpretation of Shakespeare's tragedy. It features Olivia Hussey and Leonard Whiting in the youthful roles of star-crossed lovers. Edited from the Paramount Pictures theatrical release.
Paramount 45 min Color 1973

476 Romeo and Juliet — The Words of Love. The decision made by lovers to count the world lost when they reject social mores and give themselves to love is depicted in scenes from Shakespeare's drama. A discussion of current social barriers to love follows. Produced in Canada by the Ontario Educational Communications Authority. From the *Exploring Shakespeare* series. Originally distributed by NBC Educational Enterprises.
Films Inc. 23 min Color 1969

477 Seven Authors in Search of a Reader (A Sunday Afternoon on the Island of La Grande Jatte). Alluding conceptually to the playwright Pirandello and visually to the painter Seurat, this production develops the theme of the love-hate relationship between artist and public. In so doing, it provides material for discussion of the liberation of the mind through the power of books. Directed by Frans Weisz.
McGraw-Hill 21 min B&W 1965

478 Shakespeare: A Mirror to Man. Presents the psychodramatic motivations behind the *Macbeth* soliloquy, the comedy of *Shrew*, and the tragedy of *Othello*. Sonnets reveal even more about Shakespeare's incomparably precise use of language. The players and on-screen narrators are British actors Eileen Cox and Brian Cox. From the Western Civilization series.
Learning Corp. 26 min Color 1971

479 Shakespeare and His Stage. Scenes from the Bard's *Hamlet* reflect the evolution of Western theatre, comparing the styles of Olivier, Barrymore, and Gielgud. Like the other units of the *History of Drama* series, supplementary media are available for purchase. Director: Daniel Seltzer. Produced by Harold Mantell.
Films/Human. 45 min Color 1976

480 Shakespeare's Theater. Excerpt from the prologue of the J. Arthur Rank feature film *Henry V,* exemplifying the activity of Shakespeare's Globe Theatre around 1600. Directed by and starring Sir Laurence

Olivier; score by Sir William Walton. Edited by the National Council of Teachers of English. Originally distributed by Teaching Film Custodians.
Indiana U. 12½ min   Color   1946

481 Shakespeare's Theater: The Globe Playhouse. Through the use of a scale model and three-dimensional figures, miniature actors are animated on a stage. Excerpts from *Julius Caesar, Twelfth Night, Romeo and Juliet, Hamlet* and *Macbeth* are dramatized by the miniature actors. Dialogue is provided off-screen, interspersed with commentary on the staging machinery and conventions of the day. Narrated by Ronald Colman. Produced by the Extension Media Center of the University of California (Berkeley).
Extension Media   18 min   B&W   1952

482 Shaw's Pygmalion. Excerpt from the feature film based on G.B. Shaw's play. Follows the transformation of a cockney flower girl into a young woman who passes as a duchess at an ambassador's reception. Directed by Anthony Asquith, with Leslie Howard and Wendy Hiller. Selected and edited by the National Council of Teachers of English. Originally distributed by Teaching Film Custodians.
Indiana U.   18 min   B&W   1938

483 Shaw vs. Shakespeare, Part I: The Character of Caesar. George Bernard Shaw, portrayed by Donald Moffatt, analyzes Shakespeare's characterization of Julius Caesar, and compares it with his own treatment in *Caesar and Cleopatra*. From the *Humanities Series*.
Encyc. Brit.   33 min   Color   1970

484 Shaw vs. Shakespeare, Part II: The Tragedy of Julius Caesar. Presents the Shakespearean masterpiece as a drama of political idealism. Shaw, played by Donald Moffatt, claims that Shakespeare's portrayal of Brutus as the "complete idealist" makes this play the best political melodrama. From the *Humanities Series*.
Encyc. Brit.   35 min   Color   1970

485 Shaw vs. Shakespeare, Part III: Caesar and Cleopatra. There are four political murders in Shaw's *Caesar and Cleopatra* and, in it, Caesar's reactions are crucial. Shaw asks, through actor Donald Moffatt, "Must we go on—in the nature of 'justice,' 'peace,' and 'honor'—with crime begetting crime, murder begetting murder, and war begetting war?" From the *Humanities Series*.
Encyc. Brit.   33 min   Color   1970

486 Shylock. The trial scene from Shakespeare's *Merchant of Venice* shows how concepts of justice and mercy have changed since Shakespeare's day, as Portia pleads with Shylock to show mercy to a man who owes him money. From BBC-TV.
Time-Life   30 min   B&W   1969

487 Six Filmmakers in Search of a Wedding. A light-hearted study of weddings—American style—as interpreted through six different cameras. The allusion and thematic similarity to Pirandello's 1921 play about shifting realities, *Six Characters in Search of an Author*, make the film useful in literature or other groups exploring the factors of objectivity. Produced by Envision.
Pyramid 13 min Color 1972

488 The Spoils of Poynton (series). These four programs reproduce Henry James' play written during his mid-career period. In it, the property contest between mother and son reveals the playwright's special awareness of human relationships. Produced by BBC Television.
Time-Life 45 min (ea.) Color 1976

489 Stage Irishman. This excerpt, from Dion Boucicault's melodrama, *The Shaughran*, was originally produced for the British Broadcasting Company as a tribute to the 19th-century playwright. Cyril Cusack narrates highlights of the author's career and portrays the leading role in a scene with the Abbey Players of Dublin. Director: Kieran Hickey.
Sherman Films 15 min Color

490 Stanislavsky: Maker of the Modern Theatre. Shows how Stanislavsky developed his method of "truth in art" for actors. Chekhov's widow, the actress Olga Knipper-Chekhova, recalls the opening night of Stanislavsky's production of *The Seagull*. The staging of Chekhov's *Uncle Vanya*, *The Three Sisters,* and *The Cherry Orchard* are other milestones shown in the film. Narrated by Paul Rogers. Produced by Mosfilm. English version adapted by Harold Mantell.
Films/Human. 28½ min B&W 1972

491 Star Crossed Love. This documentary is the companion to National Geographic's *Romeo and Juliet*, described elsewhere in this section. It provides sidelights to the politics and mores of the era, showing how the Bard converted such events into theatrical fare. Both films were produced by the Shakespeare Birthplace Trust.
National Geographic 20 min Color 1977

492 The Stronger. This award-winner is based on the one-act play by Swedish playwright August Strindberg. An actress is sitting in a cafe. An acquaintance approaches, joins her, and begins to talk. The first woman never speaks but her wordless reactions compel the other to go on talking, finally expressing a suspicion that the silent woman has been having an affair with her husband. As the film ends, the silent woman is stunned; her adversary goes home to husband and children. Both have been profoundly affected by the encounter. Whether there is any truth to the accusation is left for the audience to ponder and to discuss. Viveca Lindfors plays both roles. Originally distributed by Doubleday. Producer-

director: Jeffrey Young.
Phoenix 18 min   Color   1970

493 The Swampdwellers. Wole Soyinka, Nigerian playwright, won international acclaim in 1958 when this play was first produced in London. In this film adaptation, directed and performed by Africans, a young African returns to his village from the city and discovers he has grown too sophisticated to accept his parents' beliefs. Disillusioned by urban life, he is caught between two conflicting cultures, unable to identify with either.
Phoenix   40 min   B/W   1973

494 The Taming of the Shrew. Act I, Scene II (excerpt): Hortensio tells his friend Petruchio of "Katharine the Curst," and Petruchio vows to woo and wed her. Act II, Scene I (excerpt): Petruchio meets Katharine who engages him in a fierce battle of wits, but he dominates and begins already to tame the shrew.
Int. Film Bureau   13 min   Color   1973

495 The Tempest. Act I, Scene II (excerpt): Miranda and Ferdinand see each other and fall instantly in love, as Prospero has planned. But he resolves to test Ferdinand. Act III, Scene I (excerpt): Miranda offers to help Ferdinand carry wood but he refuses her offer. They confess their love for each other while Prospero looks on approvingly.
Int. Film Bureau   13½ min   Color   1973

496 The Tempest. This study of Peter Brooks shows how, as a theatrical director, he conducts an encounter group with a cast of international actors in rehearsal. These exercises are part of their preparation for Shakespeare's *The Tempest*. Mr. Brooks' techniques raise a tempest of their own, challenging established theatrical principles. Should, for example, the audience be passive or participating? Film directed by Ian Wilson.
Macmillan   27 min   Color

497 The Tempest – O Brave New World. Prospero has the magical power to dispose of evil, possibly even the power to create a "brave new world." The irony of that phrase, seen in the context of the play, and the struggle of Prospero to control evil, are special concerns of this film from the *Exploring Shakespeare* series. Produced by the Ontario Educational Communications Authority. Originally distributed by NBC Educational Enterprises.
Films Inc.   23 min   Color   1969

498 Tennessee Williams: Theatre in Process. This production takes viewers backstage to rehearsals of *The Red Devil Battery Sign*. The playwright, Williams, narrates between scenes of practice and actual performance, stressing the on-going nature of script revision and im-

provements necessitated by out-of-town tryouts. A Signet Production for the *Short Play Showcase* series. Featured actors are Anthony Quinn, Claire Bloom, and Katie Jurado.
Encyc. Brit. 29 min Color 1975

499 Theatre. Dame Sybil Thorndike is one of ten star actors who describe George Bernard Shaw's contributions to their art. Produced by Jack Schoon for the Ontario (Canada) Educational Communications Authority.
Films Inc. 28 min Color 1976

500 The Theatre of Protest. Scenes from Brecht's *The Resistible Rise of Arturo Ui* reflect the evolution of Western drama. As with the other parts of the *History of Drama* series, supplementary media are available for purchase. Produced by Harold Mantell.
Films/Human. 45 min Color 1975

501 The Theatre of Social Problems. Irene Worth narrates, and professional actors perform, scenes from Henrick Ibsen's *Hedda Gabler*. The combination of talents, authentic set design, provides the 19th-century Scandinavian context that befits the realism the author was trying to achieve. Directed by Philip Hedly. Producer: Harold Mantell.
Films/Human. 58 min Color

502 The Theatre of the Absurd. Scenes from Pirandello's *Six Characters in Search of an Author* reflect his part in the evolution of Western drama. In this masterpiece, the characters try to exchange their fixed forms in art for the uncertainties of life. Bernard Shaw called this play the most original one he had ever read. Director: Ken Frankel.
Films/Human. 58 min Color 1975

503 The Time Is Out of Joint. This documentary is the companion piece to National Geographic's *Hamlet*, described elsewhere in this section. As such, it provides background information on the political and social environment of the times...the great and small events that Shakespeare himself observed. Both films were produced in cooperation with the Shakespeare Birthplace Trust of Stratford-on-Avon, England.
National Geographic 20 min Color 1977

504 Troilus and Cressida — War, War, Glorious War. Under the savage attacks of this play, no evil escapes exposure. Heroic war becomes butchery; love is exposed as lechery; integrity and honor degenerate into deception and treachery. This theme is supported by related ballads, posters, and sequences from this play. From the *Explorations in Shakespeare* series. Produced by the Ontario Educational Communications Authority. Originally distributed by NBC Educational Enterprises.
Films Inc. 23 min Color 1969

505 Twelfth Night: An Introduction. Narrative bridges connect performance of Shakespeare's scenes by English actors, a format designed to preserve continuity of action and dramatic impact. Produced by BHE Education, Ltd. and Seabourne Enterprises (United Kingdom).
BFA Educ. Films   22¾ min   Color   1969

506 A Visit with Don Juan in Hell. This excerpt from Shaw's *Man and Superman* has come to enjoy an independent life of its own as an entertaining but thought-provoking bit of stagecraft. Actors featured are Ricardo Montalban, Edward Mulhare, and Kurt Kasznar. Included are the voices of Charles Laughton, Agnes Moorehead, and even George Bernard Shaw himself. Narrated by Lew Ayres. Produced by S. Richard Krown.
North American   22 min   Color   1975

507 Waiting for Godot. Abandoning sequential action and plot, Samuel Beckett's play is theatre of the absurd at its apogee. At the same time, it is theatre in classical form, affirming everyman's claim to existence through endurance. The cast includes Zero Mostel, Burgess Meredith, and Kurt Kasznar. Narrated by Milo O'Shea. Producer: Harold Mantell.
Films/Human.   45 min   BW   1977

508 Walter Kerr on Theater. Drama critic Walter Kerr demonstrates the characteristics of theatre as compared to film. Within this format, we watch professionals as they perform key scenes from five plays of distinctive style. They are the Pulitzer Prize-winning *No Place to Be Somebody* (with original cast); Shakespeare's *Richard III* as produced by Joseph Papp; Oscar Wilde's *The Importance of Being Earnest; Prometheus* by Aeschylus; and the Open Theatre's interpretation of *The Serpent.* Film directed by Joseph Anthony. Producer: Robert Saudek Associates.
Learning Corp.   26 min   Color   1970

509 The Well of the Saints. This Irish folk drama, written in this century by John M. Synge, proposes the thesis that sometimes we're better off with our illusions than with reality. This idea is expressed through the episode of the restoration of sight to Martin and Mary Doul. From the *Short Play Showcase* series.
Encyc. Brit.   40 min   Color   1975

Fables/Fairy Tales/Folktales

These 210 fantasies are more alike than different. They're alike in these ways: they're either completely unreal or pleasingly close to it, they suggest a morality most people agree on, and they appeal to children (and to adults who admit they still are). How do they differ from the materials in the *Children's Stories* section? Mostly in their age (old, very old) and in their original authorship (many are anonymous). Another difference shows up in the production technique used: animation. Most of these works are based on artwork, allowing freer reign to creative storylines. The same material, attempted via live-action, might never match the imaginativeness of the characters or settings originally appearing in print.

510 Aesop's Fables. Television actor-comedian Bill Cosby introduces two cartoons *The Tortoise and the Eagle* and *The Tortoise and the Hare*. Participation of older viewers can be gained by having them guess the voices of the animals (Mickey Rooney? John Wayne? John Byner?) Art work by Filmation. Directed by Lee (*The Waltons*) Rich.
Prod. Unltd.   27 min   Color

511 Ali Baba. Ali Baba, a boy with a turban full of butterflies, gets the better of Mustafa and his band of thieves in this fantasy for children. Narrated in rhyme, accompanied by wind music. Produced in Italy by artist Emanuele Luzzati and animator Giulio Gianini. Previously distributed by Connecticut Films.
Distribution 16   11 min   Color

512 All in the Morning Early: A Scottish Folktale. In this traditional Scottish counting rhyme, Sandy sets forth on an errand "all in the morning early," and meets many amiable people along the way. The repetitive verse will invite participation of young viewers in recalling sequences and practicing other reading and number skills. A Stephen Bosustow animation, adapted from the book by Sorche Nic Leodhas.
BFA Educ. Media   10¼ min   Color   1969

513 Ananse's Farm. This folk tale from Ghana is about Ananse, a spider with a heart full of concern over the hostility between some friends of his. But, instead of intervening in an open way, he dreams up a scheme to patch things up, and only succeeds in making matters worse. Animated by African filmmaker John K. Ossei. Produced by the National Film Board of Canada.
Films Inc.   7 min   Color   1974

514 Anansi the Spider. Anansi, a spider with human qualities, is a folk hero of the Ashanti people of Ghana. In this adventure, Anansi faces great trouble, and is saved only by the singular talents of his six sons. Anansi then faces the problem of choosing one of the six to reward, the prize being the moon itself. Animated from the Caldecott Award book by Gerald McDermott.
Texture   10 min   Color   1969

515 The Ant and the Dove (An Aesop Fable). "One good turn deserves another" is the moral of this ancient story. It uses the character of an insect that, despite its small size, manages to save the life of a bird. Animated by Gakken Film Company (Japan).
Coronet   8 min   Color   1962

516 The Ant and the Grasshopper (An Aesop Fable). This animated fable points out that we can't play all the time, but must work and save for a time of need. While the ants labor to provide for the winter, the

grasshopper rests in the sun. When winter comes, the grasshopper finds it difficult to live, and it is the ants' turn to sing and play.
Coronet 11 min Color 1967

517 Arrow to the Sun. This tale from the Acoma Pueblo Indians of the Southwest United States is about a boy's search for his father. It leads him to a dazzling voyage—on an arrow to the sun. There, in the sky village, he passes through fierce trials until recognized by his father, Lord of the Sun. The boy returns to Earth to spread the Sun's warm delights. Animation based on Gerald McDermott's picture-book that won the Caldecott Medal.
Texture 12 min Color 1972

518 The Bear and the Mouse. This production is a variation on Aesop, in which a mouse aids in the escape of a bear in return for past favors. Designed for children, this film shows real animals doing exactly what the story requires, as though all were experienced actors. A real bear catches a mouse, and later the freed mouse chews an escape route for his trapped benefactor. Filmmaker: Mike Rubbo.
Nat. Film Board 8 min Color

519 Beauty and the Beast. An original musical score and specially made figurines highlight this adaptation of the classic fairy tale. Puppet animation tells the story of the handsome young prince who has been changed into an ugly beast by an evil witch and of the young maiden whose love for him, despite his appearance, breaks the spell.
Coronet 19 min Color 1978

520 Bluebell and the Hippo. A Russian peasant girl has a lively encounter with a wily crocodile. But when little Bluebell sounds the alarm, she discovers that her *biggest* friend is not necessarily her best. Produced by the Soyuzmultfilm Studio.
Carousel 11 min Color

521 The Brave Little Tailor. Animated puppets act out the Grimm fairy tale of a tailor who makes a belt inscribed with the words, "Seven at one blow!" referring to his execution of houseflies. When he offers his services to the king, the monarch misinterprets the belt's message, and offers the tailor marriage to the princess if he can destroy a boar, a unicorn, and some evil giants. Produced by National Educational Television.
Indiana U. 28 min Color 1973

522 The Brementown Musicians. Donkey, Dog, Cat, and Rooster, too old now to be of further service to their masters, run away and become musicians in the town of Bremen. Along the way, they come upon robbers in a cottage. Through ingenuity and teamwork, the four animals

chase the robbers from the cottage, give up their musical careers, and "live happily ever after." This "once upon a time" story by the Grimm Brothers is animated in free-form puppetry. Produced by Institut für Film und Bild (Germany).
Films, Inc.   16 min   Color   1972

523 The Cat and the Fiddler. A fiddler has a dancing cat that earns a living for them both. The king sees the cat and tries to buy it. When the fiddler will not sell, the kings takes the cat. The cat will not dance unless the fiddler plays, so the fiddler plays. The court and the king find themselves dancing and cannot stop. The king gives back the cat, the fiddler stops playing, and the court can rest at last. The fiddler and the cat set out once again on their travels. Based on the book by Jacky Jeter, illustrated by Lionel Kalish. The original illustrations are photographed in iconographic style. Executive Producer: Stelios Roccos, ACI Media.
Paramount   11 min   Color   1970

524 The Cat and the Old Rat. Cautions that common sense should govern any encounter with a new experience. An Attila-like cat pretends to be a mound of meal in order to catch unwary but curious mice. An older rat, wise in the way of the world and of cats, sees through the feline disguise. Cartoon. Based on the Aesopian fables of the 19th-century Frenchman, Jean de la Fontaine. Available in French upon request.
Twyman   13 min   Color   1969

525 The Cat, the Weasel, and the Little Rabbit. This lesson teaches care in choosing a referee to settle an argument. A weasel and a rabbit both claim the same burrow. Neither will give in, so they decide to have a wise old cat arbitrate. The cat sits in judgment but, upon accepting their petitions, feigns deafness—forcing the two adversaries to draw closer to each other in order to be heard! Cartoon. Based on de la Fontaine's 19th-century fable. Also available in French.
Twyman   13 min   Color   1969

526 The Cherry Tree Carol. Agnes de Mille's Appalachian dance troupe performs a modern folk ballet based on Christmas **legend**. In an attempt to prevent the Virgin Mary from exerting herself while pregnant, the trees bend down to let her easily taste of their fruit. **Produced** by the **Educational** Broadcasting Corporation for ACI Media.
Paramount   10 min   Color   1975

527 Chicken Little. This age-old tale about foolish chickens and a wily fox satirizes the pitfalls of believing war-time propaganda. The villain of the piece, Foxie Loxie, has a weakness for chicken dinners, and uses psychology as a means to his epicurean ends. Animated.
Disney   9 min   Color   1943

528 The Christmas Messenger. Passing through a village one Christmas Eve, a friendly stranger pauses to hear the carolers. A boy joins him. As they listen, the stranger's divine identity and message are gradually revealed. Combines animation and action sequences with well-known Christmas carols. Narrated by Richard Chamberlain. A Reader's Digest Potterton Production. Based on an English legend.
Pyramid 25 min Color 1975

529 Christmas Rhapsody. This live-action film expresses the seasonal beauty of nature by pictorially relating the story of *The Littlest Christmas Tree*. It's about the tiny fir that, compared with its oversize brothers, seems lonely and dwarfed. But a man and his two children see its true beauty, and take it home to give it a place of honor in front of the family fireplace. Anonymous.
Encyc. Brit. 11 min B&W 1955

530 Clever Hiko-Ichi. A feudal lord in medieval Japan needs a warrior to save his realm by accomplishing the tasks of weighing a giant with a tiny scale, fighting the giant with stones, and lifting a huge boulder. A little boy, Hiko-ichi, solves all three problems with a combination of applied science and personal courage. Animation.
Coronet 12 min Color 1975

531 The Cockerel, the Cat, and the Little Mouse. This is a playful reminder not to judge by appearances. A mouse meets a noisy rooster, and is frightened by its unfamiliar looks and sounds. His encounter with a cat is different. The cat resembles us, he tells his mother, who wisely warns her child that the "sweet" beast is actually the one to worry about, while the cockerel is perfectly harmless and, in fact, may be good to eat. Cartoon based on Fontaine's 19th-century fable. Also available in French.
Twyman 13 min Color 1969

532 The Country Mouse and the City Mouse (An Aesop Fable). This well-known fable is retold in cartoon style. The story of the adventures of the country mouse that visits its city cousin points to the age-old maxim that travel may be fun, but home is the best place. Produced by Gakken Film Company, Ltd., Tokyo.
Coronet 9 min Color 1962

533 The Cow-Tail Switch: A Folktale of Africa. This animated story from the Liberian rainforest dramatizes the African belief in the living spirit of nature and respect for ancestors. The African oral tradition is apparent, as the tale is told by an African mother to her children. Created by Stephen Bosustow. From the book by Harold Courlander and George Herzog.
Learning Corp. 8 min Color 1970

534 The Dancing Princess. This is an extract from the MGM production *The Wonderful World of the Brothers Grimm*, based on the fairy tale *The Twelve Dancing Princesses*. Cast: Jim Backus, Yvette Mimieux, and Russ Tamblyn. Directed by Henry Levin.
Films, Inc.   15 min   Color   1976

535 Darius Green and His Flying Machine. This is the story of a boy who dares to defy the elements of nature. It is based on early American folklore. Narrated in poetic style by Edwin Newman. Animated. Based on the Greek legend of Daedalus and Icarus.
AIMS   5 min   Color   1968

536 Dick Whittington and His Cat. Story of a poor boy whose affection for a stray cat leads to wealth and fame. Useful for language arts and story hours, the film also shows that kindness and generosity are often rewarded. Filmed in puppet animation against a background of drawings of medieval London.
Sterling Educ.   15 min   Color   1965

537 The Eagle and the Owl. This fable teaches children that beauty is in the eye of the beholder. An eagle promises not to attack an owl's babies if the owl will describe them to the eagle. The mother owl loves her offspring and describes them as being beautiful so that, when the predator spots some ugly birds, it will eat them instead. Better for the baby birds if mother were more honest! Cartoon based on Fontaine's fable. Also available in French.
Twyman   13 min   Color   1969

538 The Ears of King Midas. This animated legend introduces a tale from Greek mythology, an observation of personal qualities common to people of all ages. High atop Mount Olympus, two gods, Pan and Apollo, quarrel over who is the better musician. To settle the argument, the gods choose King Midas—known on earth for his honesty—to listen to them and to choose between them. His decision and its consequences provide a glimpse into human qualities such as jealousy, vanity, honesty, and compassion. Produced by Fred Ladd for Greatest Tales, Inc.
Encyc. Brit.   10 min   Color   1978

539 The Elves and the Shoemaker. This live-action film is an adaptation of the Grimm Brothers' classic. A poor shoemaker and his wife show kindness to a stranger and then benefit from two happy elves who spend the night cobbling. The film has authentic Bavarian exteriors that enhance the realistic sequences. Special photographic effects add to the fantasy of the elves' scenes. Produced on location in Rothenberg and Feuchtwangen (Germany) by Allan David.
Int. Film Bureau   27 min   Color   1967

540 The Emperor's New Clothes. A couple of swindlers seize their chance to make a fool of the emperor and make money at the same time. They convince the emperor that they are magic weavers whose thread becomes invisible to those who may be unusually stupid or unfit to hold office. The emperor takes the opportunity to test members of his royal court and orders the weavers to sew him a suit of clothes. However, the vain emperor's plan backfires and his stupidity is vividly demonstrated when he parades into town clad in "invisible" clothes. Produced by Greatest Tales, Inc. Animation.
BFA Educ. Media   9½ min   Color   1976

541   The Emperor's New Clothers. This interpretation of Hans Christian Andersen's story uses a combination of pantomime and modern dance to tell the story of the vain and foolish emperor who parades through his kingdom wearing nothing but an invisible suit of clothes. This adaptation of the familiar tale is set to a musical score with a simple narrative.
Coronet   11½ min   Color   1978

542 The Emperor's New Clothes. This live-action version of Andersen's famous fable should provide enjoyment plus discussion of the concept of hypocrisy, at a slightly higher age level than most fairy tales. Produced by Ake Soderquist of Denmark.
Encyc. Brit.   28 min   Color   1971

543 The Emperor's New Clothes. The Emperor of Fopdapper wants a new robe, and hires two fake tailors to make it. Later, the Emperor learns a valuable lesson from a boy in his kingdom. The Emperor, fooled, realizes he was guilty of being vain, punishes the offenders, and takes immediate action to reform. Staged by the Peppermint Players, a repertory theater group.
McGraw-Hill   16 min   Color   1966

544   The Emperor's New Clothes. Another version, with animated puppets, of Hans Christian Andersen's story of the vain emperor and his gullible courtiers. Fairy-tale motif, sets, and costumes. Produced by Progress Films. Designed and directed by Herbert K. Schultz.
Macmillan   12 min   Color   1959

545 The Emperor's Nightingale. The beloved Hans Christian Andersen fairy tale on happiness is animated by Czech artist Jiri Trnka into a lyric affirmation of love over death.
Macmillan   60 min   Color

546 The Emperor's Oblong Pancake. The story is about an emperor who tried to change all the round objects in his kingdom to an oblong

shape. After several frustrating experiences, he realizes that some things must be circular in order to function. Based on the fairy tale by Peter Hughes.
Lucerne Films   6 min   Color   1965

547 Fables of the Green Forest (series). All of the animal characters from the Thornton W. Burgess stories appear in this series of half-hour cartoons. A few representative titles are Sammy Blue Jay, Buster Bear, Joe the Otter, Johnny Chuck, Reddy Fox, The Bad Weasel, and Grandfather Frog.
Daybreak Prod.   30 min ea.   Color   1976-1977

548   Falling Star. This ancient legend, believed to have originated within the culture of the Cheyenne Indian tribe of America, is retold in animation designed to appeal to a variety of audiences and ages.
Vision Quest   14 min   Color   1975

549 Ferdinand the Bull. An adaptation of the Munro Leaf story (unfortunately out of print) about the beast that would rather smell the flowers than fight in the great Corrida de Toros in Madrid. Animated.
Disney   8 min   Color   1935

550   The Fire Flowers of Yet Sing Low. This is the fairy tale of a Chinese girl, Yet Sing Low, who befriended a sneezing dragon on the eve of the Chinese New Year. Animated.
Sterling Educ.   6 min   Color   1962

551   The Fir Tree. Dramatization of Hans Christian Andersen's tale about a fir tree with large ambitions. A film to use at Christmas time or to illustrate a fairy story using live-action motion. Produced by Ake Soderquist (Denmark).
Encyc. Brit.   27 min   Color   1971

552 The Fish and the Burning Stones. A folk tale about the discovery of coal in Pennsylvania. With appropriate music, and narrated by E.G. Marshall, this story of a boy's act of kindness to a grateful fish can evoke response and discussion with students in primary and middle grades.
AIMS 5 min Color 1968

553 The Fisherman and His Wife. A fisherman frees a flounder that is really an enchanted prince. For his kindness, the fisherman is granted a series of wishes that his selfish wife quickly accepts but, when she seeks to become ruler of the universe, she is returned to her original position as the fisherman's wife in a small cottage. Animated from the Grimms' fairy tale interpreted by Eric Carle.
Bosustow   10 min   Color   1977

554 The Fisherman and His Wife. There was once a fisherman who lived with his wife in a bare and miserable hut by the sea. One day, he hooked a huge fish. It spoke to him, saying that it was really a prince under a spell, so he threw it back into the water. When the fisherman explained this to his wife, she insisted he go straight back to the sea to ask the fish to grant them a wish. Based on Grimm. Original music by Leo Rosenbluth. Directed by Gisela Frisen and Pier Ekholm for Minimal Produkter, Stockholm (Sweden).
Weston Woods   20 min   Color   1970

555   Flight of Icarus. This production uses the collage animation of Gerald McDermott to retell the classic Greek myth about the first men to "try their wings." One flew too close to the sun, which melted the wax that had held the artifical wings onto his body. Produced by ACI Media.
Paramount   6 min   Color   1974

556   The Fox and the Jug. A fox enters a cottage in search of prey. There he finds a tiny little cock which, frightened and clumsy, tries to run. The fox decides to finish the hide-and-seek game and, when it seems that the cock has lost, the old jug falls from the oven and hits the fox on the head. The cock flees, and the fox figures out how to avenge himself. He ties the jug to his tail to drown it in the well. The jug touches the water level, begins to fill with water, and sinks to the bottom, drowning the fox. Based on Aesop's fable. Animated by Jiri Trnka of Czechoslovakia.
Phoenix   12 min   Color   1973

557   The Fox and the Rooster. This pictorial adaptation of one of Aesop's great fables points out the moral that even a clever schemer can be outwitted when good friends help each other. Real animals play all the roles. Characters are a fox, owl, rooster, possum, and dog.
Encyc. Brit.   10 min   B&W   1951

558   The Frog and the Rat. This story illustrates the fruits of trickery and crime. A rat and a frog meet at the edge of a marsh. The rat allows the frog to suggest that he join the frog for a swim. The frog, with visions of rat meat for supper, ties the rodent's legs to his own, explaining that he will support the rat in the water. When the two of them jump in, the amphibian drags the rat down to the bottom of the pond. They thrash about so much that a sharp-eyed hawk spots them, dives down, and catches them both. Cartoon based on the fable by Jean de la Fontaine. Also available in French.
Twyman   13 min   Color   1969

559   The Frog Prince. This is the fairy tale of a stubborn princess who doesn't want to keep her promise. After her father, the king, makes her honor her word, she discovers that doing the right thing can have its own

reward. Produced in animation by John Halas and Joy Batchelor, London.
Encyc. Brit. 7 min Color 1969

560 The Giant Devil-Dingo. A legendary Australian dog is transformed from mankind's bane to our helper in an authentic adaptation of Dick Roughsey's aboriginal tale. Produced in iconographic animation by Morton Schindel.
Weston Woods 10 min Color 1979

561 Glory Was – Glory Is! In ancient Greek mythology, a goddess would awaken every hundred years to watch over the southern peninsula of Peloponnesus. This film is a photographic recreation of that myth, showing a beautiful woman who awakens in a shady hollow and roams the ruins of Athens along with its modern hotels, shops, and apartments. Produced by Fred Niles.
Mar/Chuck 15 min Color 1975

562 The Golden Deer (A Tale of India). A child-princess of India dreams of a golden deer, so the king offers a reward for its capture. But the boy who captures the deer, and then decides to help it escape is given an even greater reward. Animated.
Coronet 12 min Color 1975

563 Goldilocks and the Crosby Family. The "Three Bears" becomes more than a fairy tale when the late Bing Crosby and family get into the act. Bing, out camping with his children, is telling them the Goldilocks story when daughter Mary Frances wanders off into an animated world of adventures as Goldilocks. Later she returns to her family, having lived the legend only to find a real bear cub has rummaged through their camper. The respect-for-nature theme is reflected in the song composed by the Sherman brothers,"Look Around You," while a note of brotherhood appears in the song "How Many See a People?" Produced by DePatie-Freleng in combined animation and live-action photography.
Macmillan 26 min Color 1976

564 Goldilocks and the Three Bears. Starring three real bears, this children's story is retold in a presentation that remains faithful to the incidents and characters of the original. Includes, in addition, suggestions for drawing pictures of scenes from the story and exploring other fairy tales.
Coronet 10 min Color 1953

565 Goldilocks and the Three Bears. This version of the fairy tale is produced in sign language along with a narrated soundtrack. Manual communication is by Lou Fant, Jr., leading exponent and practitioner of *Ameslan*, American Sign Language. Cleared for TV.
Joyce Media 12 min Color 1976

566 Greek Myths, Part I. Explores myth as primitive fiction, as history in disguise, and as the outgrowth of prehistoric ritual. Important myths, such as Theseus and the Minotaur, Orpheus and Eurydice, Actaeon and the goddess Artemis, and Persephone, are presented in drama, art, and animation. From the *Humanities Series*.
Encyc. Brit. 22 min Color 1971

567 Greek Myths – Part II. Shows how ancient man developed myths to explain natural phenomena and moral problems. The myth of Narcissus is a shrewd psychological diagnosis; the myth of Typhoeus imprisoned under Mount Etna, an attempt to explain volcanos; the story of Hyperion and Phaethon relates to a possible solar disturbance. From the *Humanities Series*.
Encyc. Brit. 25 min Color 1971

568 Hansel and Gretel. The Woodcutter, Hansel, Gretel, the green witch and the forest creatures come to life in this Grimm's folktale. Hansel and Gretel are courteous and industrious children who take care of their father's house in the forest. In their efforts to help, however, they learn it can be dangerous to talk with strangers or to accept food from them. A Ray Harryhausen production.
BFA Educ. Media 11 min Color 1955

569 Hansel and Gretel. A Woody Woodpecker cartoon spoofing this famous fairy tale. Despite its unusual treatment, this animated characterization remains fairly close to the Grimm Brothers' original story. Created by United Productions of America, competitors to the Disney studio.
Creative Film 7 min Color

570 Hansel and Gretel. A story of the danger and illusions of the outside world. Nothing is what it seems to be for children outwit the adults and find their way back to a loving home. Animated in England by John Halas and Joy Batchelor.
Encyc. Brit. 7 min Color 1969

571 Hansel and Gretel – An Appalachian Version. As the subtitle reveals, this version of the European fairy tale is set in America's impoverished mountain country. All roles are played by amateur actors. Narrated and directed by Tom Davenport. Winner of a CINE Golden Eagle and other awards. (Previewing suggested because of violent content.)
Davenport 16 min Color 1975

572 Hans in Luck. Such a good head for business Hans has that, when he finishes his apprenticeship with a big lump of gold, he begins a series

of trades. Each barter results in less and less value until he has nothing. But he concludes he is very lucky when Mother welcomes him home with his favorite meal. Animated from the Grimms' fairy tale as interpreted by Eric Carle.
Bosustow 7 min Color 1977

573 The Happy Prince. A transient swallow helps a bejeweled statue to share its wealth with the poor, and both are rewarded for their concern and sacrifice. Features the voices of Glynis Johns and Christopher Plummer. Animated by Potterton Productions (of Canada) for Reader's Digest Films. Based on the story by Oscar Wilde. Director: Michael Mills.
Pyramid 25 min Color 1974

574 The Hare and the Frogs. This story illustrates some of the finer points about how to get along well with others, and shows that, no matter how cowardly you think you are, there's always someone even more fearful. The hare in this fable is afraid of everyone and everything but then, one day, he discovers he has the ability to frighten others, too. Cartoon based on the Fontaine fable. Also available in French.
Twyman 13 min Color 1969

575 The Hare and the Tortoise. The proverbial hare and the legendary tortoise engage in their classic Aesopian race, as re-told by Jean de la Fontaine, the French 19th-century writer. As proven true throughout the ages, we learn again the important lesson that persistence is better than complacency, and always pays off in the end. Cartoon. Also available in French.
Twyman 13 min Color 1969

576 The Hare and Tortoise. Aesop's famous fable is portrayed by live animals in their natural habitat. Other animals such as the skunk, goose, rooster, raccoon, and owl take part in the story.
Encyc. Brit. 10 min B/W 1948

577 The Heifer, the Goat, and the Ewe. This fable by Fontaine suggests that, while there may be safety in numbers, there are dangers in unequal partnerships. Three animals form a union with a lion that doesn't work out very well for all concerned. Teaches children that trust is an important element in getting along with others. Cartoon. Also available in French.
Twyman 13 min Color 1969

578 Help, I'm Shrinking! Children occasionally feel small or helpless. Carrie's trouble is that she lets her feelings overwhelm her and she actually shrinks. Animation exaggerates the world as Carrie sees it. She becomes small enough to ride a butterfly, and learn that size doesn't

reflect ability. Each accomplishment helps her to find herself and to realize that people like her as she is. Suggested by the works of Lewis (*Alice in Wonderland*) Carroll. Producer: Barbara Dourmashkin.
Films Inc.   12 min   Color   1975

579 The House in the Wood. The Grimm Brothers' lesson on selflessness achieves a contemporary tone by the animation of Yoshtisuke Oshina. When the woodcutter's daughters try to bring him lunch, they lose their way and are drawn to the house where an old man lives with his cow and other animals. The two eldest daughters eat without feeding the animals, and are locked in a dungeon. But the youngest feeds the beasts first, and her reward is a rich and happy life with the old man, transformed into a young prince in a magnificent castle.
Macmillan   17 min   Color   1977

580 How the Elephant Got His Trunk. An elephant learns the price of curiosity and its rewards in this animated version of Rudyard Kipling's *Just-So* story. When the stub-nosed elephant (this was before elephants had trunks) asks the crocodile what it has for dinner, the crocodile replies by clamping the elephant's nose in his teeth. Pulling away, the elephant finds its nose stretched completely out of shape. But, to its surprise, it discovers the long trunk is useful. Eventually all relatives go to get their nose stretched, too. Produced by animator Stephen Bosustow.
Learning Corp.   8 min   Color   1970

581 How the First Letter was Written. Showing the advantages of written communications, this Kipling story concerns the writing of the world's first letter by a cave girl named Taffy. Taffy's father breaks his spear while hunting. The girl encounters a stranger who does not speak her language, so she draws a message on a piece of bark. The misunderstandings from her art work cause Taffy and her father to wish for a more effective way to send a message. Designed by animator Stephen Bosustow.
Learning Corp.   8 min   Color   1970

582 How the Whale got His Throat. Rudyard Kipling's *Just-So* story of how the whale got his sieve-like throat implies that the great sea-mammal was punished for gluttony. Also useful for teaching the difference between fact and fantasy in explaining natural phenomena. Animated by Stephen Bosustow.
Learning Corp.   8 min   Color   1970

583 Icarus. This animation is an artist's conception of the Greek myth in which an inventor fashions wings for his son to escape from the labyrinth in Crete. Flute music by Eldar Rathburn. Produced by the National Film Board of Canada.
Sterling Educ.   8 min   Color   1977

584 Icarus: A Flight Fantasy. Clay animation creates a variation of the Greek myth, relating it to evolution. From the hoard of androids in a primitive sea, one individualist **surfaces** and gradually perfects his movements. His efforts aren't always successful and, so, meet with derision from his peers. But eventually he frees himself of frustration, and eveyone else then follows suit.
Macmillan   10 min   Color

585 Icarus and Daedalus. This story of the boy who flew too close to the sun, despite his father's warning, can be a lesson in listening to the advice of parents. Based on the ancient Greek myth. Animated.
Sterling Educ.   6 min   Color   1963

586 The Icarus Wish. With a boy as subject, this live-action vignette is a reminder of humanity's continuing awe of flight. Multi-screen images symbolize the diversity of emotions involved. Produced by Byron Bauer.
Churchill   7 min   Color   1972

587 I Know an Old Lady Who Swallowed a Fly. This is a Canadian folktale, sung and played by guitarist Burl Ives. Using animation, the story-song explains how such an accident even came about, and how it led to swallowing a spider, bird, cat, dog, goat, pig, cow, and horse, and—ultimately—to the old lady's death! Produced by the National Film Board of Canada.
Int. Film Bur.   5½ min   Color   1963

588 Jack and the Beanstalk. One of the most famous of all fairy tales, this is the story of Jack, who climbs the beanstalk that grew overnight from magic seeds his mother threw on the ground. He captures the goose that lays the golden eggs, then meets and kills the giant.
McGraw-Hill   16 min   Color   1967

589 Jack and the Robbers. One of the many yarns from Appalachian folklore, with a brief explanatory statement by narrator Richard Chase, who assumes many voices to portray the characters. The visuals are cartoon-style drawings about how Jack runs away from home and falls in with an assortment of animal friends that fool some robbers into thinking they're being outnumbered by strong men.
Pied Piper   15 min   Color   1975

590 The Jackdaw in Borrowed Feathers. This is an Aesopian fable by the 19th-century Frenchman, Jean de la Fontaine. In it, he teaches children that they can cheat themselves when trying to be something that they are not—a good lesson for adults, too! Cartoon produced for European television. Also available in French on special order.
Twyman   13 min   Color   1969

591 John Henry. When railroads were pushing westward, men like John Henry were needed to swing the spike hammer. Unlike other steel-drivers, John Henry used two hammers instead of one, leaving the other steel-drivers far behind. This film is the story of these and other legendary exploits.
BFA Educ. Media   11 min   Color   1972

592 Johnny Appleseed. This frontier story blends the narration of Dan Blocker with appropriate American music and color animation. Fact or legend, the individuality and selflessness of Johnny Appleseed can encourage student expression and response in the elementary grades
AIMS 5 min   Color   1968

593 Johnny Appleseed. The saga of the barefoot hero of the frontier era. As a young man, Johnny left home to travel the country, planting faith and appleseeds. After walking the land for 40 years as a friend to settlers, Indians, and animals, he left a legacy of love and fruit trees.
BFA Educ. Media   11 min   Color   1972

594 Johnny Appleseed. Animation enacts the legendary character's love of God, man, and nature that results in his life long mission to perpetuate his favorite fruit. Edited from the feature film, *Melody Time*, with the singing voice of Dennis Day.
Disney   16 min   Color   1948

595 Johnny Appleseed: A Legend of Frontier Life. In this live-action film, the story of Johnny Chapman, a man of peace whose goal in life was to make the world a better place for all creatures, is enacted against the background of pioneer America. We see how Johnny's love of God and nature started him on a mission that was to last all his life, and make his name known throughout the land.
Coronet   13½ min   Color   1954

596 The Kind-Hearted Ant. This version of de la Fontaine's fable uses a minimum of words in animating story of a generous insect that unintentionally disrupts the harmony and order of the ant hill. Produced by Zagreb Film of Yugoslavia.
Int. Film Bur.   10 min   Color   1956

597 The King and the Lion. This is another in the series of films featuring Spots and Stripes, the puppets. It is based in part on Aesop's fable, "Androcles and the Lion." Spot plays a deposed King, enslaved by Stripes. A third puppet, Reggie, King of the Forest, is the captured lion that surprises everybody by having a friendly reunion with Spots in the arena. Spots' explanation is, "Kindness begets kindness—even from lions." Produced by Alfred Wallace and Martin Stevens. Originally distributed by Pictura Productions.
Salzburg Enterprises   15 min   Color   1954

598   King Arthur. Cartoon character, Mr. Magoo, as Merlin the Magician, joins the Knights of the Round Table at Camelot during the reign of England's King Arthur. Among the brave knights performing their valorous deeds are Lancelot, Sir Galahad, Gawain, and Prince Valiant. Produced by UPA Pictures. Previously released by Macmillian Films.
Mar/Chuck   24 min   Color   1965

599 King Midas. The fable of King Midas is interpreted through modern crayon and watercolor resist. It's the old story of a king and his wish to turn all he touches to gold. Stresses that monetary values alone are not the most important.
AIMS   5 min   Color   1968

600 King Midas and the Golden Touch. Marionettes portray the king enraptured with the gift of the golden touch, his horror when he turns his daughter into gold, and his happiness when the beauty of life is restored to her.
Coronet   10½ min   Color   1950

601   Legend. This folk tale, from a Western Canadian Indian tribe, is about a young woman whose vanity leads to her disfiguration by the Spirit Woman. The characters look, dress, and speak in modern ways but with optical effects they become symbolic representations. **Produced** by the National Film Board of Canada.
Pyramid   15 min   Color   1970

602   The Legend of John Henry. In this jazz interpretation, Roberta Flack sings the story of frontier courage, strength, and perseverance of man against overwhelming odds. Animated by Stephen Bosustow.
Pyramid   11 min   Color   1973

603 The Legend of Paul Bunyan. The tall tales concerning this legendary hero spring from his confrontation with Hela Helsun, Bull of the Woods, and his adventures with Babe, his Blue Ox. Both are told in this film animated by Stephen Bosustow.
Bosustow   13½ min   Color   1973

604 The Legend of the Cruel Giant. An innocent fisherman releases a genie and is rewarded with jewels and gold. But when he sees the genie grow into a giant that brings plague and war into the world, he tricks the genie back into the bottle. Produced by the Soyuzmultfilm Studio, Moscow. Based on the Russian fairy tale.
Carousel   11 min   Color   1971

605 The Legend of the Magic Knives. After an old Indian chief realizes that carvings of an apprentice are superior to his, he throws a knife at the guardian of these carvings, but strikes himself. Dying, he is

permitted to choose any form of life after death, however, and elects to be a river always flowing close to his native tribe.
Encyc. Brit.   11 min   Color   1971

606 The Legend of the Pied Piper. "Keep your word," is the theme of this Robert Browning fairy tale of the master musician of Hamelin. Classes and informal groups can enjoy this film for its entertainment value and for the understanding of a story for later reading.
Coronet   10½ min   Color   1949

607 The Lion and the Mouse. The classic Aesopian fable is non-verbally reinterpreted here in the animated cut-out artwork of Evelyn Lambart, producer at the National Film Board of Canada. Original music supplies the background.
Benchmark   5 min   Color   1976

608 The Lion and the Mouse. Through cartoon interpretation of an Aesop fable, children can learn that size alone does not determine how helpful a person can be. The King of the Jungle laughs at the idea that a mouse could ever help him. But when a speck of dirt gets in the lion's eye, it is the mouse that removes it and proves to be a friend after all. Produced by Films for Children, Inc.
Coronet   10 min   Color   1960

609 The Lion and the Rat. This fable is about the rewards of kindness. The king of beasts spares the life of a rat that ran right into his clutches. Sure enough, when the lion becomes entrapped later on, the rodent repays the favor by gnawing away at the net, setting the regal beast free. Cartoon based on Fontaine's Aesopian fable. Also available in French.
Twyman   13 min   Color   1969

610 The Little Match Girl. This is the sentimental and seasonal story by Hans Christian Andersen about the poor street vendor who freezes to death on New Year's Eve. From the *Classic Tales Retold* series. Animated. Produced by Greatest Tales, Inc.
BFA Educ. Media   8¾ min   Color   1977

611 The Little Match Girl. This adaptation of the Hans Christian Andersen tale uses puppet animation and the author's words to tell the tragic story of the girl whose cruel father forced her to sell matches on the city streets. On New Year's Eve, despite the cold and snow, she wanders all night trying to sell her wares. But the insensitivity of those she encounters leaves her with a full load, no money, and a broken spirit. In a futile attempt to warm herself, she lights some of her matches and experiences heartwarming visions in the glow of the flame. As a reward for her suffering, the child is taken into heaven — never to suffer again.
Coronet   17 min   Color   1978

612 The Little Match Girl. This adult adaptation of the Hans Christian Andersen story was produced in live-action photography in 1928, and re-released in 1975. Its moral suggests the dangers of confusing fantasy with reality. Produced by Jean Renoir and Jean Tedesco.
Phoenix   29 min   B&W   1928

613 The Little Mermaid. Animated version of a story by Hans Christian Andersen. The daughter of the Mer-King falls in love with a prince she rescued from a shipwreck. To be with him, she goes to the Enchantress who gives her a human form in exchange for her voice. When the prince marries someone else, the Mermaid faces the prospect of becoming seafoam as the Enchantress predicted. Because of the sacrifices she makes, though, Death does not claim her. And although she loses the prince, she gains a human soul and everlasting happiness. A Reader's Digest Presentation by Potterton Productions. Narrated by Richard Chamberlain.
Pyramid   25 min   Color   1973

614 The Little Red Hen. This combination of animated artwork and live-action photography is an adaptation of the classic fable of the industrious fowl and her lazy barnyard companions. Also useful in familiarizing children with chickens, ducks, cats, and pigs.
Coronet   10 min   Color   1950

615 Little Red Riding Hood. With its animation and musical style, this classic fairy tale will help teach children never to stray from the proper path. While primarily an educational film, it is also designed to entertain children with its modern dialog and charming little forest animals. Adapted from Grimm.
Coronet   17 min   Color   1978

616   Little Red Riding Hood. Animated hand-puppets enact the storyline within a relatively modern setting that includes telephones, gas ranges, and piano. But the basic plot and characters are faithful to the original figures of the innocent girl, villainous wolf, heroic woodsman, and sweet old grandmother.
Encyc. Brit.   9 min   Color.   1958

617 Little Tom Thumb. A boy's dream of escaping from poverty and unhappiness comes true in a typically impossible but inspiring way. Tom becomes a hero by saving himself and his six brothers, and then returning home with treasure and magic boots. Based on Grimm. Produced and animated by John Halas and Joy **Batchelor** (London).
Encyc. Brit.   8 min   Color   1969

618 The Loon's Necklace. Brings to life the Indian Legend of how the loon, a Canadian water bird, received its **distinguishing** neckband. Cer-

emonial masks, carved by Indians of British Columbia, establish the characters of the story, and portray Indian sensitivity to nature. Produced by Crawley Films, Limited, of Toronto.
Encyc. Brit. 10 min Color 1949

619 The Magic Horse. The first full-length Russian color cartoon is based on one of their favorite folk tales. Castles, enchanting forests, and music provide the decor for this simple story of a boy and his tiny horse's magical powers. Directed by I. Vano. Produced by the Soyuzmultfilm Studios, Moscow. Based on the story *The Little Humpbacked Horse*. English dialogue.
Macmillan 57 min Color 1941

620 The Magic Tree. A folktale from the Congo about a youngster on a symbolic journey. The boy, Mavungu, releases a magic people held captive in the leaves of a bizarre tree. He then marries a fairy princess and creates a marvelous kingdom of his own. Produced in animation based on Gerald McDermott's picture-book.
Texture 10 min Color 1970

621 The Magic Well. Gretchen, an unselfish girl, falls into a magic well and finds herself in an enchanted land where kindness is rewarded. Later, her selfish step-sister makes the same trip...but with completely different results. Puppet characters and art backgrounds visualize this animated version. Adapted from a Grimms' fairy tale.
Coronet 14 min Color 1977

622 Many Moons. An adaptation of James Thurber's rendering of the old truth that a child and a fool may be wiser than learned men. When a princess named Lenore desires the moon, none of the king's counselors can obtain it for her. Ironically, it is the court jester who finds a way to fulfill her wish. A Rembrandt Film.
Macmillan 10 min Color 1973

623 The Master Thief. Animates a puppet version of the fairy tale about the series of conditions a count requires before granting freedom to a thief. No matter how many times his skill is challenged, the master thief succeeds in tricking the count and becoming free. Produced by National Educational Television (NET).
Indiana U. 15 min Color 1973

624 Mean, Nasty, Ugly Cinderella. Using the fairy tale *Cinderella* as frame of reference, this film demonstrates how character influences storyline. A small class responds to situations designed for the creation of new stories. Projector-stops allow viewers to write individually between segments. From the *Communication Skills* series.
Churchill 16 min Color 1972

625 The Mermaid Princess. An adaptation of the Hans Christian Andersen fairy tale, using animated puppetry along with three-dimensional sets and music. It tells the tale of the sea witch who unsuccessfully tries to enchant a handsome prince by making a mermaid human. When the prince marries someone else, the mermaid becomes a brilliant circle of skylight.
Coronet 13½ min Color 1976

626 The Monkey and the Crab. A variation of Aesop's "Grasshopper and the Ant." Farmer Crab is tricked out of his rice by Mischievous Monkey. After eating the best fruit from Crab's magically grown persimmon tree, Monkey gets his just deserts at the hands of Crab's friends. Enacted in puppet animation. Produced in Japan.
Coronet 13½ min Color 1975

627 The Musicians in the Woods. Animated puppets enact the Grimm fairy tale about animals that set out to make their way in the world. The adventure in which the donkey, dog, cat, and rooster outwit a band of thieves and gain a fortune is told here by Gakken Film Co., Ltd., Tokyo.
Coronet 13½ min Color 1962

628 The Mythology of Greece and Rome. The myths of ancient Greece and Rome were about gods invented to explain natural phenomena and behavior. They often taught a moral lesson. The stories of Ceres and Proserpina, Apollo and Daphne, and Bellerophon and Pegasus, are retold in this film and abridged. The more familiar Latin names are used.
BFA Educ. Media 16 min Color 1969

629 Narcissus. This abstract animation retells the story of the beautiful youth who became so enamored of his reflection that he scorned the love of Echo. Based on the classical Greek myth. Directed by Peter Foldes. Produced by Les Films de la Pleiade (France.)
Films, Inc. 6 min Color 1975

630 The North Wind and the Sun (An Aesop Fable). This animated film tells the story of a contest between the elements. "You can sometimes do more by being gentle than you can by using force," is the lesson children can gain from this film. Produced by Gakken Film Company, Ltd., Tokyo.
Coronet 7 min Color 1962

631 The Nutcracker. E.T.A. Hoffman's original tale is well-known around the world as a children's story and a ballet. This version is set to Tchaikovsky's music and narrated by Hans Conried. Produced in Russia by the Soyuzmultfilm Studio.
Barr Films 26 min Color 1978

632 The Nutcracker. This dance interpretation of E.T.A. Hoffman's mid-19th-century fairy tale features Edward Villella as the Nutcracker and Melissa Hayden as the Sugar Plum Fairy. The story was set to ballet, later that century, by Tchaikovsky whose music is also the foundation of this classical yet contemporary version. Choreography by Kurt Jacoby. Director: Karl Heinz Elsner.
Warner Bros. 60 min Color 1965

633 The Oak and the Reed. Teaches children one of the advantages of personal "flexibility." An oak tree brags to the reeds about his strength, claiming that they should all be like him or at least let him protect them. Things work out just the other way around, though, when a strong wind comes along and blows down the oak, while the supple reeds survive because of their adaptability to change. Cartoon based on the fable by de la Fontaine. Soundtrack also available in French.
Twyman 13 min Color 1969

634 Orfeo. This animation in sand is a subjective interpretation of the classic Greek myth of Orpheus and Eurydice. In its non-verbal film form, the story can be construed to suggest the lonely life and sacrifice of artists. Produced by Caroline Leaf.
Pyramid 11 min Color 1971

635 Orpheus and Eurydice. As an introduction to Greek Mythology, this animated film tells of the minstrel Orpheus and his descent into Hades in search of his lost bride. Orpheus finds his wife but cannot resist temptation, and he loses her forever.
Sterling Educ. 10 min Color 1963

636 Paul Bunyan. Tall tales of the great work-giant of the timber industry who conquered the American wilderness. His story is told with broad humor, designed for the elementary grades and junior high school.
BFA Educ. Media 11 min Color 1970

637 Paul Bunyan. This is the legend of a larger-than-life character who, as a baby in a cradle, was ten axe-handles high. When he ran out of trees in Maine, he headed West. During the Great Blizzard, Paul found Babe, an ox frozen blue. After he thawed Babe out, the pair became the greatest logging team in the West. Along with their other exploits, 'tis said they more or less accidentally created Minnesota's ten thousand lakes, the Grand Tetons, and Yellowstone Park. Animated.
Disney 17 min Color 1971

638 Paul Bunyan and the Blue Ox. This film retells the tall story of a fabled frontiersman and Babe, the blue (because frozen) ox he found, thawed out, and then put to work as his logging partner. Produced in

animated puppetry.
Coronet 6 min   Color   1952

639 Paul Bunyan: Lumber Camp Tales. This animated film recounts
famous tall tales of the American folk-hero: the bunkhouse with beds
stacked 137 high, the gigantic flapjack griddle, the popcorn blizzard, and
the ingenious method by which Paul and his great blue ox straightened
out the Big Onion River.
Coronet 10½ min   Color   1962

640   Petronella. Things never change much in Skyclear Mountain
where traditionally the son of the King and Queen would always leave
home and rescue a princess. That was the way it was until King Peter and
Queen Blossom. Their only child turns out to be a girl, Petronella, who
carries out the tradition by setting out to rescue a prince! Based on the
book by Jay Williams. Produced by Barbara Dourmashkin.
Film Fair 13¼ min   Color   1978

641 The Pied Piper of Hamelin. Robert Browning's narrative poem of
this familiar legend, symbolizing the conflict between greed and honor, is
translated to animated film and narrated by Peter Ustinov. Produced by
Argo Sight & Sound, Ltd.
BFA Educ. Media   16¾ min   Color   1970

642 The Pied Piper of Hamelin. The fable of the mysterious stranger
who agrees to rid Hamelin of its rats by leading them into the sea with his
magical music. When the town refuses to pay for the task, the Piper leads
the village children into happy oblivion through the mountainside,
leaving the townspeople to rue the day they broke their word. Produced
by Rembrandt Films from the story by Robert Browning. Directed by Al
Kousel. Narrated by Eli Wallach.
Macmillan 5 min   Color   1970

643 The Princess and the Pearls. From *The Arabian Nights*, this story
depicts Sinbad the Sailor shipwrecked in a storm, and his meeting with a
fish that gives Sinbad a string of pearls for sparing his life. But when the
Sultan's palace is robbed, Sinbad is accused of having stolen the pearls.
He is saved by the Sultan's daughter, and the tale ends happily as he gains
acceptance into the Sultan's court. Animated by Karel Zeman. Produced
by Short Film, Prague (Czechoslovakia).
Learning Corp.   14 min   Color   1973

644 Prometheus XX. Can humanity afford to turn away from opportunity? This is the question posed by this animated version of the ancient
Greek legend of Prometheus who once braved the gods themselves in order to bring the miracle of fire to earth. Produced by Gene Feldman.
Wombat 6 min   Color

645 Puss in Boots. Uses animated puppets to enact Charles **Perrault's** fairy tale, *The Master Cat, Puss in Boots*. Tells the story of a clever pet that manages to win its master a fortune, a royal title, and marriage to a beautiful princess. Produced in Germany.
Encyc. Brit. 16 min B&W 1957

646 Raccoon Story: A Menomini Indian Folktale. Originating from the Menomini tribe, Wisconsin, this film centers about a typical figure of many folktales, the trickster. It combines American Indian culture with lessons in honesty, self awareness, and responsiblity. The cast consists of life-size puppets. Teacher's-guide suggests activities such as role-play, group discussion, creative writing, art projects, reading, library skills, and research projects.
Xerox Films 9 min Color 1974

647 The Rainbow Serpent. How did the serpent Goorilla create Australia's geography and wildlife? Dick Roughsey's aboriginal legend, recreated in iconographic animation, explains the playful theory behind this fable from "Down Under."
Weston Woods 11 min Color 1979

648 Rapunzel. This is the Grimm story of Rapunzel the golden-tressed, imprisoned in a tower by a wicked witch. Her plight is discovered by a handsome prince who dares to climb the tower to rescue the lovely maiden. A Ray Harryhausen Film.
BFA Educ. Media 11 min Color 1955

649 Rapunzel, Rapunzel. This is an Americanized version of the Grimm Brothers' fairy tale, its treatment paralleling that of *Hansel and Gretel—An Appalachian Version*: filmed in live-action photography, with emphasis on the adult-level human relationships. It borrows from another Tom Davenport production for the 19th-century Shaker music that provides part of the background. Produced by Tom and Mimi Davenport.
Davenport 16 min Color 1978

650 The Rat and the Oyster. A country rat decides to leave home and to explore the world at large. Making his way to an unknown land, he discovers some oysters on the ocean shore. Thinking they look good enough to eat, and being willing to experiment, he starts to do just that when one of the oysters decides the same thing about him! Cartoon based on de la Fontaine's fable from 19th-century France. Also available in French.
Twyman 13 min Color 1969

651 The Rat That Retired from the World. This story illustrates the meaning of false piety. A world-weary rat decides to get away from it all permanently and withdraws into a life within an enormous Holland

cheese that becomes both his home and his food supply. While in his oblivious refuge, an enemy cat invades his former nest. The other rats come to him, begging for his help and protection against the invader. The recluse rodent refuses any material aid, but, instead, promises to pray for them. Cartoon based on de la Fontaine. Also available in French.
Twyman 13 min Color 1969

652 Reflections: A Japanese Folktale. In this story, designed to probe perception, a young man buys a box with a mirror on the bottom. In it, he sees the face of his dead father. His wife sees, not her father-in-law, but a beautiful rival for her husband's love. A holy woman, when solicited for her judgment, perceives another holy woman, and decides the box is meant for her. Where is the truth? Are our perceptions distorted by selfinterest?
Encyc. Brit. 19 min Color 1975

653 The Remarkable Rocket. David Niven narrates this animated adaptation of Oscar Wilde's story about the fate of fireworks prepared to be set off during a royal wedding ceremony. Music by Howard Blake. A Reader's Digest-Gerald Potterton coproduction.
Pyramid 26 min Color 1975

654 Return to Oz. This animated featurette is based on Frank L. Baum's *The Wizard of Oz*. After receiving a letter from her old friends in Munchkinville, Dorothy puts on her magic slippers and returns to Oz. Surprises are in store after she learns that the letter wasn't written by Strawman, Lion, and Tinman, but by her old enemy, the Wicked Witch of the West!
Macmillan 57 min Color 1969

655 The Roc Bird and the Rescue. In this adventure from *The Arabian Nights*, a parrot helps Sinbad escape from the palace, where he had been condemned to death for daring to love the sultan's daughter. But Sinbad falls into the clutches of the monstrous roc bird, and winds up on an island. A quirk of fate frees him, and he sets off to sea with some new-found friends. Animated by Karel Zeman. Produced by Short Film, Prague (Czechoslovakia).
Learning Corp. 15 min Color 1973

656 The Rug Maker: A Folktale of Africa. This East African story shows that even a chief's son can benefit from a trade. Mama Seminigi, the village's best storyteller, recalls how Kamalo, son of a chief, did not learn an occupation. But when he wanted to marry Chinowana, he became a rug-maker to please her. When Kamalo and a hunting party were captured by enemies, Kamalo's rug-making brought about their rescue. The film ends with Mama Seminingi urging listeners to learn a trade, too. Animator: Stephen Bosustow. From the collected stories

When Stones Were Soft, by Eleanor B. Heady.
Learning Corp. 9 min Color 1970

657 Rumpelstiltskin. This is the Grimm Brothers' story of the fair Juliana, her task of spinning straw into gold, and the little man who lost his temper.
Coronet 10 min Color 1949

658 Rumpelstiltskin. This is the Grimm Brothers' story of the evil dwarf who, when the queen's page guessed his strange name, was frustrated in his plot to take the woman's child. Animated by Halas and Batchelor (London, England).
Encyc. Brit. 8 min Color 1970

659 Rumpelstiltskin. A troupe of Connecticut school children, the "Ha' Penny Players," act out all the parts in this live-action performance. Conceived as a way of stimulating interest in classroom production. Based on Grimm.
Sterling Educ. 11 min Color 1963

660 Sand. The sand images of producer-sculptor Caroline Leaf photographically interpret the fable of "Peter and the Wolf" as a shadow world where a boy's fear of the unknown is finally resolved. Besides providing a story line, *Sand* is an example of the graphic possibilities of a common substance usually taken for granted or ignored. Produced by Caroline Leaf.
Phoenix 10 min B&W 1969

661 Sasha, Yasha, Yakov and the Wolf. Sasha the hare, Yasha the pig, and Yakov the little black lamb lend meaning to the word "sharing" as they put winter hunger and a sneaky wolf to flight. Produced by the Kiev-Popular Science Films Studio. Based on a Russian legend.
Carousel 11 min Color 1971

662 The Selfish Giant. A giant builds a wall around his castle to keep children from playing there. For being so nasty, the giant is tormented by snow, frost, wind, and hail that finally force the giant into accepting the children. In fact, he helps a mysterious child climb a tree and receives a hug for his kindness. Long after, when the giant is old and gray, the mysterious child—the Christ child—returns and leads the giant to another garden, the garden of Heaven. A Reader's Digest presentation. Animated by Murray Shostak and Peter Sander. From the fairy tale by Oscar Wilde.
Pyramid 27 min Color 1972

663 The Selfish Giant. This 19th-century fairy tale is reinterpreted in Oscar Wilde's words, supplemented by music and the animated drawings of Gertrude and Walter Reiner of Germany. Produced by Mor-

ton Schindel.
Weston Woods   14 min   B&W   1964

664 The Seven Ravens. The famous Grimm fairytale of revenge and love is recreated in this film by a team of European animators. The heroine is a 7-year-old girl who sets out to free her seven brothers from a witch's curse that has turned them into blackbrirds. Directed by Christel Wiemer.
Learning Corp.   22 min   Color   1971

665 The Seventh Mandarin. Can an emperor rule a people he's never met? This one does...until...one night the seventh mandarin takes his turn at flying the great kite said to be the Emperor's spirit. A wind snatches the kite away. In pursuit, the mandarin sees ramshackle huts and hears the groans of the **poor**. Next day, he reports his findings to the emperor who has seen the same visions in a dream. The walls around the palace are leveled, the king rides out to see his people, and rules them wisely till the end of his days. From the storybook by Jane Yolen. Animation by Steve Bosustow.
Xerox Films   12½ min   Color   1973

666 Seven with One Blow. The little tailor kills 7 flies with a blow of his yardstick and decides he was made for better things. Through sleight of hand, he is rewarded with marriage to the princess. He finally becomes king and rules the country wisely ever after. Animated from the fairy tale series by Eric Carle, based on Grimm.
Bosustow   10 min   Color   1977

667 Shoemaker and the Elves. Animated puppets tell the story of the elves who slip into the shoemaker's shop and make shoes for him. This film, based on the Grimms' fairy tale, tells what happens when the shoemaker and his wife leave new clothes, food, and sweets for the elves one night. Produced by Gakken Film Company, Ltd., Tokyo.
Coronet   13 min   Color   1962

668 The Shoemaker and the Elves. A shoemaker has his misfortunes reversed by the midnight magic of a pair of cobbler elves. The poor man and his wife discover their tiny helpers and express their gratitude by leaving two sets of new clothes on the workbench. The elves are so delighted that they dance out the window, leaving behind the message: "Long life–Happiness–Peace." Animated in free-form puppetry by Institut für Film und Bild (Germany).
Films Inc.   15 min   Color   1972

669 The Singing Bone. This is one of the fairy tales from the MGM production of the *Wonderful World of the Brothers Grimm*. It features Terry-Thomas, Buddy Hackett, and Conrad Nagel. Direction by Henry

Levin.
Films Inc.   13 min   Color   1976

670 Sioux Legends. Sioux and Blackfeet Indians in North Dakota re-enact scenes from the daily life of their ancestors, along with legends of tradition and religion that influenced these Plains tribes before the arrival of white men. A Nauman production for ACI Media.
Paramount   20 min   Color   1973

671 Sleeping Beauty. Costumed actors re-enact this age-old fairy tale against a medieval background. It's the story of the princess, doomed with all her subjects to sleep for 100 years. A handsome prince awakens her with a kiss, and wins her hand in **marriage** – to the approval of the entire kingdom, naturally!
Coronet   13½ min   Color   1952

672 Sleeping Beauty. A story of revenge – with the usual happy, fairy tale ending. The wicked old witch lays a curse on the baby princess, but the good fairy is able to protect her and the royal court. Animated by Halas and Batchelor Films, Ltd., England.
Encyc. Brit.   7 min   Color   1970

673   The Sleeping Beauty, Brier Rose: A German Folktale. Animated puppets dramatize this fairy tale about the Princess Brier Rose, who is cursed to die of a spindle prick. However, the curse is softened by another sorceress who predicts that Brier Rose will not die, but sleep for 100 years. A valiant prince breaks the spell, and everyone lives happily ever after! An Omega Production.
BFA Educ. Media   15 min   Color   1970

674 Snow White With Mr. Magoo. The beloved Grimm fairy tale is brought to life in this film about a lovely princess and her cruel step-mother who casts her out and makes threats upon her life. Magoo plays all seven of the dwarfs who protect Snow White. Cartoon animation. Originally distributed by McGraw-Hill.
Macmillan   52 min   Color   1965

675   The Staunch Tin Soldier. A birthday party for a boy provides Hans Christian Andersen with an opportunity to tell the story of the toy soldier that falls out the window, is eaten by a fish, and finally returns to his first home. Produced in Denmark by Ake Soderquist for Filmkonsult AB, Copenhagen.
Encyc. Brit.   27 min   Color   1971

676   The Steadfast Tin Soldier. This is the bitter-sweet fairy tale of the one-legged toy that falls in love with a ballet doll. From the classic by Hans Christian Andersen. Narrated by Don Hammer. Animated puppetry. A Danish Film Culture production by Ivo Caprino.
Macmillan   14 min   Color   1955

677 The Stonecutter. This ancient Japanese fable of envy and greed is vivified by Gerald McDermott's graphic designs. The simple narrative serves as counterpoint to the stylized images. Music performed on the koto provides authentic Japanese background. Animated by Gerald Mc-Dermott.
Weston Woods 6 min   Color   1975

678 A Story—A Story. Long ago, there were no stories on earth. All stories belonged to the Sky God. Ananse, the Spider, then spun a web up to the sky in order to bargain with the Sky God. Colored woodcuts and music performed entirely on African instruments add authenticity to this folktale. Based on the Caldecott Award-winning book, written and illustrated by Gail E. Haley. Animated by Gene Deitch.
Weston Woods   10 min   Color   1974

679 The Strange Story of the Frog that Became a Prince. Who wants to be a prince? Not this hapless frog that runs up against a witch. A click of her fingers triggers the disastrous change from frog to prince. But no amount of finger-snapping (or even backward magic words) can restore him to his froghood. All ends happily, however, as viewers discover. Being just what you are is the nicest thing of all. From the story by Elinor Lander Horwitz. Animated by Stephen Bosustow.
Xerox   11½ min   Color   1973

680 The Swineherd. A spoiled Princess scorns the love of an honorable prince. She does not value his precious gifts of a rose and a nightingale, but is willing to kiss a swineherd 100 times for a silly toy. The swineherd, of course, is the clever prince in disguise. Illustrated by Bjorn Wiinblad. **Animated by Gene Deitch. Producer: Morton Schindel. Based on Hans** Christian Andersen.
Weston Woods   13 min   Color   1975

681 The Tale of King Midas. This fable goes beyond the well-known curse of the golden touch, and portrays Midas' later punishment: sprouting donkey ears. Such a secret is one that can't be kept from the barber, who eventually breathes it into the earth where nature and fate spread the word. Filmed in live-action photography.
Encyc. Brit. 18 min   Color   1974

682 The Tale of Rumpelstiltskin. As a live-action interpretation of the traditional fairy tale, touches of humor encourage children to use their own imaginations and create fantasy tales of their own. Based on Grimm.
Encyc. Brit. 21 min   Color   1974

683 The Tale of the Ugly Duckling. This is the fairy tale, by Hans Christian Andersen, of a little swan that was raised with a brood of ducklings and rejected because it did **not** conform to the appearance of a

duck. Finally, after many discouraging experiences, the ugly duckling discovers its true identity as a swan of beauty and dignity. Animated in England by Joy Batchelor and John Halas.
Encyc. Brit.   8 min   Color   1953

684 A Tale of Till. This story is one of many based on the German folk character, Till Eulenspiegel. It opens with Brueghel's art of the Dark Ages, and then dissolves into a puppet show about the court jester, Till, who helped his king settle a dispute between people who claimed to have lost the same purse of money. Accompanied by music of the period. Narrated by Barry Sullivan. Produced by Marianne Meyerhoff.
Film Fair   11¼ min   Color   1975

685 Tara, the Stonecutter. An adaptation from a Japanese folk story written in the 1300's. This film is designed to stimulate self-expression and consciousness of values among children in the primary and middle grades. Animation is based upon the authentic Japanese prints of Uta Maru. An original musical score by Billy May.
AIMS   8 min   Color   1962

686 Theseus and the Minotaur. Theseus, a young prince of Athens, was a great warrior even as a boy. How he outwitted Minos, the cruel King of Crete, and slew the monster Minotaur is the subject of this classic Greek folk tale and legend. The moral of the story: "Good always triumphs over evil." Produced in animation by Alfred Wallace and Wan-go Weng. Originally distributed by Pictura Productions.
Salzburg   5 min   Color   1954

687 Three Fox Fables. Using real animals, this film recaptures the spirit of three of Aesop's best fables: *The Fox and the Grapes, The Fox and the Crow*, and *The Fox and the Stork*. Collaborator: Grace Storm.
Encyc. Brit.   11 min   B&W   1948

688 Three Gifts. This legend from Czechoslovakia is about a man who received magic presents from three lodgers, and about the punishment received by the bailiff and the miller who tried to steal the gifts. Produced in puppet animation by Short Film, Prague.
Phoenix   16 min   Color   1974

689 Three Golden Hairs. When the evil queen hears a prophecy that a baby will become queen, she attempts to drown the baby in the river. Furious that all her attempts to do away with the girl fail, the queen sends her maid to fetch three golden hairs from the devil's beard. The young lady succeeds and, using the queen's greed for gold, tricks her into becoming the eternal ferryman. Animated from the Grimms' fairy tale interpreted by Eric Carle.
Bosustow   12½ min   Color   1977

690 The Three Little Pigs. Uses a fairy tale moral to emphasize the importance of budgeting time in order to finish necessary chores and still have time to play. From the Primary Guidance Project, tested in the Chicago schools. Animated.
Disney 9 min Color 1956

691 The Three Little Pigs: Background for Reading and Expression. To stimulate interest in telling and reading animal stories, this children's classic is retold in film. The elements of the original story, all of which are retained, are suggested by the use of real animals.
Coronet 10 min Color 1956

692 Three Little Woodpeckers. This cartoon, starring Woody Woodpecker, is a parody of the fairy tale, "The Three Little Pigs."
Creative Film 7 min Color

693 Three Stone Blades. A dramatization of an Eskimo legend from the Bering Strait region. When a husband goes on a hunting trip and fails to return, his wife goes to his brother for food. The brother's wife gives her, instead, three stone blades. When the brother finds out what his wicked wife has done, he leaves her to become the provider for his dead brother's family. Cinematography by Ira Latour. Directed by Orville and Dorothy Goldner.
Int. Film Bureau 15½ min Color 1971

694 Thumbelina. This story by Hans Christian Andersen is about a tiny girl who escapes from a toad and finds refuge with a field mouse. When it tries to arrange a marriage with the mole, she escapes on the back of a swallow she nursed to health. Produced by Coronet Films.
Perspective 11 min Color 1970

695 Ti-Jean Goes Lumbering. A French-Canadian folk tale presents the superhuman exploits of Ti-Jean, a boy who performed feats dwarfing those of the hardiest lumberjack at a Quebec lumber camp. Produced by the National Film Board of Canada.
Int. Film Bureau 15½ min Color 1953

696 Tikki Tikki Tembo. In this ancient fairy tale, we learn why Chinese parents today give their children short names instead of long ones. This story is also a delicate satire of social customs and pretensions the world over. Written by Arlene Mosel. Illustrated by Blair Lent. Adapted and directed by Gary Templeton. Iconographic.
Weston Woods 9 min Color 1974

697 The Tinder Box. This is a live-action adaptation of Hans Christian Andersen's fairy tale. As in the original, a handsome soldier wins a beautiful princess with the help of dogs that guard the magic tinder box.

Produced by Ake Soderquist for Filmkonsult AB (Denmark).
Encyc. Brit. 25 min Color 1971

698 Tom Thumb. No bigger than your thumb, Tom proves he's clever beyond his size. After escaping from men who want to exhibit him, he thwarts a robbery, is swallowed by a cow, then eaten by a wolf. Tom is saved by persuading the wolf to enter his father's pantry where it is slain after over-eating. Animated from the Grimms' fairy tale series interpreted by Eric Carle.
Bosustow 9½ min Color 1977

699 Tom Thumb in King Arthur's Court. This animation traces the career of the fabled little hero, from his birth within the heart of a rose to the day he is made a Knight of the Round Table. Tom's adventures are designed to teach the lesson that courage is not a matter of size but of spirit. Based on Grimm.
Coronet 19 min Color 1963

700 Tom Tit Tot. This is the English version of "Rumpelstilskein," narrated by Margaret Lott. Costumed actors perform the story in silhouette and pantomime against sylized background to music of the 13th-century setting of the story. Produced by Flora Mock. Music by the Pro Musica Antiqua, played on authentic antique instruments.
Creative Film 13 min Color

701 The Tortoise and the Hare. This version of Aesop's fable illustrates the desirability of perseverance and the **objectionable** qualities of boasting and showing off. From the Primary Guidance Project, tested in the Chicago schools. Animated.
Disney 8 min Color 1954

702 The Ugly Duckling. The Hans Christian Andersen story is retold in live-action style. Filmed in Europe, the tale takes on authenticity as we follow the misfortunes of the unwanted "duckling" that grows into a beautiful swan.
Coronet 11 min Color 1953

703 The Ugly Duckling. This is the Hans Christian **Andersen** story about the cygnet that grows up among ducklings. No matter how hard he tries to please, he is rejected. He wanders in desolation through the woods, searching for someone who will love him. As he sits crying on the river bank, a beautiful mother swan and her babies show him that he has a place in their family and a right to be happy and proud. Animated art. Non-narrated.
Disney 8 min Color 1955

704 The Ugly Duckling. Adapted from the classic by Hans Christian Andersen, this film uses real animals to tell the story of the baby swan. Collaborator: Grace Storm.
Encyc. Brit.   11 min   Color   1952

705 The Ugly Duckling. Animated puppets tell one of Hans Christian Andersen's most beloved stories in a setting designed by Zenon Wasilewski.
Macmillan   15 min   Color   1959

706   The Ugly Duckling. This animation originates from the illustrations of Otto S. Svend, whose imagery is combined with music to express the feelings of a being that suffered because it was "different." Animated by Gene Deitch. Producer: Mort Schindel.
Weston Woods   15 min   Color   1975

707   Valiant Hans. Animated puppets play the role of ghosts, a banished princess, and her courageous prince. Based on the fairy tale by the Brothers Grimm.
Indiana U.   16 min   Color   1973

708 The Wave: A Japanese Folktale. Ojiisan and his grandson Tada lived on a mountainside above a fishing village. One day, Ojiisan saw a huge wave racing toward the village, so he set fire to the village ricefields. Tada did not know what to think. Had grandfather gone mad? Enraged, the villagers raced up the hill to save the rice. Suddenly the old man cried, "Look!", pointing toward the sea. They saw the wave engulf their village, and realized Ojiisan had burned the rice to save their lives. Stephen Bosustow, producing consultant.
BFA Educ. Media   9 min   Color   1968

709 What's Red Riding Hood Without the Wolf? With the fairy tale *Little Red Riding Hood* as frame of reference, this film shows how plot and protagonist are related. A small demonstration class responds to situations designed to encourage creative writing. Projector-stops allow viewers to write between segments. From the *Communication Skills* series.
Churchill   16 min   Color   1972

710 Whazzat? Six clay figures jump into and out of new shapes as they skip, crawl, stumble, and flow over one another on their way toward an elephant. But, colorful as they are, these characters can't see. And so, when they touch the beast, each one thinks he's describing something different. Only by pooling their information do they recognize the animal

for what it is. Based on the 11th-century East Indian folktale, "The Six Blind Men and an Elephant." This animated version is non-verbal. Made by Crocus Productions.
Encyc. Brit. 10 min Color 1974

711 White Seal. This animation is based on a tale from Rudyard Kipling's *The Jungle Book*. It's about a young seal that learns to distinguish friend from foe, eventually leading the seal pack to the most dangerous species of all—man. The narrator is actor Roddy McDowall. Produced by Chuck Jones Enterprises.
Xerox Films 26 min Color 1976

712 Why the Sun and the Moon Live in the Sky. This legend from eastern Nigeria is brought to life by collage animation and a specially composed score. Long ago, when the Sun and Moon lived on earth, they invited their friend, the Water, to visit them. The water warned them he would bring his family with him, so they built a big new house for the party. But when the Water arrived with his people, they flooded out the Sun and the Moon, who had to take refuge in the sky. Storybook by Elphinstone Dayrell. Executive producer: Stelios Roccos, ACIL Media.
Paramount 11 min Color 1970

713 The Wild Swans. This is a Hans Christian Andersen story about a girl's devotion to her 11 brothers who have been turned into swans. Shows how her endurance and courage break this spell and changed the swans into men again. Produced in animation by Greatest Tales, Inc.
BFA Educ. Media 9 min Color 1976

714 William Tell. This animated film, in a 12th-century Swiss setting, presents the legend of the archer who must shoot an apple from his son's head to save the boy and himself. The story of Tell's refusal to be humbled before the tyrant Gessler marks the independent spirit of a great people.
Coronet 10½ min Color 1960

715 William Tell. Mr. Magoo is the brave Swiss peasant who saved his life by shooting an apple off his son's head with an arrow. He then went on to kill the tyrant oppressor, and led the revolt against the Austrians. The Swiss, inspired by Tell's courage, overthrew their invaders and established their independence in the 14th century. Cartoon. Formerly distributed by McGraw-Hill and Macmillan Films.
Mar/Chuck 24 min Color 1965

716 The Wisest Man in the World. This iconographic film retells one of the legends of the wisdom of Solomon, the visit of the Queen of Sheba and her attempts to outwit him. She sets up a number of tests, but

Solomon solves each problem. At last he is almost baffled, but receives help from an unexpected source, a honeybee. The Queen acknowledges his wisdom, and the two courts celebrate together. The story told here is not in the Bible, but is based on the book by Benjamin Elkin, and illustrated by Anita Lobel. A Thomas Sand film, produced for ACI Media.
Paramount   11 min   Color   1970

717 The Wolf and the Seven Kids. "Once upon a time, a goat and her seven kids lived happily in a house in a meadow. In the woods nearby lurked a hungry wolf..." So begins this animated tale from the *Grimm Brothers'* collection. The dangerous predicament of the seven kids and the resourcefulness of their mother can act as a springboard for interest in folktales from different regions and cultures. Produced in animation by Fred Ladd for Greatest Tales, Inc.
Encyc. Brit.   10 min   Color   1978

718 The World Tree: A Scandinavian Creation Myth. Depicts the creation of the earth according to the Scandinavian myth "Voluspa." Portrayed are the frost giant, the ice cow, trolls, the first man and woman, and finally the world tree and its importance in the universe. The animation is based on Scandinavian cave drawings.
Int. Film Foundation   10 min   Color   1977

719 The Youth Who Wanted to Shiver. Poor, stupid Jack! Try as he might, he can't learn to shiver. Ghost stories, scary places, and morbid company all fail to make him react. Jack strikes a bargain with the king to break a spell on the princess and is rewarded with marriage. To Jack's surprise, the princess proceeds to teach Jack how to shiver. Animated from the Grimms' fairy tale interpreted by Eric Carle.
Bosustow   8½ min   Color   1977

Nonfiction

Rachel Carson...deTocqueville...Frederick Douglass...John F. Kennedy...Buckminster Fuller...Thoreau. Go over those names again. You'll realize that these uncommon authors have something in common: their writings are not only a record of their achievements but an actual part of them. As a result, their works are useful on two levels, informational and literary. These same virtues make their works worthy of conversion into films, a medium that—with its unique capacity for reality—is especially valid as an instrument of documentation. These **232** productions will show another quality shared by book and film talents: facts don't *have* to be boring.

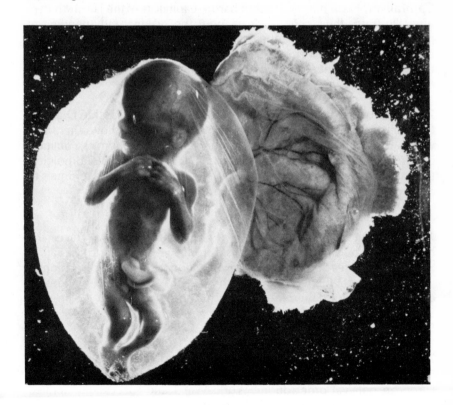

720 The Age of Uncertainty (Series). This 13-part series outlines the political and economic history of the world since about 1800. The on-camera narrator is the book's author, John Kenneth Galbraith, former advisor to John F. Kennedy and ambassador to India. Produced for BBC by Adrian Malone and Richard Gilling in cooperation with public station KCET-TV, Los Angeles.
Films, Inc. 56½ min (each) Color 1977

721 The Age of Uncertainty #1: Prophets and Promise of Classical Capitalism. Recounts the birth of classical capitalism in England and France, and explores the thinking of its early theorists, Adam Smith and David Ricardo. Also depicts the acceptance of capitalist theory in the US in the latter half of the 19th century.
Films, Inc. 57 min Color 1977

722 The Age of Uncertainty #2: Manners and Morals of High Capitalism. Examines the "robber baron" capitalists of the late 19th century. Illustrates their curious ideas about the making and spending of money—termed "conspicuous consumption" by the innovative economist Thorstein Veblen. Galbraith also demonstrates how these attitudes affect current economic practices.
Films, Inc. 56 min Color 1977

723 The Age of Uncertainty #3: Karl Marx – The Massive Dissent. Galbraith explores the work and thought of Karl Marx. Shows that Marx was a learned man who excelled in sociology, economics, political philosophy and journalism. Censorship, police persecution and political upheavals in France gradually changed him from a moderate reformer to a revolutionary.
Films, Inc. 57 min Color 1977

724 The Age of Uncertainty #4: The Colonial Idea. Traces the history of colonialism and imperialism from the Crusades to the fall of Saigon. Compares Spain's ruthless exploitation of its American colonies with the more benevolent British system in India. Includes a dramatization of a day in the life of a British official in the Indian Civil Service.
Films, Inc. 57 min Color 1977

725 The Age of Uncertainty #5: Lenin and the Great Ungluing. Depicts how Lenin accurately predicted the breakup of the old European political order during World War I and successfully applied Marxist theory in making a socialist revolution in Russia.
Films, Inc. 56 min Color 1977

726 The Age of Uncertainty #6: The Rise and Fall of Money. Galbraith employs a carnival setting to illustrate the importance of a cen-

tralized banking system to a stable economy. He also explains the history and function of money, and examines the cycles of instability and inflation that plague the capitalist system.
Films, Inc. 56 min Color 1977

727 The Age of Uncertainty #7: Mandarin Revolution. Reviews the worldwide depression that followed World War I. Demonstrates how the theories of John Maynard Keynes overturned many traditional ideas about capitalism, and offered the industrialized nations an alternative to revolutionary socialism.
Films, Inc. 56 min Color 1977

728 The Age of Uncertainty #8: The Fatal Competition. Investigates the origins and development of the "military-industrial complex" and its effects on the U.S. economy from the end of World War II to the present. Also analyzes the continuing rivalry between the U.S. and the Soviet Union.
Films, Inc. 57 min Color 1977

729 The Age of Uncertainty #9: The Big Corporation. Galbraith examines the history, sociology, and future development of the big corporation, the institution "that most changes our lives." He emphasizes the role of corporations in encouraging government intervention in the economy.
Films, Inc. 56 min Color 1977

730 The Age of Uncertainty #10: Land and the People. Illustrates the role of land distribution in determining wealth and poverty. Galbraith visits the U.S., Mexico, Canada, Pakistan, and Singapore—all examples of countries with at least some success in breaking the "equilibrium of poverty."
Films, Inc. 56 min Color 1977

731 The Age of Uncertainty #11: The Metropolis. Portrays the difficulties of industrial nations by examining the problems of the urban metropolis, the most visible facet of modern society and the one that best reflects its uncertainty and crises.
Films, Inc. 57 min Color 1977

732 The Age of Uncertainty #12: Democracy, Leadership, and Commitment. Galbraith considers the processes and operation of democracy, commenting on world leaders he has known: Franklin D. Roosevelt, Gandhi, John F. Kennedy, and Martin Luther King, Jr. He emphasizes the role of individual responsibility in preserving democracy.
Films, Inc. 57 min Color 1977

733 The Age of Uncertainty #13: Weekend in Vermont. World

leaders gather at Galbraith's Vermont home to discuss current economic, social, and political issues: Nuclear weapons, Third-World nations, environment, the relationship of the individual to corporate organization, etc. Guests include former British Prime Minister Edward Heath, historian Arthur Schlesinger, Soviet academician Gyorgy Arbatov, and former Secretary of State Henry Kissinger.
Films, Inc.   56 min   Color   1977

734 America (Series of 13). These programs coproduced by BBC-TV and Time-Life, feature *America* author Alistair Cooke as on-screen narrator. He outlines this land's discovery, colonization, revolt, expansion, imperialism, and contemporary status.
Time-Life   52 min (each)   Color   1973

735 America (Film I): The New Found Land. It is one of the last untamed continents: rich, fertile, widely varied in landscape and animal life, populated only by small tribes of Indians. Suddenly: Fifth Avenue, New York City. Alistair Cooke explains how the white man got to North America and what he was seeking. The continent's two "great losers," the Spanish and the French, arrive and spread—conquistadores, traders, trappers and missionaries. The Spanish rancho culture develops in the Southwest. French traders push out from Quebec and New Orleans. But then the British arrive and a whole new world begins.
Time-Life   52 min   Color   1973

736   America (Film 2): Home Away from Home. Merchants and social dissenters pour in from Elizabethan England to settle America's East Coast. Regional character evolves as Puritans, Pilgrims, and Quakers struggle with the rocky North while a landed gentry prospers in the highly productive feudal South. From the first Plymouth struggle to a modern Massachusett's Thanksgiving, and from the early Jamestown hardships to current Virginia **tobacco** farms, contrasting American ideals show up in all **their** variety.
Time-Life   52 min   Color   1973

737   America (Film 3): Making a Revolution. The colonies draw together in common complaints against the mother country. Blunders in London, inept colonial governors and costly British frontier wars drain the colonists and push them to fight— a pragmatic struggle fired not by ideologies, but by the character of men such as Washington, Jefferson, and Henry. From the Concord Bridge and antique long rifle, to the modern National Rifle Association, Alistair Cooke traces our tradition of turning to arms in the face of trouble.
Time-Life   52 min   Color   1973

738   America (Film 4): Inventing a Nation. It takes a decade to hammer out a constitution based on what Alistair Cooke calls our three

great principles: "compromise, compromise, compromise." The secret Independence Hall debates involving Hamilton, Mason and Madison set **precedents** for modern politics, while a visit to Jefferson's Virginia home, Monticello, gives insight into the mind that created our Bill of Rights. Then a westward surge follows Daniel Boone across the Appalachians, expanding the character of the new republic "beyond the imagining of the learned and graceful men of the 18th century."
Time-Life 52 min Color 1973

739 America (Film 5): Gone West. In 1803, the Louisiana Purchase is made. Lewis and Clarke are sent on a reconnaissance mission to the Pacific, while rivermen explore the distant reaches of waterways like the Missouri. Expansionist whites force whole Indian nations—Chickasaw, Choctaw, Creek, Cherokee—west of the Mississippi, and red vs. white war is common. Then the Gold Rush hits, and 49'ers by the thousand trek to California by wagon train.
Time-Life 52 min Color 1973

740 America (Film 6): A Fireball in the Night. From Robert E. Lee's old home, the view today is across the graves of the Kennedy brothers and into the Lincoln Memorial. Great splits in our nation's past and present are summarized in the causes, splendors, and miseries of the Civil War, and in the racial wounds that still trouble the land. From early slave importation to present Southern shanty towns, and from Eli Whitney's development of the cotton gin to modern Northern assembly lines and Southern fields, **Alistair** Cooke's accounting sums up conflicts that are still mostly unresolved.
Time-Life 52 min color 1973

741 American (Film 7): Domesticating a Wilderness. The nation again turns West, draining off war-bred tensions. Mormons make the Utah desert bloom. A transcontinental rail link is driven across awesome terrain. Abilene's railhead becomes a cowboy's Mecca, while **European** immigrants populate the midlands and bring in the barbed wire that will impose order on vast empty spaces. The Indians' last desperate struggle **explodes in the Custer massacre and the Battle of Wounded Knee, a** prelude to the present-day poverty of reservation life.
Time-Life 52 min Color 1973

742 America (Film 8): Money on the Land. Modern Chicago dissolves into the **countryside** it grew from: a "gorgeous deposit of raw material ready for mass cultivation and shipping and processing," ready **for exploitation by opportunistic turn-of-the-century industrialists.** Early inventors like Edison, as well as lucky prospectors, find the methods and resources. Then the Rockefellers, Carnegies, and **Vanderbilts** move in, as the focus of America shifts from the farmer, "for better or worse, to the cities."
Time-Life 52 min Color 1973

743　America (Film 9): The Huddled Masses. From the beckoning torch of the Statue of Liberty, the camera pulls back to reveal the Manhattan skyline. Alistair Cooke visits ships' holds, Ellis Island, the Lower East Side, garment factory sweat shops—all recalling turn-of-the-century immigration. Old photographs of the poor newcomers' plight contrast with oil portraits of tycoons who got fat at their expense. Then it is the present—Coumbus Day with Chinese, Puerto Rican, and black children all saluting the flag.
Time-Life 52 min Color 1973

744　America (Film 10): The Promise Fulfilled and the Promise Broken. To veterans returning from the "War to End All Wars," the promise of unlimited prosperity is symbolized by a Model-T Ford and a mail order catalog. The 20's boom with speakeasies, rumble-seat sex, saxophones and a best-seller called *The Man Nobody Knows*, depicting Jesus Christ as a super salesman. And then, the Crash. Alistair Cooke shows how the Depression came and what the New Deal meant. The mills stay closed until we return to war.
Time-Life 52 min Color 1973

745　America (Film 11): The Arsenal. "The American Way of War," from colonial Williamsburg to the modern traditions of the armed forces. Roosevelt's dream of an "arsenal of democracy" is fulfilled as World War II elevates America into the world's power elite. Alistair Cooke plots developments up to the present: the United Nations Security Council, the Los Alamos atomic laboratories and the underground Strategic Air Command War Room.
Time-Life 52 min Color 1973

746　America (Film 12): The First Impact. A record of one immigrant's sojourn here provides a revealing look at how we first appeared to outsiders. "A personal interlude," says Alistair Cooke, "a memoir of how I came to America and the people, places, institutions, and landscapes that I admired enough to make me want to stay; from the New England fall and New Orleans jazz to the Mayo Clinic, San Francisco, and H.L. Mencken."
Time-Life 52 min Color 1972

747　America (Film 13): The More Abundant Life. "America today. What, in its experience, has been fulfilled and what betrayed?" A potpourri of impressions: Hoover Dam from the confident 30's, neon Las Vegas in the glittering 70's, Los Angeles strangled with motor cars, Hawaii showing racial harmony amid pollution and over-development. A summary of our nation's present status and our prospects for the near future.
Time-Life 52 min Color 1973

748　America and the Americans. Based on John Steinbeck's study,

this film is a parallel evaluation of our nation and its many social problems. Crucial subjects analyzed are civil rights, big business, pollution, waste of resources, and political-military privilege. Narrated by Henry Fonda. Produced by NBC-TV News.
McGraw-Hill 51 min Color 1968

749 America, I Know You. Through historical pictures, live-action scenes, and selected readings, young viewers can see the symbols of our national life that may provide social cohesiveness and rallying points in spite of conflicts of interpretation. Based on the book by Bill Martin, Jr. Produced by Sargon Tamimi.
Film Fair 6¼ min Color 1971

750 An American Indian Speaks. This documentary gives the Indians' views about their people, their heritage, the white man and the future. Scenes include a Creek ceremonial dance, a Sioux rodeo and interviews with the Nisqually who tell of their struggles for fishing rights. Actual scenes of their arrest are included. Based on *The New Indians* by Stan Steiner.
Encyc. Brit. 23 min Color 1973

751 Annapurna. Filmed as it happened, this is the 1950 documentary of the preparation for, the ascent and the agonizing descent of Annapurna, one of the great mountains of the earth. "The conquest of your soul," said author Herzog, "is as important as the real physical victory." Photography by Marcel Ichac. Narrated (in English) by Maurice Herzog and Edward Byrne.
Macmillan 57 min Color 1952

752 Aristotle's Ethics: The Theory of Happiness. One of four lessons, each independently valid, on the philosophical and poetic contributions of ancient Greece. Dramatized scenes are interpreted by Mortimer Adler. Part of the *Humanites Series*, directed by John Barnes. Based on Aristotle's *Nichomachean Ethics*.
Encyc. Brit. 28 min Color 1963

753 The Art of French Cooking. In this adaptation of Fernande Garvin's best-seller, the author reveals some of her culinary secrets. She demonstrates five special recipes, using common ingredients and ordinary utensils.
RH Media 16 min Color 1975

754 Ascent of Man (series). These 13 programs are narrated by the late Dr. Jacob Bronowski, author and anthropologist. They were coproduced by BBC and Time-Life Films and have been widely televised over Public Broadcast Service stations. A discussion guide is available.
Time-Life 52 min (each) Color 1975

755   Ascent of Man #1: Lower Than the Angels. A multitude of evolutionary changes—anatomical and intellectual—gives rise to man's superiority among other animals. Computer techniques illustrate evolution, while x-ray and slow-motion photography of an Olympic athlete show the interweaving of mind and body.
Time-Life   52 min   Color   1975

756   Ascent of Man #2: The Harvest of the Seasons. Man domesticates plant and animal life. With the Neolithic cultivators come the nomads and warfare. Cameras capture the life style of the Bakhtiari tribe of Iran, and re-create the war games of Genghis Khan.
Time-Life   52 min   Color   1975

757   Ascent of Man #3: The Grain in the Stone. Man splits a stone and reassembles the pieces to build a wall, a cathedral, and a city. From the temples of Paestum and the cathedrals of France to the expressways of Los Angeles, this film expresses man's faith and fancy as architect and builder.
Time-Life   52 min   Color   1975

758   Ascent of Man #4: The Hidden Structure. The bronze crafts-men of China and the Samurai swordsmiths of Japan are the starting point for this journey that leads from the beginnings of chemistry to Dalton's atomic theory and our knowledge of the chemical elements.
Time-Life   52 min   Color   1975

759   Ascent of Man #5: Music of the Spheres. Traces the evolution of mathematics, the relationship of numbers to music, astronomy, and perspective in painting. Follows the spread of Greek ideas through the Islamic empire to Moorish Spain and Renaissance Europe.
Time-Life   52 min   Color   1975

760   Ascent of Man #6: The Starry Messenger. The story of man's early attempts to map the forces that move the planets. Dr. Bronowski traces the origins of the scientific revolution through the conflict between fact and dogma, culminating in the trial of Galileo.
Time-Life   52 min   Color   1975

761   Ascent of Man #7: The Majestic Clockwork. In the drama of physics, Newton and Einstein occupy center stage. This film explores the revolution that ensued when Einstein's theory upset Newton's description of the universe.
Time-Life   52 min   Color   1975

762   Ascent of Man #8: The Drive for Power. Industrial and political revolutions altered man's concept of power during the 18th century. Dr. Bronowski shows why these developments were as important as the

Renaissance in man's progress.
Time-Life 52 min Color 1975

763 Ascent of Man #9: The Ladder of Creation. The camera journeys from Wales to the Amazon to explore the controversy around a startling new theory of evolution developed simultaneously by Alfred Wallace and Charles Darwin.
Time-Life 52 min Color 1975

764 Ascent of Man #10: World Within World. Commencing with a visit to an ancient Polish salt mine, Dr. Bronowski looks at the world inside the atom. He traces the history of the ideas that made 20th-century physics "the greatest achievement of the human imagination."
Time-Life 52 min Color 1975

765 Ascent of Man #11: Knowledge of Certainty. Dr. Bronowski offers his view of the moral dilemma that confronts today's scientists. He contrasts humanist traditions with the inhumanities of the Nazis, the harnessing of nuclear energy with the development of the atomic bomb.
Time-Life 52 min Color 1975

766 Ascent of Man #12: Generation Upon Generation. Examines the complex code of human inheritance—from the experiments of geneticist Gregor Mendel to today's sophisticated laboratories.
Time-Life 52 min Color 1975

767 Ascent of Man #13: The Long Childhood. In this closing film, Dr. Bronowski draws together the many threads of the series, as he takes stock of man's complex and precarious development.
Time-Life 52 min Color 1975

768 Autumn Across America. Why do we still offer bounties on certain animals? Why do we destroy the awesome redwoods? Why is the elk near extinction? The questions are aimed at awakening respect for all living things. One answer is clear: every species depends on other species for survival. Producer: Hobel-Leiterman. Based on the book by Edwin Way Teale.
Xerox Films 50 min Color 1970

769 Awakenings. About the L-dopa treatment of survivors of the 1920's encephalitis epidemic in the Bronx. The central figure is an English neurologist but equally remarkable are his hospitalized patients. Based on the book by Dr. Oliver Sacks. Produced by Yorkshire (England) Television.
Internat'l Rehab. 41 min Color 1977

770 The Battered Child. This documentary on infant abuse is based on the book by Drs. C. Henry Kempe and Roy E. Helfer. This pair of

physicians formed a team of Colorado psychiatrists, pediatricians, and social workers. Their purpose: to study the causes of maltreatment and to treat the children subjected to it. Their work is based on the theory that emotional therapy, not penal commitment, is the best long-term solution for parents and children. Produced by National Educational Television.
Indiana Univ.　58 min　B&W　1969

771 The Beginning of Life. This film uses the still pictures of Swedish photographer Lennert Nilsson, as shown in his book *A Child Is Born*. Demonstrates the changes in the human fetus during gestation. Also shows sperm movement, ovulation, and other processes in a non-technical manner. Notes that life really begins with conception and exists for 38 weeks prior to birth. Produced by the Swedish Broadcasting Company.
Benchmark　29 min　Color　1969

772　Behavioral Interviewing With Couples. Demonstrates one method of interviewing couples during initial counseling. Joan and Marvin, the overadequate/underadequate couple observed in the companion film, *Three Styles of Marital Conflict*, are featured together with their therapist, Dr. John Gottman, author of *A Couple's Guide to Communication*.
Behavioral Images　14 min　Color　1976

773　Behind the Scenes. A "back-stage" look at the animation of Kenneth Graham's book *The Reluctant Dragon*, showing how the process develops from concept to motion picture. The storyline involves humorist Robert Benchley in a tour of the Disney studio in 1941, the "Golden Age" of cartoon classics such as *Snow White, Pinocchio, and Fantasia*. This film begins in black-and-white but switches to color to introduce Donald Duck, Pluto, Goofy and other fantasy characters.
Walt Disney　26 min　C/B&W　1952

774　Between Man and Woman. This is a TV interview with author Everett L. Shostrom, depicting marital roles people play. A professional actor and actress roleplay modes of reacting. They then attempt to demonstrate an actualizing or rhythmic relationship as described in Dr. Shostrom's book.
Psych. Films　33 min　Color　1974

775　Birth Without Violence. Why must childbirth be such an abrupt introduction to life? The French obstetrician, Frederick Leboyer, believes life need not be traumatically begun and, in his own film production, shows delivery in a peaceful setting without glaring lights, loud sounds, upside-down dangling, or immediate severing of the umbilical cord. Non-narrated. Background music is provided by a Japanese flute.
New Yorker　21 min　B&W　1975

776 Black Dimensions in American Art. Features the important creations of America's most celebrated black artists (nearly 50 of them), representing every major style in painting today. Based on the book, *Black Dimensions in Contemporary American Art*, by Bernie Casey.
AIMS   11 min   Color   1971

777 Bob Knowlton Story. A case study on communications. Shows the disastrous effects of poor organizational development and planning on production, communication, and interpersonal relations in business. Based on the real-life case reported by Dr. Alex Bavelas, it shows how psychological barriers, often self imposed, can interrupt communication and job performance.
Roundtable   28 min   Color   1967

778 The Book of Kells. The Book of Kells exemplifies the Golden Age of Ireland. Dating from the 9th century, it contains some of the finest items of early Christian art, preserved as the illumination of the Gospels written in Latin. Now in the Library of Trinity College in Dublin, this rare volume is seen in detail as the Archbishop of Armagh turns the pages of decorative print and pictures. Produced by Ulster Television Limited.
Pictura   20 min   Color   1973

779 The Brotherhood of Man. The book, *Races of Mankind* by Drs. Ruth Benedict and Gene Weltfish, provides the basis for this animated film. It stresses the equality of all people and their need for unity. Produced by United Productions of America for the United Automobile Workers. A Contemporary Films release.
McGraw-Hill   10 min   Color   1946

780 The Burks of Georgia. The subjects are a poor but proud family for whom survival is everything. Arlon and Grace live on five acres beyond the Dalton city dump. Ten of their 13 children are living nearby with wives, husbands, and children in a collection of small houses and trailers. Poor education and menial jobs keep them chronically poor, but the Burks refuse to accept welfare. Theirs is a solid loving family even when violence is a common form of expression. The Clan has inherited a strong sense of togetherness from Grace and Arlon. From the book, *Six American Families* by Paul Wilkes. Filmmakers: Albert and David Maysles.
Carousel   59 min   Color   1977

781 Carl Rogers on Education. Dr. Rogers describes situations in which people attain optimum learning, and indicates the directions education must take in order to have a positive influence on children. The film is available in two separate parts. Based on Rogers' book, *Freedom to Learn*.
American Personnel   60 min   Color   1973

782 The Cave. An exercise in distinguishing reality from appearance, shadow from substance. Inspired by *The Allegory of the Cave* from Book VII of Plato's *Republic*. Narrator: Orson Welles. Animated by Steve Bosustow.
Counterpoint   9 min   Color   1973

783 Charles Darwin. One of a series of three films on great scientists. In this one, Professor Richard Eakin portrays the "father of evolutionary theory" towards the end of his life (1809-1882), with special attention to Darwin's observations as entered into his *Journal of the Voyage of the Beagle*. Explains his observations in *Origin of the Species*, and quotes from his *Autobiography*. Produced by the University of California (Berkeley).
Extension Media   24 min   Color   1975

784 A Chemical Feast. In chef's clothes and surrounded by an array of chemicals and modified foods, comedian Marshall Ephron merrily concocts a synthetic "lemon pie" using ingredients listed on its label. Then he takes four food products, notes their additives, their unproductive ingredients, and calculates their exorbitant price by the ounce. Suggested by the book, *The Chemical Feast*, by Jim Turner.
Benchmark   11 min   Color   1972

785 The Children of Bet Alpha. This look at Israel's communal approach to raising children was shot entirely at Kibbutz Bet Alpha, the locale of Professor Melford Spiro's classic analysis of child development, *Children in Kibbutzim*. Focuses on four age groups: infants, three, seven, and 12-year olds. Produced by Tue Ritzau and Herbert Krosney.
Phoenix   27 min   Color   1974

786 Cipher in the Snow. True story of a school boy nobody thought was important. Based on Jean Mizer Todhunter's award-winning story in the National Education Association's 1964 Teachers Writing Contest. Film produced by the Motion Picture Department, Brigham Young University, Provo, Utah.
Brigham Young U.   24 min   Color   1973

787   Civilisation (Series of 13). Kenneth Clark, author of the *Civilisation* book, serves as on-screen narrator of these 13 television programs. He spans the history of the world, with emphasis on Western achievements, and surveys the relationship among art, science, government, and religion. Produced by BBC.
Time-Life   52 min each   Color   1970

788 Civilisation #1: The Frozen World. Kenneth Clark describes the ideal that was inherited from 5th-century Greece and lasted more than 600 years. After the fall of Rome, Europe was left to the pagan wanderers.

At last, Charlemagne, the first great man of action to emerge from the darkness, reestablished contact with the ancient cultures.
Time-Life 52 min Color 1970

789 Civilisation #2: The Great Thaw. In this film, Clark describes the hundred marvelous years in which the great abbeys and cathedrals—Cluny, Canterbury, Winchester, Vezelay, Moissac, Autun and Chartres—reflected the belief that God could be approached through beauty, gentleness and compassion.
Time-Life 52 min Color 1970

790 Civilisation #3: Romance and Reality. Here is the Gothic world, a world of chivalry, romance, courtly love and worldly happiness, depicted by the Lady with the Unicorn tapestries and the Très Riches Heures. It is the period of St. Francis, the poetry of Dante, the art of Giotto, and the emergence of woman as an ideal.
Time-Life 52 min Color 1970

791 Civilisation #4: Man—The Measure of All Things. The great names of this film are Botticelli, Masaccio, Bellini, Giorgione, and Van Eyck. The time is early 15th century—the era of discovery of modern man, not as God's servant but personified in the motto of the Florentine architect, Alberti: "A man can do all things if he will." The architecture of the Pazzi Chapel exemplifies humanism.
Time-Life 52 min Color 1970

792 Civilisation #5: The Hero as Artist. About the year 1500, Rome exploded into an expanse of imperial splendor. Over Michelangelo, Raphael and Bramante stands the dominant power of Pope Julius II. We also see the aging Leonardo da Vinci and his scientific view of humanity.
Time-Life 52 min Color 1970

793 Civilisation #6: Protest and Communication. At the close of the 15th century, Gutenberg's printing press was becoming a major influence. The writings of Luther, Erasmus, and Thomas More spread to a wider audience through the medium of print. And the invention of printed woodcuts gave the works of Dürer even greater impact.
Time-Life 52 min Color 1970

794 Civilisation #7: Grandeur and Obedience. The Rome of the Counter-Reformation, of Michelangelo, Bernini, and Sixtus V is the most grandiose piece of town planning ever attempted. The works of Titian, Rubens, and Bernini appeal to universal emotions—the uniting of flesh and spirit, dogma and sensuality, obedience and freedom.
Time-Life 52 min Color 1970

795 Civilisation #8: The Light of Experience. The Dutch were the

first to replace divine authority with experience, experiment and obser-
vation. Kenneth Clark travels from the Holland of Frans Hals, Rembrandt,
Vermeer and Saenredam to the London of Isaac Newton and Christopher
Wren. The spirit of free enterprise begins to make itself felt.
Time-Life   52 min   Color   1970

796   Civilisation #9: The Pursuit of Happiness. The music of the
18th century—Bach and Handel (the *St. Matthew Passion* and the *Messiah*
respectively) and Mozart and Haydn (*Don Giovanni* and the *Creation*
respectively)—rings out in this film with melodious flow, complex sym-
metry and decorative invention. These qualities are also reflected in architecture in the rococo style.
Time-Life   52 min   Color   1970

797   Civilisation #10: The Smile of Reason. With notable excep-
tions—the etchings of Hogarth, for one—this is an age happy in its belief
that, through reason and moderation, the millenium is at hand. David,
DeTroy, and Houdon all reflect the optimism of Voltaire and the En-
cyclopedists who would advance mankind by conquering ignorance.
Time-Life   52 min   Color   1970

798 Civilisation #11: The Worship of Nature. A belief in the divinity
of Nature is a new force in the 18th century. Locations include Wordsworth's Tintern Abbey, Grasmere, and Fountains Abbey in Yorkshire.
"Civilization, which for so long had been dependent on great
monasteries or palaces or well-furnished salons, could emanate from a
cottage," in the words of Kenneth Clark.
Time-Life   52 min   Color   1970

799 Civilisation #12: The Fallacies of Hope. The beautiful dreams of
the 18th century are blasted by the betrayals of the 19th. The chief
figures in this period of romanticism from 1789 through the 19th century
are Byron, Beethoven, Blake, David, Delacroix, Rodin and Daumier—a
new reality, cynicism discovering and depicting the harshness of the
world.
Time-Life   52 min   Color   1970

800 Civilisation #13: Heroic Materialism. The final episode takes us
from the Industrial Revolution to the present state of Western civilization.
We are the world of the moon shot, the atomic bomb and the computer.
Kenneth Clark also discusses humanitarian reformers like Wilberforce
and Lord Shaftesbury, the conscience of Dickens, the paintings of the Im-
pressionists, and his own beliefs. In his own words, "one may be optimistic, but one can't exactly be joyful at the prospect before us." Despite
atomic blasts and doomsday machines, civilization continues to inch
ahead "like a rock climb, three steps up, two steps down—but in the
end—an ascent."
Time-Life   52 min   Color   1970

801 Color It Living. Shows naturalist-artist Arthur Glenn Loates in the process of capturing North American wildlife in action. His sensitivity of subject and his attention to detail, à la Audubon, lend special awareness to the importance of preserving our environment. Based on the November 1973 *Reader's Digest* article by Anker Odum, "The Silent Zoo of Glenn Loates."
Mar/Chuck   30 min   Color   1974

802 The Color of Man. A series of three films based on the paper-back book by Robert Carl Cohen. In examining the various aspects of racial identity, it attempts to explain the emotional connotations involved. Produced in association with the United Nations.
American Educ.   Approx. 60 min   Color   1973

803 The Cooking of Germany. Robust cookery prepared in the German tradition is the subject, as adapted from the Time-Life *Foods of the World* series. Dining is shown to be a basic part of the social life of Germans. The film concludes with traditional food prepared and served for Christmas. Book written by Nika S. Hazelton.
RH Media   23 min   Color   1974

804 The Cooking of Italy. A tour of Italy suggests the differences in environment that have resulted in a variety of basic dishes. Milan, Bologna, Turin, and Venice are seen and their favorite dishes are prepared and served with style and pride. Adapted from the Time-Life *Foods of the World* series. Author: Waverly Root.
RH Media   22 min   Color   1975

805 Coping With Technological Change. Environmentalists, young people, the futurists, business executives, and members of the scientific community are raising questions about the nature of technological society. In recognition of this re-evaluation, DeCarlo and Drucker raise questions about the roles of industry and government in the area of technological change. Dr. DeCarlo is former director of automation research for IBM. Peter Drucker is the author of *Age of Discontinuity*, on which a series of nine films is based. (This is number 3.)
BNA Films   30 min   Color   1971

806 Cosmic Zoom. Based on the science book *Cosmic View* by Kees Boeke, this animation probes the magnitude of space and the microcosm of matter. The camera achieves this effect by "zooming" into and out of its center of reference—a human being. Non verbal, with original music. Produced by the National Film Board of Canada.
McGraw-Hill   8 min   Color   1969

807 Days of Discovery. The concepts in this film are based upon the book, *Your Child's Intellect*, by former U.S. Commissioner of Education

Dr. T.H. Bell, who appears in the Introduction. Photos of parent-teacher-children interaction shows the rationale behind home-based early childhood education. Includes examples of successful techniques of pre-school instruction.
Olympus   20 min   Color   1975

808   The Death of Socrates. Based on Plato's *Dialogues, The Crito,* and *Phaedon.* Produced in modern dress, this film underlines the fact that political persecution has persisted for the 2500 years since Socrates' execution. Socrates was killed by an Athenian tribunal for "subversive" teaching because he spoke against the existing powers. From BBC-TV.
Time-Life   45 min   B&W   1969

809   Diet for a Small Planet. This treatment of Frances Moore Lappé's bestseller emphasizes the global need to reduce the consumption of meat — an extravagance that's denying millions of people their minimum nutrition. Features the author herself with fellow writer Ellen Buchanan Ewald (*Recipes for a Small Planet*) and biochemist Kendall King. Produced by Winifred Scherer and John Abrahall.
Bullfrog Films   28 min   Color   1973

810   Ellis Island. Between 1900 and 1910, the wave of immigrants reaches tidal proportions. As they sight the Statue of Liberty, their optimism explodes with joy. Less than one-half mile from the welcoming lady lies the reality of Ellis Island. After Ellis, they face an even sterner reality — trying to make it in a strange land without money, friends, or knowledge of its language. Narrated by Richard Basehart. Producer: Metromedia Producers Corporation/Wolper. From the Book by John F. Kennedy, *A Nation of Immigrants*.
Films Inc.   12 min   B&W   1972

811   Elsa and Her Cubs. In this personal documentary film, the coauthors of *Born Free*, Joy and George Adamson, record their friendship with a lioness, Elsa, in Kenya. It covers the time when Elsa is a cub until she in turn has cubs of her own.
Benchmark   25 min   Color   1970

812 Emperor and Slave: The Philosophy of Roman Stoicism. Marcus Aurelius, a Roman emperor, and Epictetus, an emancipated Greek slave, epitomize the way of life required by the stoic philosophy that claimed virtue to be an invincible armor against outrageous fortune. A dramatization from the EBE *Humanities Series*. Directed by John Barnes. Based on *Meditations* by Aurelius.
Encyc. Brit.   29 min   Color   1964

813   Everything about Bicycles. This adaptation of the National Safety Council's handbook includes not only information on maintenance and riding techniques, but also a brief history and prediction of the future

of the bicycle. Animated by **Farmhouse** Films.
Pyramid   15 min   Color   1975

814 Excerpts from Walden. This look at Walden as if through the eyes of Thoreau reveals his reason for leaving the comfort of mid-18th-century Concord, Massachusetts, and seeking a life in the wilderness. It also shares the harvest of ideas he reaped during his two-year exile. Original music enhances the mood. Narrative passages are read by actor Arthur Hill.
Counterpoint   19 min   Color   1976

815   Exploring the Spectrum. Records the scientific methods behind Dr. John Ott's observations of the correlation between plant-animal life and exposure to the visible and invisible rays of the electromagnetic spectrum. These findings have contributed to the developments of a new scientific discipline, photo-biology. Based on Ott's book, *Health and Light*. Coproduced by Henry Ott Films for **Environmental Health**.
Int. Film Bureau   46 min   Color   1975

816   Fast Is not a Ladybug. A film about the meaning of "fast" and "slow," centered on how long it takes to go from here to there. As a subjective way of thinking about fast and slow, the concept of relative speed is developed in a child-oriented way. Based on the book by Miriam Schein and illustrated by Leonard Kessler.
BFA Educ. Media   11 min   Color   1959

817   Favela: Diary of a Slum. A visual chronicle of people living in a Brazilian *favela* (a slum). Their life of poverty and misery is spent scavenging for mere existence, without hope for the future. Based on *Diary of Poverty* by Carolina Maria de Jesus. Produced by Institut für Film und Bild.
Films, Inc.   17 min   Color   1974

818   The Flower of the Tales. Photographed from the Burgundian miniatures, this film examines the intricate illustrations that adorn the medieval manuscripts in the Royal Library of Belgium. Under the patronage of Philip the Good and his son, Charles the Bold, the form and content of the printed page developed into a fine art. The camera captures gold leaf designs flickering in the light, recalling an age when books were cherished from generation to generation. Produced by F. Geilfus for the Ministry of Education and Culture, Belgium.
Int. Film Bureau   17½ min   Color   1976

819   Frankl and the Search for Meaning. In this film, psychiatrist author Viktor Frankl describes our search for meaning as a form of "height" psychology, contrary to the Freudian theory, which is described as "depth" psychology. Frankl conceives meaning as a personalized

valuing that each person must have in order to give life validity. Based on the American edition of Dr. Frankl's book, *Man's Search for Meaning*.
Psych. Films   30 min   Color

820   Free to Be ... You and Me. This exploration of self-awareness concentrates, in a light-hearted way, on the uniqueness of the individual. Marlo Thomas, as MC, introduces a series of entertaining profiles by artists such as Harry Belafonte, Alan Alda, Roberta Flack, Tom Smothers and Roosevelt Grier. Produced for television by the Ms. Foundation. An extension of the book by Carole Hart.
McGraw-Hill   42 min   Color   1973

821   The Future of Technology. To be effective, today's manager must be aware of the many forces—social, economic, religious, political and technological—that have impact on **organizations**. Charles DeCarlo, president of Sarah Lawrence College and formerly director of automation research for IBM, discusses with Peter Drucker the nature of technology, pointing out areas where technology must direct its attention. Drucker is the author of *Age of Discontinuity*, the inspiration for the *Managing Discontinuity*, series, of which this is the first film.
BNA Films   28 min   Color   1971

822   Future Shock. A visual examination of contemporary Western Society, and a projection of industrialized mankind on a collision course with tomorrow. Based on the observations of futurist Alvin Toffler. On-screen narrator: Orson Welles. Produced by David Wolper/Metromedia.
McGraw-Hill   42 min   Color   1972

823   The Georges of New York City. The bread-winner is a black policeman whose dangerous job has brought material rewards but also put a strain on family life. Bob and Peggy and their three children live in a pleasant neighborhood far from the high crime district that is his beat. Peggy is a supervisor in an insurance company. Bob loves the excitement of his job but Peggy fears for his safety. The Georges have reached into the middle class but, as blacks, are still painfully aware of second-class citizenship. From the book *Six American Families* by Paul Wilkes. Filmmaker: Arthur Barron.
Carousel   59 min   Color   1977

824   The Glory of Their Times. This nostalgic documentary provides rare footage from the golden baseball age of John McGraw, Christy Mathewson, Babe Ruth, and others of that era. Narrator is Alexander Scourby. Based on the book by Lawrence S. Ritter.
Macmillan   50 min   B&W   1968

825   A Good Sign. In this examination of outdoor signs, billboards, and displays, Dr. R. James Claus parallels his book, *Visual Environment*. He surveys advertising as an art form in Las Vegas and as an indispensable

help at the airport. Dr. Claus also draws attention to the blight it can create.
Klein   15 min   Color

826 Gotterdammerung: Fall of the Third Reich. In the second year of World War II, Hitler is a hero in his homeland. Repeated military victories have silenced opposition. But his appetite is insatiable. Ignoring the warnings of his generals, he commits Germany to the invasion of Russia. Four years later, his grandiose dreams lie buried in the rubble of cities. The Reich that was to last a thousand years is demolished. Producer: M-G-M Documentary and David Wolper. Based on *The Rise and Fall of the Third Reich* by William L. Shirer.
Films, Inc.   28 min   B&W   1972

827 The Greenbergs of California. A "perfect" marriage is on the rocks. Jackie and Arne Greenberg had everything going for them: a beautiful home in a San Francisco suburb, two attractive children, and money to live comfortably. But Arne, a lawyer, has moved out and is now a weekend father. The children express their feelings about living with separated parents and wish the family could be together. From the book *Six American Families* by Paul Wilkes. Filmmaker: Mark Obenhaus.
Carousel   59 min   Color   1977

828 Group Dynamics: "Groupthink". Dr. Irving Janis, author of *Groupthink*, itemizes eight factors that contribute to compulsive consensus. The dramatized case-study is about a management decision on whether to run more tests before marketing a new drug. The same principles involved there are applied to famous American military situations such as Pearl Harbor, Korea, the Bay of Pigs and the Cuban missile crisis. Produced for *Psychology Today* by Steve Katten.
McGraw-Hill   22 min   Color   1973

829 Hey, Cab! A dramatization of a true experience of black journalist Bob Teague. A cab bypasses the black man stranded on a rainswept curb. Another goes by within splashing distance. A third cab is finally stopped—by a traffic light. The cabbie doesn't want to chance the ghetto at night; the black man needs a ride. Who is right? And where does it stop? Based on *Letters to a Black Boy*.
BFA Educ. Media   10½ min   Color   1970

830 Hinduism and the Song of God. This documentary portrays the India that bred the Hindu concepts expressed in the *Bhagavad Gita*: man's purpose in life, the equitable law of Karma and the four stages of life. Produced by Elda Hartley.
Hartley   30 min   Color   1974

831 How Could I Not Be Among You? This is a film that inspired a

book, published by Braziller, with an introduction by Robert E. Neale and with photographs by Thomas Reichman. Like the film, it's based on the words of the late poet Ted Rosenthal, as he writes of his feelings about the disease-induced death he's about to face. Originally distributed by Eccentric Circle Cinema.
Benchmark   29 min   Color   1971

832 How to Say No to a Rapist and Survive. This film is a presentation of the rape-prevention techniques developed by Frederic Storaska, director of the National Organization for the Prevention of Rape and Assault (NOPRA). No real-life or dramatized scenes of rape appear in this film, which focuses on the author's personal demonstrations before his audience. Storaska is the author of the book that prompted this film.
Learning Corp.   52 min Color 1975

833 How to Use the Reader's Guide to Periodical Literature (One Detecive, a Spy, a Thief, Four Clues, and You). The H.W. Wilson research tool is presented within a storyline designed to interest young library users. It was produced by the Nassau (N.Y.) Library System under a grant from the Library Services and Construction Act of HEW. Originally distributed by ACI Media.
Paramount   12 min   Color   1969

834 I Am Joe's Heart. Based on the *Reader's Digest* article, this anatomy "tour" combines live-action and animation of three-dimensional models. Narrated by Henry Morgan. Idea conceived by author J.D. Ratcliff.
Pyramid   26 min   Color   1973

835 I Am Joe's Lung. It's an inside view of an average adult lung. Shows why smog, dust, and smoke can literally take your breath away. "Most of my neighbor organs can absorb an enormous amount of abuse," says Joe's lung. "I can't," it continues. "That's why lung diseases have reached epidemic proportions." Adapted from the *Reader's Digest* medical series by J.D. Ratcliff. Narrated by Richard Basehart.
Pyramid   25 min   Color   1975

836 I Am Joe's Spine. Through animation and the voice of Burgess Meredith, Joe's spine shows and tells what's happening to it as Joe twists, bends, lifts, stretches, and stoops in the process of cleaning out his attic. A *Reader's Digest* production. Based on the magazine article by J.D. Ratcliff.
Pyramid   25 min   Color   1974

837 I Am Joe's Stomach. Shows what really happens when we get "sick" from over-indulgence. Gives a graphic on-the-spot lesson in ulcer prevention, designed to teach observers to treat their stomach with more respect. Adapted from the *Reader's Digest* medical series by J.D. Ratcliff.

Narrated by John Forsythe.
Pyramid   25 min   Color   1975

838 The Identity Society. This film-record tells why so many students are uninvolved in their own education, and suggests what to do about it. Its analysis of why failure doesn't scare students anymore is based on Dr. William Glasser's book. Production consultant: William Knittles, Ph.D.
Media Five   28 min   Color   1972

839 The Immigrant Experience: The Long, Long Journey. The problems and dreams of immigrants to America are dramatized through this story of a turn-of-the-century Polish family. Through the eyes of the boy in the family, Janek, the saga of his uprooted parents, grandmother and sister is presented as contemporary history. The format is an interview with Janek today. Having retired after 52 years at the same slaughterhouse where his father began, Jack is content with the opportunities his grandchildren have, but nostalgically muses on his own youth. Based on *The Immigrant Experience: The Anguish of Becoming American*, edited by Thomas C. Wheeler.
Learning Corp.   31 min   Color   1973

840 Immigration in the 19th Century. In the mid-19th century, social unrest sweeps Europe in protest to centuries of oppression. The lavish promises of a distant nation are translated into a dozen tongues: Scandinavian, German, Irish, Chinese, Czechoslovakian, Lithuanian. In 1886 the Statue of Liberty begins her vigil above the waters of New York Harbor. Her promise of opportunity is visible for miles. Producer: Metromedia Producers Corp. and David Wolper. Narrator: Richard Basehart. Based on *A Nation of Immigrants* by John F. Kennedy.
Films Inc.   13 min   B&W   1972

841 Immigration in the 20th Century. Fear of foreigners reached its height in the 1920's with the Red Scare, the resurgence of the KKK and restrictive quota laws stifling all but the "elite" Nordics and Anglo-Saxons. Finally in 1965 President Johnson, fulfilling a pledge to John F. Kennedy, eliminated the prejudice of a national **origins** quota system. Narrated by Richard Basehart. Producer: Metromedia Producers Corp. and David Wolper. From the book by John F. Kennedy, *A Nation of Immigrants*.
Films Inc.   13 min   B&W   1972

842 The Incredible Bread Machine Film. This series of dramatizations provides an illustration of the harmful effects of government regulation of the marketplace. It cites examples of official errors, and concludes with a discussion between economists, Walter Heller and Milton Friedman. Based on the book by R.W. Grant, *The Incredible Bread Machine*.
World Research   55 min   Color   1976

843 In Search of Ancient Astronauts. Could visitors from other planets be responsible for many of the unexplained phenomena on earth today? This picture, narrated by Rod Serling, examines the theory that the earth once had visitors from outer space. Based on Erich von Däniken's bestseller, *Chariots of the Gods?*, the film explores the "clues" of ancient monuments, artifacts, and documents of the Mayan civilization and the Egyptian pyramids.
Xerox Films　52 min　Color　1973

844 Introduction to Confucius. The tenets of Confucian social and political thought, given in his classic *Great Learning*, are presented with ancient Chinese music and many quotes from Confucius. The visual material, photographed in the Republic of China, includes art treasures and sequences from the colorful ceremony celebrating the birthday of Confucius. Produced and directed by Sumner Glimcher. Photographed and edited by Warren Johnson. Written by Joan Glimcher.
Int. Film Foundation　12 min　Color　1975

845 Is It Always Right to Be Right? This award-winning film, with its quick-tempo pace, is designed to provoke discussion about the importance of active listening as a technique for settling differences. Animation by Stephen Bosustow. Narrator is Orson Welles. Book by Warren Schmidt.
Bosustow　8 min　Color　1972

846 John Muir's High Sierra. This tribute to Muir's passion for conservation is also a tribute to the spirit of his letters, journals and books. More than any other person, he is credited with the creation of our National Parks system and with public appreciation of Yosemite and the Sierra Nevadas where he lived between 1880 and 1910. Produced by Dewitt Jones, himself a respected naturalist and writer.
Pyramid　27 min　Color　1973

847 Journals of Lewis and Clark. This program covers the terrain traveled by Meriwether Lewis and William Clark, the virgin Northwest, in the development of the American frontier. It points out the problems of conservation and of the treatment of Indians that followed these explorations. Narrated by Lorne Greene. An NBC-TV production. Also available in the original 53-minute television edition.
Encyc. Brit.　27 min　Color　1966

848 Journey Into Summer. The drama of Edwin Way Teale's book is heightened by the contrast of unspoiled and spoiled nature. We first see nature at her zenith of color and life, then the camera zooms in on Lake Erie. Other threatened sites and doomed animals are also recorded together with a note of hope. Awards: Bronze Medal, Atlanta Festival; Chris Award, Columbus Festival. Producer: Hobel-Leiterman.
Xerox　51 min　Color　1970

849 The Kennedys of Albuquerque. Father is a crusader for retarded children but spends so much time traveling, he has little time for his own son. He designs nuclear weapons and his wife Joan, at 40, is making an effort to enlarge her experiences beyond the home. Oldest daughter Nancy feels challenged to live up to her father's high expectations. She's unhappy about being 15th in a class of 700: "It's not number one." From the Book *Six American Families* by Paul Wilkes. Filmmaker: Bill Jersey.
Carousel   59 min   Color   1977

850 Latin-American Cooking. A visit to Latin-America and a reminder of the many foods that originated with the Indians. Traditional and modern techniques are used to prepare the same basic recipes. Adapted from the Time-Life *Foods of the World* Series. Also available with Spanish narration. Author: Jonathan N. Leonard.
RH Media   22 min   Color   1975

851   Learning to Live 1. Ego States. The Parent, Adult and Child aspects of our personalities are explored to show why we act and react the way we do. One of 8 films on Transactional Analysis. Study-guide available. Based on *Born to Win* by James and Jongeward. Producer: Jeffrey Weber.
Mass Media   30 min   Color   1974

852   Learning to Live 2. Transactions. When two people relate—"transact"—the three ego states are involved. How do my ego states "hook" yours? One of 8 films on Transactional Analysis. Study-guide available. Based on *Born to Win* by James and Jongeward. Producer: Jeffrey Weber.
Mass Media   30 min   Color   1974

853   Learning to Live 3. Strokes. We all need recognition—i.e. "strokes." How can we be less afraid to ask and to accept recognition and love? One of 8 films on Transactional Analysis. Book by James and Jongeward: *Born to Win*. Study-guide available. Producer: Jeffrey Weber.
Mass Media   30 min   Color   1974

854   Learning to Live 4. Time Structures. How time affects the priorities in our lives. How can we gain better control or direction in our use of time? One of 8 films on Transactional Analysis. Study-guide available. Book by Dr. Muriel James and Dr. Dorothy Jongeward. Producer: Jeffrey Weber.
Mass Media   30 min   Color   1974

855   Learning to Live 5. Feelings. We all collect hurt and angry feelings. What can we do to be more honest in accepting and expressing our real feelings? One of 8 films on Transactional Analysis. Study-guide available. Based on the book *Born to Win* by Muriel James and Dorothy

Jongeward. Producer: Jeffrey Weber.
Mass Media   30 min   Color   1974

856 Learning to Live 6. Games. Some of the "games" people play are frustrating and destructive. How can we stop playing such games? One of 8 films on Transactional Analysis. Study-guide available Based on *Born to Win* by James and Jongeward. Producer: Jeffrey Weber.
Mass Media   30 min   Color   1974

857 Learning to Live 7. Acquiring Life Scripts. We all adopt life plans or "scripts" early in life. How are these scripts acquired? One of 8 films on Transactional Analysis. Study-guide available. Based on *Born to Win* by Muriel James and Dorothy Jongeward. Producer: Jeffrey Weber.
Mass Media   30 min   Color   1974

858 Learning to Live 8. Changing Life Scripts. Some of us have life scripts that thwart our fulfillment as a person. How can we change? Based on *Born to Win* by Dr. Muriel James and Dr. Dorothy Jongeward. One of 8 films on Transactional Analysis. Study-guide available. Producer: Jeffrey Weber.
Mass Media   30 min   Color   1974

859 Let's Make a Film. Under the direction of Yvonne Andersen, children from 5 to 18 have been making animated films for more than seven years at the Yellow Ball Workshop in Newton Mass. In this film, students can see children their own age working with movable cutouts, clay, toys, painted film, constructed forms, and live actors—all parts of the filmmaker's language. In her book, *Teaching Film Animation to Children*, Ms. Andersen tells how to guide children in exploring these techniques. Photographed and directed by Yvonne Andersen.
Van Nostrand   13 min   Color   1972

860 The Limits to Growth. This is a report from the Club of Rome, an international society dedicated to solving present predicaments and preventing future ones. Its projection of facts shows that the cumulative effects of population growth, depletion of natural resources, and ecological deterioration argue for a halt to unchecked "progress." Produced by Potomac Associates and Thames of England. Contributors to the study: Dr. Dennis Meadows, William Behrens III, and others.
Raymond, Ltd.   60 min   Color   1975

861   Lincoln's Gettysburg Address. Culminating with Charlton Heston's delivery of this immortal speech, this film can serve the study of language and history. Original art, photographs, graphics of the period and battle scenes trace the breach between North and South, the elections of 1858 and 1860 and highlights of the Civil War. Produced by Art Evans.
Paramount   15 min   Color   1970

862 The Living Earth. In his essay, *Walden*, Henry David Thoreau describes "this curious world...more wonderful than it is convenient, more beautiful than it is useful". The camera attempts to parallel this vision with an assemblage of natural imagery accompanied by Eddie Albert's reading of passages from Thoreau's masterpiece. Produced by Fred Hudson.
Pyramid 9 min Color 1971

863 Lovesick. A lonely and frustrated intellectual, in his pursuit for love on the streets of New York, follows the out-of-context advice of Rollo May's *Love and Will* and Erich Fromm's *Art of Loving*. His efforts in "winning over" a neighborhood prostitute are sad reflections of urban alienation. Produced by Drew Denbaum.
Phoenix 28 min B&W 1976

864 The Manager as Entrepreneur. One way for managers to look at themselves is by asking, how do they respond to the complex demands made by the outside world? Do they think and behave in ways that support innovation and self-renewal? John Humble and Peter Drucker discuss the managerial staffing required by today's and tomorrow's organizations. Humble is a director of Urwick, Orr, and Partners, Ltd.; Drucker is the author of *Age of Discontinuity*, the book that inspired the *Managing Discontinuity* series, of which this is the ninth film.
BNA Films 31 min Color 1971

865 Man and the State: Machiavelli on Political Power. The political principles of Niccolò Machiavelli have had tremendous impact on our Western society. In this open-ended film, Machiavelli is forced to debate his ideas. In his a politics of realism? Does he show the world as it is today? Is his Renaissance philosophy much different from ours? Related reading: *The Prince*. A Bernard Wilets Film.
BFA Educ. Media 28¼ min Color 1973

866 Man and the State: The Trial of Socrates. The trial and death of Socrates (as given in Plato's account) is important in the history of Western civilization. It poses questions that are still troubling our society: How far should we go in suppressing people and ideas? Should a person obey laws he/she feels are unjust? A Bernard Wilets Film.
BFA Educ. Media 28½ min Color 1973

867 Max Made Mischief: An Approach to Literature. Demonstrates a curriculum developed by Sonia Landes. By using Maurice Sendak's classic children's book, *Where the Wild Things Are*, two teachers guide their third grade class in exploring plot structure, the nature of poetry, and the use of illustrations. The teachers discuss their progress between classes and, at the end of the film, meet with author Sendak to learn about his intentions in writing the book and his statement that "fantasy

only makes sense when rooted ten feet deep in reality."
Doc/Learning   30 min   Color   1978

868 Meeting in Progress. Takes viewers through a problems-solving conference, demonstrating ways to deal with situations crucial to the success of a meeting. After each key point there is an opportunity for viewers to respond to three alternatives when asked, "What would you do if you were the leader?" Based on the programmed guide-book, *Conference Leadership: The Critical Functions*, by psychologist Dr. Oliver D. Fowler and management consultant Malcolm **Macurda**.
Roundtable   43 min   Color   1970

869 Meet Your Parent — Adult — Child. In light-hearted style, this animation explains the principles of Transactional Analysis, particularly Dr. Thomas Harris's analogy of each individual's P-A-C (Parent-Adult-Child) ego states. One of two films in a series. See also **We're OK.**
BFA Educ. Media   8¾ min   Color   1975

870 The Middle Years. An examination into the period between youth and old age, the middle years characterized by change that is sometimes disturbing, sometimes fulfilling. Based on *Passages* by Gail Sheehy. Produced by the Canadian Television Network.
Films, Inc.   23 min   Color   1976

871 Mr. Chairman (The Fundamentals of Parliamentary Law). Presents the principles of group regulation in a series of animated sequences. Shows why rules of order are essential to democratic discussions and decision-making, and also suggests how parliamentary procedure can be adapted to the needs of a specific group. Based on the *Rules of Order* by Henry Martyn Robert.
Encyc. Brit.   13 min   Color   1959

872 Mr. Symbol Man. "Blissymbols" are pictorial figures designed by Charles Bliss as a form of language for the handicapped or for aliens. This film tells the story of this Australian and his creation of a new system of pictographs, believed in some quarters to be equivalent to the invention of braille. A coproduction of the National Film Board of Canada and Film Australia. Based on *Semantography* by Bliss.
Benchmark   49 min   Color   1976

873 Movement Education. Pointing out the importance of exercise for school-age children, including the hyperactive, this film theorizes that "movement education" can promote cooperation, discipline and enjoyment. It shows youngsters at the Frostig Center of Educational Therapy in activities calculated to improve coordination, balance, strength, and endurance. Based on the text by Marianne Frostig, Ph.D. and Phyllis Maslow, Ph.D.
AIMS   27½ min   Color   1977

874 The Multinational Corporation. One of the most controversial business developments of this century is the multinational corporation as a mechanism for producing, distributing and marketing goods and services worldwide. It looks upon the global economy as one market, despite the existence of nationalism, unions and other business interests. Dan Seymour, executive of J. Walter Thompson Company, joins Peter Drucker to explore the effectiveness of the multinationals. Drucker is the author of *Age of Discontinuity*, the model for the *Managing Discontinuity* series, of which this is the seventh film.
BNA Films 32 min Color 1971

875 The Music of Auschwitz. In this *60 Minutes* segment, Morley Safer interviews an Auschwitz survivor, Fania Fenelon, in Paris and at the site of the deadly concentration camp. Documentary footage reveals the existence of a prison orchestra, composed of women, formed for the bizarre enjoyment of their Nazi captors. Based on Ms. Fenelon's account which was translated into English as *Playing for Time*. Production by CBS News.
Carousel Films 16 min Color & BW 1978

876 A Nation of Immigrants. Based on John F. Kennedy's account of immigration to America, this film is built from the raw materials of history: photographs, motion-pictures, music of the period and the people themselves. Narrated by Richard Basehart. **Producer: David Wolper/Metromedia.**
Films Inc. 53 min B&W 1972

877 Nazi Germany: Years of Triumph. In the thirties, Naziism flourishes in Germany. The freedom of 67 million people is subverted by a dictator. This is the triumph of Hitler whose lust for power turns outward. Austria, Czechoslovakia, then Poland. And England stands alone. Producer: M-G-M Documentary and David Wolper. Based on *The Rise and Fall of the Third Reich* by William L. Shirer.
Films Inc. 28 min B&W 1972

878 99 Days to Survival. Walter Schirra, one of the first seven astronauts, hosts this re-creation of Major John Wesley Powell's 1869 exploration of the Colorado River and Grand Canyon. TV actor E.G. Marshall reads from Powell's journal, while Schirra and a crew of river runners make the same challenging journey. Sponsored by the Smithsonian Institute.
Pyramid 52 min Color 1972

879 Nobody Ever Died of Old Age. Dramatizes the lives of resourceful senior citizens who are struggling to combat, with dignity, the social odds against them. Combines praise for old people with outrage at the dehumanization they experience at the hands of society. Based on the

book by Sharon Curtin. Produced and directed by Herbert Danska.
Films, Inc.   58 min   Color   1976

880 No-Nonsense Delegation. This production features the author of
the book, Dale McConkey. He explains his techniques for over-coming
problems related to delegation of authority and suggests ways of improving managerial effectiveness in achieving results. A training-leader's
guide and course manual is available.
Didactic   30 min   Color   1973

881   Non-Verbal Communication. This film is the basis of a
multimedia management training program designed to make executives
aware of the impact of unspoken language in their business relations.
Deals with posture, voice inflection, facial expression and other unspoken signals. Narrated by Dr. Albert Mehrabian of UCLA, author of
Silent Messages, the source material for this production.
Salenger   17 min   Color   1978

882 North from Mexico. This film, based on *North from Mexico: The
Spanish Speaking People of the United States* by Carey McWilliams, creates
a portrait of Mexican-Americans and the Southwest. It makes a
statement about their contributions, concerns, and expectations. It also
tries to bring Anglo-Hispanic relations into perspective, and examines
the moral basis for the struggle of the Chicano to attain long-denied
human rights. Produced and directed by Sumner Glimcher
Mass Comm. Inc.   20 min   Color   1975

883 North with the Spring. The camera conveys a panoramic survey
of Edwin Way Teale's views of the rebirth of spring. Covers the passage of
spring on a 17,000 mile journey from the Flordia Everglades to the
Canadian Arctic. As the camera moves northward, we see migratory birds,
the start of the reproductive cycle in a mountain stream and a wild pony
in foal. Producer: Hobel-Leiterman.
Xerox Films   52 min   Color   1970

884 Notes on the Port of St. Francis. In this portrait of San Francisco,
natural sounds and unusual camera angles reveal the lesser known side
of the city. The commentary quotes at length from an essay written by
Robert Lewis Stevenson when he visited San Francisco in 1888. Narrator
is Vincent Price. Produced by Frank Stauffaucher.
Film Images   23 min   B&W   1952

885 The Now Employee. Traces the history of the N.O.W. (New
Orientation to Work) group whose program is designed to help em-
ployers to understand young people just entering the work force.
Package consists of film or videotape, manual, workbook, and a copy of
David Nadler's original book.
Didactic   25 min   B&W   1973

886 The Nuremberg Chronicle. Explores the woodcuts of this anonymous German book published in 1493, recounting world history as perceived in that period of turmoil and change. Produced at Wesleyan University by John Frazer and Russell T. Limbach, with the cooperation of the Davison Art Center.
Conn. Films   22 min   B&W   1967

887 The Occult: An Echo From Darkness. Links the monoliths at Stonehenge, the pyramids of Egypt and the Tower of Babel with mankind's attempts to substitute Satan for God. The current interest in the occult is analyzed as a continuation of the struggle between the powers of light and dark. Practitioners of the occult are interviewed and several ceremonies are filmed. Ends with an appeal for Christian faith in the forces of good. Based on Hal Lindsey's *Satan Is Alive and Well on Planet Earth*. Produced by Mal Couch. Directed by Tom Doades.
Pyramid   51 min   Color   1973

888 Of Time, Work, and Leisure. A documentary presentation of the concepts set forth in Sebastian de Grazia's provocative study by the same name. In our work-oriented, clock-dominated society, we have won "time off" but we have lost the ability to appreciate true leisure. Produced by National Educational Television.
Indiana U.   29 min   B&W   1963

889 One Day at Teton Marsh. This nature study is based on the book of the same name by Sally Carrighar. It describes the wildlife ecology of a peaceful swamp, where animals and birds adapt freely without the intrusions of mankind. The film is divided into two complete reels.
Disney   47 min   Color   1966

890 Parliamentary Procedures in Action (2nd Edition). Rules and regulations keep a meeting moving in a democratic and orderly way. Step-by-step events of a meeting are paralleled by explanations of key concepts: duties of officers, order of the agenda, activities of committees, and the various motions. Based on Henry Martyn **Roberts'** *Rules of Order*.
Coronet   16 min   Color   1965

891 The Pasciaks of Chicago. The subjects are a blue-collar Polish-American family whose ethnic roots are challenged by the lifestyle of their children. Oldest son Gary refuses to follow his father into the Department of Sanitation. He has gone to Hollywood to be an actor. The other children wait to see what will happen, while the parents find it's hard to let go of old traditions. From the book *Six American Families* by Paul Wilkes. Filmmaker: Mark Obenhaus.
Carousel   59 min   Color   1977

892 Patrick Henry's Liberty or Death. Film and television star Barry

Sullivan delivers the narration of Patrick Henry's "Liberty or Death" speech recreating the ferment of the pre-Revolutionary period. Graphic techniques review the historic events that preceded independence: the Boston Tea Party, the Quartering Act, the division of the colonists, and the Boston Massacre. Mr. Sullivan concludes with a forceful delivery of the famous oration. Produced by Art Evans.
Paramount   15 min   Color   1970

893 The Peter Principle. The Peter Principle states that "In any hierarchy, employees tend to rise to their level of incompetence, and that's where they stay." The advocate of this axiom, Dr. Laurence J. Peter, examines its implications individually and organizationally. Discussion-guide available. Produced by BBC-TV.
Time-Life   25 min   Color   1973

894 Plato's Apology: The Life and Teachings of Socrates. Mortimer Adler, with the aid of dramatized excerpts from *The Dialogues* of Plato, expounds the philosophy of Socrates as recorded by his disciple, Plato. Part of the *Humanities Series*. Produced and directed by John Barnes.
Encyc. Brit.   28 min   Color   1963

895 Plato's Cave. This dramatization from Book VII of *The Republic* follows Socrates' "script" on the nature of human perception and the distinction between symbol and substance. The philosopher is played by Victor Izay. Music by Jaime Mendoza-Nava. Producer: Arthur Gould.
Pyramid   20 min   Color   1974

896 Plimpton: The Great Quarterback Sneak. George Plimpton, writer, joins the National Football League Baltimore Colts for preseason training, and then guides the team as quarterback for four plays against the Detroit Lions in an exhibition game. George involves himself in all aspects of his subject as he trains for the quarterback's job describing the preparation for the job and his attempts to play various positions. The script is patterned after Plimpton's book, *The Paper Lion*. William Kronick, who guided Plimpton through three other films, acted as producer-director on this one. Producer: The Wolper Organization.
Films Inc.   52 min   Color   1974

897 Police Dog. Joseph Cotten narrates the step-by-step training of a "K-9," with examples of its utilization in searches for bombs, narcotics, and lost children. Available in two separate parts. Produced by Leo Handel, author of the book on which this film is based, *A Dog Named Duke*.
Handel Film Corp.   50 min   Color   1972

898 Pollution Control — The Hard Decisions. Robert V. Hansberger, formerly president of Boise Cascade Corporation, points up the responsibilities of business in relation to the environment. These issues are all a

trade-off, says Peter Drucker, of risks against benefits. Viewers are encouraged to think twice about environmental betterment. Drucker wrote *Age of Discontinuity*, the book that generated the *Managing Discontinuity* series of which this is the fifth film.
BNA Films 28 min Color 1971

899 Pregnancy After 35. Deals with the physical and emotional factors of belated motherhood. Includes real-life situations of a variety of women and quotes statistics relating to Down's syndrome and other birth defects sometimes associated with later child-bearing. This aspect is balanced by a reminder that postponed parenthood has its own special joys and advantages. Narrated by Carole McCauley, author of the book of the same name. Directed by Gwen Brown. Producer: Alvin Fiering.
Polymorph Films 22 min Color 1978

900 Rag Tapestry. This study records the process of making a rag tapestry in an experimental workshop with 24 children in the Metropolitan Museum of Art in New York. The subject is the City of New York. Original drawings by children were transferred to a piece of rug backing. Then the 8- to-12-year-olds poked their brown shuttle hooks to create a colorful woolen mural of the city. Filmed by George and Sherry Zabriskie. Directed by Ann Wiseman, author of *Rag Tapestries and Wool Mosaics*.
Int. Film Foundation 11 min Color 1974

901 Remedy for Riot. Traces the rise of urban revolt in America, and probes the problem of racism and its results. Reviews the findings of the National Advisory Commission on Civil Disorders (the Koerner Report), and suggest ways of improving relationships between the black and white communities. Produced by CBS Television News.
Carousel 36 min B&W 1968

902 The Rise of Hitler. Uses documentary footage from the late 1930's and traces the life of Hitler from his childhood to his ascension as Chancellor of Germany. Greatest emphasis is placed on the building of the Nazi party and Hilter's ability to play on the hatreds and fears of the German people. A David Wolper MGM Documentary production. Based on William L. Shirer's *The Rise and Fall of the Third Reich*.
Films, Inc. 20 min B&W 1972

903 Run Dick, Run Jane. Based on the best-selling *The New Aerobics* by Kenneth Cooper, this production shows how the habit of exercise can provide insurance against America's leading killer, heart disease. Featured are a marathon runner with no feet and a 103-year old waiter who used to run six miles every morning before work. Also available with sound-track in Spanish.
Brigham Young U. 20 min Color 1971

904 Saint Augustine. In his *City of God*, St. Augustine provided the classic analysis of the relationship between man in time and man in eternity. It was written soon after the sack of Rome when the pagan world was in as great disarray as ours. Malcolm Muggeridge finds the comparison alarming. He sees our decline exemplified in erotic movies, violence on television, cult groups, and great wealth ignoring extreme poverty. His interpretations on screen parallel those expressed in his book *A Third Testament* upon which this film was based. Produced for PBS television by BBC.
Time-Life 57 min Color 1977

905 Seashore. Live-action photography, relating sea and earth to each other, conveys a subtle message: either we change our wasteful ways of living or destroy our planet's fruits. Inspired by Loren Eisley's *The Immense Journey*. Produced by Fred Hudson.
Pyramid 8 min Color 1971

906 The Silent Witness. A photographic investigation of the shroud with Christ-like resemblance in Turin, Italy. Analyzes both the evidence and the tradition behind this linen, trying to verify its authenticity as claimed since discovery in the 1350's. Based on *The Shroud of Turin* by historian Ian Wilson who coscripted this documentary. Produced by Screenpro Films (London).
Pyramid 55 min Color 1979

907 Slavery and Resistance. Colonial to Civil War accounts of how the black Americans endured and resisted slavery at the risk of life. Documented are some of the achievements of famous runaway slaves, including poet Phyllis Wheatley, novelist and playwright William Wells Brown and anti-slavery orator and writer Frederick Douglass. Produced for the New York Times.
Coronet 24½ min Color 1969

908 A Slave's Story: Running a Thousand Miles to Freedom. This film is based on an authenticated narrative by William and Ellen Craft and is introduced by their great-granddaughter. The dramatization of the Crafts' escape from slavery in 1848 follows their journey from the Deep South to Philadelphia. Their plan was made successful by the fact that Ellen was sufficiently light-skinned to pass as white. So with Ellen disguised as a man traveling with his slave (William), the young couple set out on their trip, eventually crossing the Mason-Dixon line. Director: John Irvin.
Learning Corp. 29 min Color 1972

909 Social Needs as Business Opportunities. Executive Hansberger and author Drucker discuss the social responsibilities of business, touching on subjects such as education, vocational training, employing

the disadvantaged, community rebuilding and the relocation of obsolete plants. They agree that good intentions are no substitute for competence and that businessmen should resist being pushed into projects merely because there is nobody else to do it. Robert Hansberger is past president of Boise Cascade Corporation. Peter Drucker is author of *Age of Discontinuity*, the source of the *Managing Discontinuity* series of which this is the sixth film.
BNA Films   32 min   Color   1971

910 Stained Glass. Shot entirely in England, this film provides a look into the world of stained glass. Using images and music, the film reveals the subject's craftsmanship and human achievement, and shows the different steps of making stained glass from artist's sketches to the finished product. Lawrence Lee author of *The Appreciation of Stained Glass*, served as technical advisor.
Skye Pictures   15 min   Color   1978

911 The Stephenses of Iowa. They are a third-generation farm family whose good life is threatened by inflated costs of land and equipment. For Carl and Lois and their six children, farming is in their blood. All the Stephenses want to stay on the farm but see family farming and rural values threatened by an overwhelmingly urban society. From the book, *Six American Families* by Paul Wilkes. Filmmakers: Arthur Barron and Mark Obenhaus.
Carousel   59 min   Color   1977

912   Sticky My Fingers, Fleet My Feet. Exposes the stubborn American myth that athletic prowess represents masculinity. Norman is a forty-ish executive, religiously addicted to his weekly touch football game in Central Park. But his self-esteem is considerably lowered when spectacularly out-performed by a 15-year-old boy. Based on the *New Yorker* article by Gene Williams, who plays the part of Norman. Produced under a grant from the American Film Institute.
Time-Life   23 min   Color   1969

913   The Story of a Book. This chronicle follows Canadian author Holling C. Holling through the demanding process of creating *Pagoo*, the story of a hermit crab. Shows the steps of originating an idea, doing research, writing and re-writing, illustrating, planning the lay-out, and printing.
Perennial Education   11 min   Color   1962

914   Strictly Speaking. Based on Edwin Newman's witty bestsellers, *Strictly Speaking* and *A Civil Tongue*, this film makes a case for clear and concrete expressions as opposed to jargon, redundancy and gobbledygook. Newman is a winner of the Peabody and Emmy awards for

TV excellence as an NBC correspondent, commentator, and critic. (There is a charge for preview, applicable toward purchase within 60 days.)
Cally Curtis　27 min　Color　1979

915　Summerhill. Here is a school without fixed rules, where students are their own masters. A co-educational English boarding school, Summerhill, was founded by Alexander Neill in 1917. In the film, he explains his objectives and, from the activities of the children, can be seen how his methods work. School, he says, should put preparation for life ahead of learning. Produced by D. Dennis Miller and P. Cecily Burwash.
Nat. Film Board　28 min　Color　1967

916　Symbol Boy. This segment, part of the 49-minute film entitled *Mr. Symbol Man*, is an animated cartoon that uses "Blissymbols," the basic nonverbal figures designed by Charles K. Bliss. A coproduction of the National Film Board of Canada and Film Australia. Patterned after Bliss's book *Semantography (Blissymbolics)*.
Benchmark　3½ min　Color　1976

917　Tales from a Book of Kings: The Houghton Shah-Nameh. The semi-mythical *Book of Kings* (Shahnameh) traces Iran's ancient Persian Empire from the time of its legendary birth to its downfall in the 7th century. Iranian rulers had the book copied and illustrated by the best artisans, and the Houghton manuscript is the finest example surviving, made in the 16th century. It contains 258 miniature paintings. Produced by the Metropolitan Museum of Art in New York.
Time-Life　26 min　Color　1974

918　Talking with Thoreau. Guided by the writings of Henry David Thoreau, the film creates a visual impression of his life at Walden Pond. Suggests that his 19th-century ideas on nature, conscience and privacy are relevant to the 20th century. Filmed by Signet Productions.
Encyc. Brit.　29 min　Color　1975

919　Terra Sancta: A Film of Israel. A review, through the eyes of an Israeli citizen, of the 4000-year history of the land that spawned three of the world's great religions. Includes references to Old Testament predictions of an eventual Jewish homeland and state. Written and narrated by Chanoch Jacobsen. Produced by Harry Atwood.
Int. Film Bureau　31 min　Color　1968

920　This is Israel. The live-action camera travels over super-highways built on ancient sands through a land of camels, Cadillacs, pomegranates and oil pipelines. Shimmering panoramas of many hues reveal the Biblical glory of Israel's past and the hope of its future. Narrator: Gila Almagor. Photographer: Edward English. Produced by Sonny Fox and Morton Schindel. Based on the picture book by Miroslav Sasek.
Weston Woods　12 min　Color　1963

921 This Is Marshall McLuhan: The Medium Is the Message. A graphic exploration of the ideas of Dr. McLuhan and reactions to his controversial theories in *Understanding Media*. Clarifies, through discussion and visual interpretation, such ideas as the medium is the message, media are extensions of man, new patterns of thought are required by new realities, and artists have, in their forms of expression, forecast vast changes in human outlook. An NBC television film with Marshall McLuhan as the communicator.
McGraw-Hill 53 min Color 1967

922 Three Styles of Marital Conflict. The three case-studies that comprise this film are based on clinical actuality and research. Each of the vignettes illustrates a conjugal conflict that frustrates constructive solution. Each dramatization also displays the reciprocal nature of such situations along with verbal and nonverbal behavior of individuals. Based on *A Couple's Guide to Communication* by Dr. John Gottman.
Behavorial Images 14 min Color 1976

923 A Time of Migration. A glimpse of the mystery and majesty of ocean life, based on naturalist John Hay's book, *The Run*. Each spring, hundreds of alewife fish rush into the streams of Cape Cod. They battle currents, predators, and marshes as they swim their way to the spawning pools and back again to the Atlantic. No one knows how they communicate or how they are guided year after year. Directed by Nicholas Noxon. Produced by Potomac Films.
Macmillan 13 min Color 1962

924 A Time of Wonder. In poetic prose and watercolor paintings, the author describes the wonders of nature on a Maine island. Based on the picture-book by Robert McCloskey. Producer: Morton Schindel.
Weston Woods 13 min Color 1961

925 The Time of Your Life. Based on Alan Lakein's *How to Get Control of Your Time and Your Life* this film outlines his six practical steps for managing ourselves more effectively. Shows people doing things the wrong way and the right way, then presents their defense of poor practices, followed by persuasive rebuttals. Features actor James Whitmore. Produced for the Cally Curtis Company by the University of California (Berkeley).
Extension Media 28 min Color 1974

926 de Tocqueville's America. Reviews the treatise *Democracy in America*, by Alexis de Tocqueville, the 19th-century French observer. Includes the prediction that the abolition of slavery would result in racial strife if blacks were not given true equality under law. Format is based on exchange of comments among four U.S. Senators within the context of

contemporary social and political crises in the U.S. Produced by the Canadian Broadcasting Company.
Indiana U.   60 min   BW   1970

927 To Defeat the Doomsday Doctrine. John Maddox, author of *The Doomsday Syndrome*, argues that pessimism about the environment and human survival are largely unfounded. He cites as evidence British progress in cleaning the air and the Thames, and a Swedish aeration system for purifying lake water. Produced by Hobel-Leiterman, Ltd. (Canada).
Document Assoc.   22 min   Color   1974

928 To Die, to Live — Survivors of Hiroshima. Between scenes of the 1945 atomic attack and of the rebuilt Japanese city, the voices of witnesses describe their experiences and feelings. Based on the book *Death in Life: Survivors of Hiroshima* by Robert Jay Lifton, M.D.
Time-Life   60 min   Color & BW   1976

929 To Die Today. An in-depth outline of Dr. Elisabeth Kübler-Ross's principles on the humane care of the terminally ill. On camera, she describes the four stages of death awareness: denial, anger, depression and grief. She then interviews a healthy-looking patient with Hodgkins disease, and later discusses his condition with medical students at Chicago's Billings Hospital. Roughly parallels Dr. Kübler-Ross's book, *On Death and Dying*. Produced by the Canadian Broadcasting Corporation.
Filmakers   50 min   B&W   1971

930 Tomorrow's Customers. Vermont Royster, former editor of *The Wall Street Journal*, discusses with Peter Drucker the importance of innovative marketing as a means of reaching future buyers. What cultural forces will influence purchasing patterns? How should organizations respond to rapidly changing fads, trends and counter-trends? These questions form the outline of this second film in the *Managing Discontinuity* series, featuring Drucker, author of *The Age of Discontinuity*.
BFA Films   33 min   Color   1971

931 To Solve the E.S.P. Mystery: Extra-Sensory Perception Is No Dream. E.S.P. is slowly emerging from the shadows where it once stood side by side with the occult. It continues to defy our known laws of time and space. But, scientists are now capturing E.S.P. effects in the laboratory, and the future will surely produce additional understanding of this extraordinary faculty. This film features psychiatrist Montague Ullman, president of the American Society of Psychical Research and author of the book, *Dream Telepathy*. Producers: Hobel-Leiterman, Ltd.
Document Assoc.   24 min   Color   1973

932 Total Fitness in Thirty Minutes a Week. This is an adaptation of

the best-selling book by Dr. Laurence Morehouse. It demonstrates ways of achieving physical benefits with a minimum of effort. Besides explaining the principle of pulse-rated exercise, the author himself outlines a five-point program for total health. Produced by Denis Sanders.
Pyramid 28 min Color 1975

933 Touching. This subject consists mainly of a camera conversation with socio-anthropologist Ashley B. Montagu on the often neglected concepts of tactile awareness. Based on content covered in depth in his book, *Touching*.
Psych. Films 35 min Color 1975

934 Transactional Analysis. Based on *TA in Psychotherapy* by Eric Berne, M.D., this film shows the two-fold claims made for "TA": an easily understood theory of behavior and a practical blueprint for individual and organizational change. Uses a combination of production techniques: interviews, animation, live-action cutaways and diagrams. Produced by Joan Owens.
CRM Educ. Films 31 min Color 1975

935 Truth and the Dragon. A metaphorical exposé of propaganda, especially as practiced in commercial advertising. The "dragon" of falsehood assumes seven disguises, including glittering generalities, testimonials, the folksy approach and bandwagon psychology. Based on the book by Elsa Bailey.
Perennial 10 min Color 1969

936 The Two Faces of Group Leadership. Counselors, under the direction of Dr. Marilyn Bates, apply leadership techniques within realistic conditions. Starting with the pre-group interview and moving quickly through the various stages of group counseling, this film gives a view of two basic functions: mobilizing and managing. Dr. Bates is co-author of *Group Leadership: A Manual for Group Leaders*.
Psych. Films 30 min B&W

937 Uncle Ben. A young widow dies, leaving her three children uncared for. Her brother Ben, against tremendous odds, decides to keep the family together. Overcoming his alcohol problem and the struggle to be a father proves that it is possible for a person to change for the better. Based on a true story by Kenneth McFarland.
Brigham Young 27 min Color 1978

938 Union Maids. This is a documentary about three unusual American women who, in the face of fierce oppression, became labor organizers during the Depression of the 1930's. Their determination led to improved working conditions in the pharmaceutical, meatpacking,

and laundry industries. From the book, *Rank and File*, by Stanton and Alice Lynd. Produced by Julia Reichett, James Klein, and Mike Mogulesque.
New Day Films 45 min B&W 1976

939 Up the Organization. Robert Townsend, who wrote the book that outraged the corporate community, appears here and gives his very individualistic views on such topics as chief executives, personnel departments, management consultants, computers, public relations, and coercive conformity. Produced for BBC Television by Peter Riding.
Time-Life 30 min Color 1972

940 Vanishing Cornwall. Based on Daphne du Maurier's book, this film is narrated by Sir Michael Redgrave, and is taken directly from the text. Ms. du Maurier has lived in Cornwall for over forty years. It is the setting for several of her novels (*Rebecca, Jamaica Inn, Frenchmen's Creek, The King's General, My Cousin Rachel*) and, in this film, we share her knowledge of what has given Cornwall its history and flavor.
Sterling Educ. 54 min Color 1969

941 Walden Pond. The beauty and simplicity of Walden Pond (near Concord, Mass.) provided inspiration for this philosopher's "radical" writings—and actions—in the late 19th century. Discussion-guide available. Produced for BBC-TV by Lawrence Gordon Clark.
Time-Life 15 min Color 1975

942 Wandering Through Winter. A 20,000-mile trail, beginning just below San Diego, brings us to the extreme Northeast above the Caribou in Maine. Deer forage in the thicket. Ducks wing their way south. The days lengthen, and the sun returns. Life quickens everywhere and the seasons come full cycle. Based on the observations of Edwin Way Teale. Produced by Hobel-Leiterman, Ltd. (Canada).
Xerox 50 min Color 1970

943 Washington's Farewell. Television performer William Shatner delivers a concise version of the better known portions of the "Farewell Address" in which President Washington reviewed the precedents established during his administration, and offered advice that would guide a new nation for generations. Original artwork and period graphics provide political and personal atmosphere. A reproduction of the printed Farewell Address accompanies each print of this film. Produced by Art Evans.
Paramount 15 min Color 1970

944 We're OK. This is the other film in the series of two on Transactional Analysis. It is, as such, an extension of Dr. Thomas Harris' approach to human relations as reflected in the phrase *I'm OK—You're OK*.

Animated with humor. (See also **Meet Your Parent-Adult-Child.**)
BFA Educ. Media 8½ min Color 1975

945 Who's Gonna Collect the Garbage? A discussion panel about various segments of the work force, their problems and how they can be handled. This is film number four of the *Managing Discontinuity* series based on Peter Drucker's *Age of Discontinuity*. Drucker himself acts as on-camera moderator.
BNA Films 44 min Color 1971

946 Why Do I Feel Guilty When I Say No? Based on Dr. Manuel J. Smith's bestseller on assertiveness training, *When I Say No, I Feel Guilty*. This film includes author Smith, June Lockhart, consultant Fred Sherman. It teaches viewers how to cope with everyday problems and conflicts at work or at home, using verbal skills that can help to deal with criticism and manipulation. Purchase or rental includes "Meeting Guide" written by Mr. Sherman.
Cally Curtis 30 min Color 1977

947 Why Me? A probing look based on Rose Kushner's book, into breast cancer. Highlighted is a demonstration of self-examination for early detection of this disease. Ten women who have had mastectomies tell of the ordeal and its psychological side-effects. Produced by KNXT-TV, Los Angeles.
Carousel 57 min Color 1974

948 William Withering and Digitalis. An "on location" dramatization of the success of the 18th-century English doctor who discovered a cure for dropsy. Against the advice of colleagues, Withering analyzed the formula of a folk remedy, and isolated the key ingredient, digitalis, still a major medication for heart disease today. From the book, *Historic Medical Classics*, by Dr. John C. Krantz, Jr. Film epilogue by Dr. Helen Taussig, "blue baby" authority, of Johns Hopkins University.
Cine-Men 40 min Color 1976

949 Yes, Virginia, There Is a Santa Claus. This animation is based on the true story of the girl, Virginia O'Hanlon, who wrote to her newspaper for an honest answer to the perennial question of Christmas. Jim Backus narrates this version of Francis Church's classic editorial answer. Teacher's guide is available. Production by the David Wolper Organization.
Films Inc. 27 min Color 1975

950 The Young Alcoholics. A realistic look at the scope and seriousness of early drinking problems, based on new data and the author's experiences working with young alcoholics. The foundation for

this film is a study conducted in Orange County, Calif., where the author works as a counselor. From the book of the same name by Tom Alibrandi.
Film Forum 18 min Color 1978

951 The Young Art: Children Make Their Own Films. This is a film-and-book introduction to film-making for the classroom teacher. In the pages of *Children as Film Makers* by Yvonne Anderson, teachers will find basic information for film-making. *The Young Art* shows students using the techniques described in the book. It was shot entirely by students of the Collegiate School in New York.
Van Nostrand 16 min Color 1972

Novels

These 140 films are either excerpts from or abbreviated versions of a novel. This literary form is more than any other a narrative vehicle, a fact that does much to explain its compatibility with film, which is quite a story-telling medium itself. Their mutual subjects are as diverse as *Tillie's Punctured Romance* and *Roots*. Yet, despite this polarity of topic and treatment, these two "competing" arts share an affinity for expansive and complex themes, paradoxically helping us—through fiction—to understand reality.

952 The Adventures of Huckleberry Finn. Mark Twain's classic novel is brought to life with much of the pathos and humor of the original masterpiece. In a carefully re-created mid-19th-century Mississippi Valley, Mickey Rooney plays the role of Huck in this re-edited version of the original production by Metro-Goldwyn-Mayer. Directed by Richard Thorpe. Originally released by Teaching Film Custodians with the cooperation of the National Council of Teachers of English.
Films Inc. 44 min B&W 1939

953 Alice in Wonderland. This is a condensaton of Paramount's presentation of the fantasy by Lewis Carroll (Charles Lutwidge Dodgson). Characters included are: White Rabbit, Dodo, Duchess, Cheshire Cat, Mad Hatter, March Hare, Queen of Hearts, and Mock Turtle. Originally distributed by Teaching Film Custodians in conjunction with the NCTE.
Indiana U. 40 min B&W 1942

954 The American West: A Dying Breed. A study in conflict of values and of generations. In the face of potential disaster, a man's ethics win out over the son's opportunistic solution to the problem of contaminated cattle. Based on Larry McMurtry's novel, *Hud*. Extracted from the Paramount feature *Hud*, with Paul Newman, Melvyn Douglas, and Brandon de Wilde. Directed by Martin Ritt.
Films, Inc. 23 min BW 1976

955 ...And I Want Time. Edited from the motion picture *Love Story* as a study on death and dying. The life of a young couple is traced from the time of their marriage to the untimely death of the young wife. Ali McGraw and Ryan O'Neal portray the ill-fated pair. Based on the novel by Eric Segal.
Paramount 28 min Color 1977

956 Anna Karenina. Tolstoy's brilliant novel of Czarist Russia is brought to the screen with the artistry of Greta Garbo, Fredric March, and Basil Rathbone. Provides a prologue to understanding events that shaped current world politics. From the full-length production by Metro-Goldwyn-Mayer. Directed by Clarence Brown. Re-edited in cooperation with the National Council of Teachers of English. Originally distributed by Teaching Film Custodians.
Films Inc. 40 min B&W 1935

957 Arrowsmith. Excerpt from the MGM Hollywood feature based on the Sinclair Lewis novel about the social and medical ethics of using an unproven serum to fight bubonic plague in the West Indies. Directed by John Ford; with actors Ronald Colman and Helen Hayes. Edited for non-theatrical use by the National Council of Teachers of English. Originally distributed by Teaching Film Custodians.
Indiana U. 13 min B&W 1931

958 Authority and Rebellion. Focusing on the first part of *The Caine Mutiny*, this film traces the disintegration of Captain Queeg and the dilemma of his Executive Officer. The commentary of Orson Welles compares Herman Wouk's novel to other works of literature. Edited from the Columbia Pictures feature *The Caine Mutiny* with Humphrey Bogart.
Learning Corp. 31 min Color 1972

959 Bardell Vs. Pickwick. In this scene from Dickens' *Pickwick Papers*, Mr. Pickwick's landlady is convinced her tenant is proposing marriage when, actually he is only discussing the possibility of hiring a man servant. The resultant confusion is not only complex but comic. Produced by Desmond Davis with the Dickensian Society of London.
Perspective 24½ min B&W 1962

960 The Battle at Elderbush Gulch. The story of two urchins whose pet dogs innocently start a battle between American settlers and Indians. The innovative technique of director D.W. Griffith allows parallel action to maintain the suspense of two or three simultaneous episodes. Silent production with music added. Based on Kemp Niver's illustrated book, available from the distributor.
Pyramid Films 24 min BW 1913

961 Books Alive: A Portrait of Jennie. The love story of a painter and his mysterious subject. Written by Robert Nathan, the novel introduces viewers to an unreal time element. As a young artist paints her portrait, Linda Marsh, as the heroine Jennie, promises to be as old as he is. Produced by Turnley Walker.
BFA Educ. Media 6 min Color 1969

962 Books Alive: Moby Dick. Jeff Corey plays the part of Ahab, Herman Melville's whaling ship captain. Ahab reveals his monomania, as he declares the purpose of the voyage is to capture the great white whale Moby Dick. Does he at long last capture the seemingly charmed white whale? Or vice versa? Produced by Turnley Walker.
BFA Educ. Media 6 min Color 1969

963 Books Alive: The Caine Mutiny. An unseen narrator welcomes Captain Queeg as he steps out of the pages of Herman Wouk's novel. The captain, played by Paul Richards, reveals he is weak, given responsibilities beyond his capacity, and a man who will not face the truth about himself. Produced by Turnley Walker.
BFA Educ. Media 6 min Color 1969

964 The Boston Tea Party. Dramatizes the historical role played by a colonial youth who becomes involved in events that precipitated the American Revolution. An excerpt from the feature film *Johnny Tremain*. Based on the book by Esther Forbes.
Disney 30 min Color 1966

965 Bound For Freedom. This is the story of two boys brought from Europe in the 1770's to work as indentured servants. Background material provides an authentic picture of colonial America. Based on the book by Ruth Chessman. Directed by David Tapper. Released by Tapper Productions.
Films, Inc. 52 min Color 1976

966 Captain Kidd. Cartoon figure, Mr. Magoo, plays the lead in this Robert Louis Stevenson classic. Kidd fought bravely in the war between Britain and France, and was awarded a King's commission. But later he was accused of piracy, was caught, tried, and hanged in England. In 1699, treasure found in New York was said to be part of Kidd's hidden loot.
Macmillan 26 min Color 1965

967 Charles Dickens: Characters in Action. The four dramatic sequences selected were taken from the following works of Dickens: *Tale of Two Cities* (condemnation of Charles Darnay), *A Christmas Carol* (Scrooge before reform), *Great Expectations* (Pip's first visit to Miss Havisham), and *David Copperfield* (the exposure of Uriah Heep's forgery). Original productions by Loew's, MGM, and Universal Pictures. Study-guide prepared by National Council of Teachers of English and by Teaching Film Custodians.
Indiana U. 21 min B&W 1958

968 A Charles Dickens Christmas. A dramatization of the visit of Mr. Pickwick and his companions to Dingley Dell Farm. From the chapter "A Good-Humored Christmas" in Dicken's novel *The Pickwick Papers*. Produced by John Barnes.
Encyc. Brit. 22 min Color 1954

969 The Charles Dickens Show. Photographed "on location," Victor Spinetti plays the part of a traveling barker with a magic lantern show in 19th-century England. Along with references to the novelist's life, here are some of his fictitious characters recreated in costume: Fagin, Oliver Twist, David and Dora Copperfield, Uriah Heep, and Ebenezer Scrooge. A Seabourne Enterprises Production by Piers Jessop.
Int. Film Bureau 52 min Color 1973

970 Civil War: A Poor Man's Fight. This is an excerpt from MGM's 1950 film of Stephen Crane's novel, *The Red Badge of Courage*. In it, actor and war hero Audie Murphy plays the part of the young soldier who panics during combat, then realizes he's not the only one confused about the reasons for war. Supporting actor: John Huston, the director.
Films Inc. 25 min B&W 1976

971 The Count of Monte Cristo. The hero of this tale of 18th-century

France, a young sailor, is accused unjustly of aiding the exiled Napoleon, and is imprisoned. He escapes by feigning death, returns to the cavern of Monte Cristo, and digs up a fabulous treasure. Mr. Magoo, as the cartoon hero of Dumas' classic, then uses the fortune to punish his tormentors.
Macmillan 26 min Color 1965

972 Crime and the Criminal. How different is the criminal from the rest of us? Does society have the right to take his life? Truman Capote explored these questions in his nonfiction novel, *In Cold Blood*. Orson Welles extends that exploration in this film, and compares Truman Capote's study of the criminal mind to that of other writers: Sophocles' saga of *Oedipus*, Dostoevsky's *Crime and Punishment*, and Stevenson's *Dr. Jekyll and Mr. Hyde*. Specially edited from the Columbia Pictures feature *In Cold Blood*, directed by Richard Brooks.
Learning Corp. 33 min B&W 1972

973 David and Betsey Trotwood. Betsey Trotwood dislikes donkeys and small boys. She is outraged that David is born a nephew and not a niece. But, years later, the runaway David finds a pleasant haven with her. From the novel *David Copperfield* by Charles Dickens. Produced in association with the Dickensian Society of London, by Desmond Davis.
Perspective 24½ min B&W 1962

974 David and Dora. David's courtship of Dora, his employer's daughter, is marked with tenderness, amusing misunderstandings, and treachery by Miss Murdstone. From the novel *David Copperfield* by Charles Dickens. Produced by Desmond Davis in collaboration with the Dickensian Society, London.
Perspective 24½ min B&W 1962

975 David and Dora Married. Honeymoon happiness dwindles before Dora's childlike management of the household. But David's decision to accept Dora for what she is gives them some months of happiness before her death. From the novel *David Copperfield* by Charles Dickens. Produced by Desmond Davis with the London Dickensian Society.
Perspective 24½ min B&W 1962

976 David and His Mother. Young David is happy with his widowed mother and Peggotty. But misery enters their lives when his mother marries Mr. Murdstone, and Miss Murdstone comes to manage the house. Misery becomes sorrow when David's mother dies. From the novel *David Copperfield* by Charles Dickens. Produced, with the cooperation of the Dickensian Society (London, England), by Desmond Davis.
Perspective 24½ min B&W 1962

977 David and Mr. Micawber. Robert Morley plays the insolvent but optimistic Mr. Micawber, who befriends young David on his arrival in London. From the novel *David Copperfield* by Charles Dickens. Produced by Desmond Davis in conjunction with the Dickensian Society of London.
Perspective 24½ min   B&W   1962

978 David Copperfield: The Boy. Shows the formative years of Dickens' literary hero, along with the environment and personalities of 18th-century England that influenced the boy's development. Characterizations by film greats Lionel Barrymore, Edna May Oliver, Basil Rathbone, and W.C. Fields. Produced by Metro-Goldwyn-Mayer. Directed by George Cukor.
Films, Inc.   42 min B&W   1935

979 David Copperfield: The Man. This sequel picks up David's life as he completes his schooling and sets off to make a career for himself. More of Dickens' characters come to life as David meets Dora Spenlow, Little Em'ly, and Steerforth. Produced by Metro-Goldwyn-Mayer. Directed by George Cukor. Originally distributed by Teaching Film Custodians.
Films, Inc.   40 min B&W   1935

980   Dear Lovey Hart: I Am Desperate. This live-action story is based on Ellen Conford's novel about a teenager assigned to write her school's lovelorn column. Her advice as a journalist brings results that force her to examine issues of honesty and responsibility. From the *After School Special* TV series. Producer: Martin Tahse.
Disney   32 min   Color   1977

981   Drums Along the Mohawk. Excerpt from the 20th Century-Fox feature depicting pioneer life along the Mohawk River in New York State during the Revolutionary War. Directed by John Ford, with actors Henry Fonda and Claudette Colbert. Prepared in collaboration with the Audio-Visual Committee of the National Council for the Social Studies. Originally distributed by Teaching Film Custodians. Based on the novel by Walter Edmonds.
Indiana U.   31 min   B&W   1939

982 Due Process of Law Denied. Excerpt from the Hollywood feature film *The Ox-Bow Incident* based on the novel by Walter Van Tilburg Clark. Portrays the lynching of three innocent men by a Nevada vigilante group in 1885. With actors Henry Fonda, Anthony Quinn, and Dana Andrews. Produced by 20th Century-Fox. Directed by William Wellman. Originally distributed by Teaching Film Custodians.
Indiana U.   29 min   B&W   1942

983   Early Victorian England and Charles Dickens. This is the

second film in the series on *Great Expectations*. In it, with representative enactments by the Old Vic players, Clifton Fadiman describes the mentality and morals of the era, and how Dickens was motivated by his middle-class observations of the inequities of splendor and squalor, prosperity and poverty. From the *Humanities Series*. (The next series film is entitled *Great Expectations I*; prior film is *The Novel: What It Is*.)
Encyc. Brit. 30 min Color 1962

984 Faithful Departed. The action of James Joyce's novel, *Ulysses*, is set in Dublin on the 16th day of June, 1904. From a collection of 40,000 photographs of the period, director Kieran Hickey has recreated Dublin and its inhabitants—the "faithful departed" of the title—as they were on that now famous day. Photography by Sean Corcoran and Roland Hill. Music by Somerville-Large.
McGraw-Hill 10 min B&W 1970

985 Fight. This is the John Steinbeck story, filmed in "Steinbeck country." It traces dramatic events in the Torres family and especially the life of the eldest son who accidentally killed a man in Monterey (Calif.) at the turn of the century. The author himself introduces the film. Music composed by Laurindo Almeida. Director: Louis Bispo. Production by San Francisco Films. (Original 81-minute edition available for rental only.)
Kit Parker 40 min B&W 1961

986 Flatland. This animation, based on the short novel by Edwin A. Abbott, depicts the tale of a square that lives in Flatland, satirizing the difficulties encountered in trying to convince a two-dimensional society of the existence of a third dimension. Produced by John Gardner. A Contemporary Films release.
McGraw-Hill 12 min Color 1965

987 Francesca, Baby. This dramatization, based on the novel by Joan L. Oppenheimer, is meant to demonstrate the family problems caused by a parent's alcoholism. As a realistic portrayal of fact, this story offers helpful direction for youngsters so involved. From the *After School Special* TV series. Producer: Martin Tahse.
Disney 46 min Color 1977

988 Gaucho. Gaucho, a fatherless preadolescent in New York's "El Barrio," feels betrayed by the marriage of his brother, who promised to take Gaucho and his mother back to Puerto Rico. Resolving to earn the money himself, Gaucho becomes withdrawn from his family, finally becoming the unwitting dupe of a petty criminal. Only after a brush with the police does he see how his obstinacy has isolated him from those who love him. Based on the book by Gloria Gonzalez. Produced by Martin Tahse.
Time-Life 47 min Color 1978

989 The Good Earth. A reflection of the depth and humanity of Pearl Buck's novel—a classic portrait of peasant life in prerevolutionary China jolted by the upheaval of civil war. A shortened version of the Hollywood feature, starring Paul Muni, Luise Rainer, and Keye Luke. Produced by Metro-Goldwyn-Mayer. Directed by Sidney Franklin. Originally distributed by Teaching Film Custodians.
Films Inc. 42 min B&W 1937

990 Goshawk. A thorough but poetic view of one person and the training of a bird of prey. Based upon T.H. White's book of the same name, this account blends the love of man with the stubborn intelligence of the bird into a story of dignity and respect mutually attained. Produced by Robert Baumstone.
Institutional Cine 52 min Color 1975

991 Grass Roots. Records and compares a variety of American communes, including Twin Oaks in Virginia, founded in 1966 on the basis of B.F. Skinner's behaviorism novel, *Walden Two*. Other sites include a pocket of anarchists in Maryland; a network of affinity groups in California's Mendocino County; and the Lama Foundation, a religiously oriented colony. Produced by Martinengo and Wahlberg.
Phoenix 54 min Color 1975

992 The Great American Novel: Babbitt. Many facets of Sinclair Lewis' character are revealed in this film. His feelings and his problems are shown, and his speech to the Zenith Real Estate Board is re-created by actor Pat Hingle. Produced by CBS.
BFA Educ. Media 26 min Color 1968

993 The Great American Novel: Grapes of Wrath. This is an outline of John Steinbeck's portrayal of people whose lives are disrupted through no fault of their own. It can lead to discussion of how (or whether) such Depression-era uprootings differ from the current situation of other Americans who are migrating from rural to urban areas. Richard Boone reads pertinent passages. Production by CBS-TV.
BFA Educ. Media 29 min Color 1968

994 The Great American Novel: Moby Dick. A modern-day trawler captain and his crew illustrate the universality of Herman Melville's novel. Examines the temporal and philosophical aspects of this modern voyage, creating an awareness of the timelessness of Melville's work, and suggesting that similar values exist in all great literature. Produced by CBS News.
BFA Educ. Media 25 min Color 1969

995 Great Expectations. Excerpts from the Universal Pictures full-length production. Selected scenes outline Dickens' complex plot struc-

ture and the relationships among characters. Originally re-edited and distributed by Teaching Film Custodians in co-operation with the National Council of Teachers of English.
Indiana U. 41 min B&W 1946

996 Great Expectations I. Third in a series of four films on the novel as a literary form. Selected scenes by the Old Vic actors of England establish the setting and characters of this Dickens novel, while Clifton Fadiman explains its major themes. From the *Humanities Series*. Director: John Barnes.
Encyc. Brit. 34 min Color 1962

997 Great Expectations II. Probes into the novel's underlying meanings. Interprets the dominant themes of the Kantian ideal, notes the violation of this universal law of morality and how it precipitates the tragedy of Victorian hypocrisy. This lesson and its predecessor should be preceded by films *Early Victorian England* and *The Novel: What It Is*, which are part of the *Humanities Series*. Produced by John Barnes.
Encyc. Brit. 33 min Color 1962

998 Gulliver's Travels. This is a children's version of Jonathan Swift's classic satire, designed to be viewed on the level of an adventure story of Gulliver's experiences in the miniature land of Lilliput. Narrated by Vincent Price. Animation.
AIMS 6½ min Color 1971

999 Hawaii Revisited. James Michener takes viewers on a journey to the scene of his epic novel, *Hawaii*, recounting the islands' unique history and speculating about their future. To Michener, Hawaii is "a microcosm of humanity—both a hope and a warning." Also available in a 58-minute edition. A *Readers Digest* film.
Pyramid 26 min Color 1978

1000 Heidi. This excerpt, from this 20th Century-Fox feature, dramatizes the novel by Johanna Spyri. It's the story of a Swiss orphan girl (played by Shirley Temple) whose cheerful goodness gladdens the life of her grandfather and her invalid friend. Director: Alan Dwan. Originally distributed by Teaching Film Custodians.
Films Inc. 42 min B&W 1937

1001 Heidi—The Living Legend. This production is Johanna Spyri's classic legend of Heidi told with photographs taken in Maienfeld, Switzerland, the site of the book. A look at the people and countryside of Maienfeld today, a village in the Alps where life and surroundings remain much as they were in the author's time. Produced by William Schwartz and Hugo Harper for ACI Media.
Paramount 15 min Color 1973

1002 Heroes and Cowards. The subject of Joseph Conrad's novel, *Lord Jim*, sees himself as a capable first mate. But when he must choose whether to risk his life by alerting passengers or save himself, Jim's illusions are suddenly stripped away. Concentrating on the first half of the novel, this dramatization recaptures the scene of the storm that creates the setting for Jim's moral test. Orson Welles' commentary compares the theme of heroism and cowardice in Conrad with the same theme by other writers. Specially edited from the Columbia Pictures feature *Lord Jim* with Peter O'Toole.
Learning Corp. 32 min Color 1973

1003 The Historical Dracula: Facts Behind the Fiction. Count Dracula, oddly enough, is an actual figure from history whose life inspired the Bram Stoker character. The surreal beauty of his native region and castle provide the background for this study of the nobleman so closely associated with the Frankenstein monster and the werewolf. Produced in (Where else?) Romania by Ion Bostan.
Macmillan 16 min Color

1004 Home to Stay. Henry Fonda stars as a spirited grandfather fighting off lapses into senility. His granddaughter and her friend, Joey, thwart her Uncle Frank from placing Grandpa in a nursing home. Adapted by Suzanne Clauser from the novel *Grandpa and Frank*, by Janet Majerus. Producer: David Susskind.
Time-Life 47 min Color 1978

1005 The Horrible Honchos. Hollis, a new boy in the neighborhood, becomes the butt of a gang of kids, "The Horrible Honchos." The Honchos regard Hollis as an outsider, declaring war on the newcomer even though they have no reason to be hostile. Individually the children gradually come to know and like the new boy, but the pressures from the gang make them conform. Their last prank, getting Hollis lost in the woods, comes close to disaster and sobers them to a realization of what they have been doing. Based on the novel, *The Seventeenth Street Gang*, by Emily Chaney Neville. Produced by Daniel Wilson.
Time-Life 31 min Color 1977

1006 The House of the Seven Gables. A classroom version of the Hollywood feature motion-picture based on Nathaniel Hawthorne's novel. Re-edited in conjunction with the National Council of Teachers of English. Original distributor: Teaching Film Custodians. Produced by Universal Pictures.
Indiana U. 35 min B&W 1940

1007 How Green Was My Valley. A classroom version of the theatrical full-length feature, based on the novel of the same name by Richard Llewellyn. Selected by the National Council of Teachers of

English, and originally distributed by Teaching Film Custodians. Produced by 20th Century-Fox.
Indiana U. 32 min B&W 1941

1008 Huck Finn #1: Huckleberry Finn and the American Experience. Clifton Fadiman prompts viewers to see the story of "Huck" as an experience that transcends time. Cooper's *Last of the Mohicans* and *Huckleberry Finn* are compared by means of selected dramatizations from both novels. By focusing on the epic qualities (including humor), Mr. Fadiman illustrates how *Huckleberry Finn* fulfills the basic essentials of all classic literature universality. From the *Humanities Series*. Produced by Larry Yust.
Encyc. Brit. 26 min Color 1965

1009 Huck Finn #2: The Art of Huckleberry Finn. Fadiman uses dramatizations from the novel to emphasize the recurrent motif of Reality vs. Appearance. Re-enactments along the Mississippi retain the flavor of river life in the mid-19th century. From the *Humanities Series*. Larry Yust, producer.
Encyc. Brit. 25 min Color 1965

1010 Huck Finn #3: What Does Huckleberry Finn Say? Clifton Fadiman points out that *Huckleberry Finn* can be viewed from three angles: as an adventure story, as the picture of a world, and as a drama of moral conflict. Scenes depicting the relationships among Huck, Jim, Pap, and the Grangerford and Shepherdson families delineate the structure of the novel. From the *Humanities Series*. Produced by Larry Yust.
Encyc. Brit. 27 min Color 1965

1011 Huckleberry Finn. Scenes from this novel are interspersed with actor Gordon Pinsent's impersonation of Mark Twain defending his literary theories. Produced by Susan Murgatroyd for the Ontario (Canada) Educational Communications Authority. Originally released by NBC Educational Enterprises.
Films Inc. 29 min Color 1976

1012 Islands in the Stream. Based on Hemingway's posthumous novel, this is the story of an artist who regains the love of his grown sons during a summer together at his island retreat. George C. Scott plays the lead role in this shortened version of the Bart/Palevsky production.
Paramount 40 min Color 1978

1013 It's a Mile from Here to Glory. Only when Early MacLaren, a shy 15-year-old, makes the track team does he gain the admiration of his peers for the first time. Winning begins to mean more to him than anything else. Then an auto accident leaves Early with both legs broken and his spirit severely crippled. But, with the help of a teammate and a

physical therapist, he regains the use of his legs and returns to racing with newfound spirit. Based on the novel of the same name by Robert C. Lee. Produced by Martin Tahse.
Time-Life 47 min Color 1978.

1014 Jane Eyre. Dramatizes the principal episodes from the novel by Charlotte Brontë, as produced by 20th Century-Fox, with Orson Welles as Rochester. Re-edited for nontheatrical use, and originally distributed, by Teaching Film Custodians in conjunction with the National Council of Teachers of English.
Indiana U. 41 min B&W 1946

1015 Kidnapped. This is a liberal adaptation of the Robert Louis Stevenson adventure novel, produced by 20th Century-Fox and re-edited for nontheatrical use. Originally distributed by Teaching Film Custodians in cooperation with the National Council of Teachers of English.
Indiana U. 29 min B&W 1938

1016 Kidnapped. This is the latest known visualization of the great adventure novel by Robert Louis Stevenson. Pictorially presented, it may have even more natural appeal for the audience of children for whom this story was originally intended. Produced by Robert L. Baumstone.
Institutional Cine 50 min Color 1974

1017 King Arthur's Yankee. Through three-dimensional animation, Mark Twain's *A Connecticut Yankee in King Arthur's Court* comes to the screen by way of puppets that enact the fantasy of a 19th-century scientist who finds himself in King Arthur's magic-ridden Camelot. For upper elementary and junior high school language arts students.
Counselor Films 26 min Color 1977

1018 Kipling's India. This episode from Rudyard Kipling's *Kim* recreates colonial India in 1885. It's the story of an orphan English boy befriended by a Buddhist who, for the boy's own good, arranges for his return to school. This excerpt from the full-length feature *Kim*, concludes with a series of discussion questions prepared by the National Council of Teachers of English. Originally re-edited and distributed by Teaching Film Custodians.
Indiana U. 20 min Color 1954

1019 Les Misérables. This summary of the Hollywood feature film is based on Victor Hugo's novel. Dramatizes, in the characters of a police inspector and a reformed criminal, the conflict between law and justice. With actors Fredric March and Charles Laughton. Directed by Richard Boleslawski. Originally distributed by Teaching Film Custodians for 20th Century-Fox Productions.
Indiana U. 39 min B&W 1935

1020 The Lost World – Revisited. With scenes from the 1925 production of Arthur Conan Doyle's fantasy, *The Lost World*, this film resurrects a classic of the silent era. Along with *King Kong* eight years later, this picture proved the optical genius of Willis H. O'Brien, master of special effects for the screen.
Sterling Educ. 29 min B&W 1967

1021 The Magic Moth. This dramatization originates from Virginia Lee's novel about a death in a family of five. It deals with the difficult but necessary duty of honesty and acceptance of facts, while suggesting that death need not be the end of feelings and relationships. Treatment especially suitable for children and adolescents.
Centron 22 min Color 1976

1022 Mark Twain and Tom Sawyer. Illustrates elements of the author's own life that show up in *Huck Finn* and *Tom Sawyer*. Also shows the fence episode from *Tom Sawyer*, along with Cardiff Hill, Bear Creek, Jackson Island, "the cave," and – of course – a paddle-wheel river boat.
Int. Film Bureau 11 min Color 1950

1023 Mark Twain's America. Using period photographs and engravings, this film recreates the life of Mark Twain and the age in which he lived. Prototypes of Tom Sawyer, Huck Finn, and Becky Thatcher are shown, as well as characters who traveled on the old sidewheelers. Produced by NBC-TV.
McGraw-Hill 54 min B&W 1960

1024 Mark Twain's Mississippi. A segment from MGM's *Adventure of Huck Finn* provides background for the locale and characters of the novel. Presents the episode of Huck and Jim as they run away on their raft, capsize, and are rescued by a steamboat. Mickey Rooney plays the part of Huck. Originally distributed by Teaching Film Custodians in conjunction with the National Council of Teachers of English.
Films Inc. 10 min Color 1939

1025 Me and Dad's New Wife. Twelve-year-old Nina, who has been treated maturely by her divorced parents, discovers on her first day in junior high that her math teacher is her father's new wife. She also learns that her parents' divorce was amicable, but not before she subjects her family and classmates to a series of painful emotional crises. In a classic teen conflict – peer pressure against the individual – an adult, not a teenager, becomes the alienated scapegoat. Based on *A Smart Kid Like You* by Stella Pevsner. Produced by Daniel Wilson.
Time-Life 33 min Color 1975

1026 Miss Havisham. This unique Charles Dickens character lives in the isolation of the decayed remains of her wedding banquet that never

took place. To avenge the absence of her bridegroom, she plots to use her ward Estella to break the heart of young Pip. From the novel, *Great Expectations* by Charles Dickens. Produced by Desmond Davis with the help of the Dickensian Society of London.
Perspective 24½ min   B&W 1963

1027 Mr. Hyde. A tongue-in-cheek cartoon version of Robert Louis Stevenson's *Dr. Jekyll and Mr. Hyde* tale with a twist ending. Produced by Fred Wolf of Murakami-Wolf Films. Of possible interest both as a form of satire and as an example of prototype animation style.
Creative Film 5 min Color

1028 Mr. Jingle at Dingley Dell. En route to a Christmas celebration at Dingley Dell, Mr. Pickwick and his friends fall in with the rascally Alfred Jingle. From the novel, *The Pickwick Papers* by Charles Dickens. Produced by Desmond Davis, with the cooperation of the Dickensian Society of London, England.
Perspective 24½ min B&W 1965

1029 Mr. Pickwick's Dilemma. Out to expose Jingle again and to help a friend, Mr. Pickwick stumbles into a lady's bedroom one night, is challenged to a duel of honor, and is arrested. From the novel *The Pickwick Papers* by Charles Dickens. Produced by Desmond Davis with the assistance of London's Dickensian Society.
Perspective 24½ min B&W 1963

1030 Moby Dick with Mr. Magoo. Mr. Magoo as Ishmael sails the Pacific with vengeance-driven Captain Ahab, who is determined to kill the great white whale, Moby Dick. After a lengthy search, the whale is sighted. A fierce battle lasts for three days, during which all are killed by the whale except Ishmael, who clings to a floating coffin until rescued. Cartoon animation. Originally released by McGraw-Hill.
Macmillan 26 min Color 1964

1031 Mutiny on the Bounty. *The Bounty*, a British warship, sails from London to the South Seas under the command of Captain Bligh (Charles Laughton), accompanied by Christian (Clark Gable), his executive officer. The crew revolts and sets Bligh and a group of followers adrift in a boat. Upon arriving in England, Bligh sets out in another ship in search of the *Bounty*. Christian, on Pitcairn's Island, burns the *Bounty* to protect the survivors of the mutiny. Edited from the MGM production based on the novel by Charles Nordoff and James Hall. Director: Frank Lloyd.
Films Inc. 42 min B&W 1935

1032 My Father, Sun-Sun Johnson. Based on the book by C. Everard Palmer, this story of family upheaval is set in Jamaica. Rami finds it hard to accept his parents' divorce, and is even more disturbed when his

mother marries his father's long-time rival. Father and son work together at building up a small farm but, just when it seems the family might be reunited, a twist of fate takes Sun-Sun's life.
Learning Corp. 28 min Color 1977

1033 1900: Passing of an Age. This is an excerpt from the 1942 movie, directed by Orson Welles, of Booth Tarkington's *The Magnificent Ambersons.* In it, Anne Bancroft and Joseph Cotten dramatize scenes suitable for discussion of male-female roles and the impact of the auto on our quality of life. The narration is by Henry Fonda. Originally released by RKO Pictures.
Films Inc. 25 min B&W 1976

1034 The Novel: What It Is, What It's About, What It Does. First in a series of four films in the *Humanities Series.* Through his own recitations and with the aid of the Old Vic Company, Clifton Fadiman introduces the literary concepts of style, characterization, mood, and motivation. This prologue leads to the opening of *Great Expectations* by Charles Dickens. (The next film in this series is *Early Victorian England and Charles Dickens.*)
Encyc. Brit. 30 min Color 1962

1035 Nureyev's Don Quixote (series). Four complete ballet excerpts from the full-length film version of Cervantes' classic novel. The four films are: *The Market Place in the Port of Barcelona* (16 min.), *Basilio and Kitri, the Lovers* (17 min.), *A Tavern Celebration* (20 min.), and *The Wedding Reception: The Grand Pas de deux* (20 min.). The four films are not dependent upon each other. Each contains individual ballet sequences of Nureyev with Lucette Aldous and the company of dancers of the Australian Ballet. Codirected by Sir Robert Helpmann and Rudolf Nureyev.
Sterling 73 min (Series total) Color 1972

1036 The Okies – Uprooted Farmers. Dust storms and drought in the early thirties spelled disaster to country folk of Oklahoma already under financial pressure. Many took to the road, looking to the promise of California. This story of dignity and endurance in the face of exploitation provides background to the great Depression and the New Deal. Extract from the 1940 feature film, *Grapes of Wrath*, based on the novel by John Steinbeck. Opening and closing statements by Henry Fonda who appears as the main character, Tom Joad. Directed by John Ford for 20th Century-Fox.
Films Inc. 24 min B&W 1975

1037 The Old Soldier. A crisis in the lives of Dr. Strong and his young wife Annie is caused by the thoughtless interference of her mother, "the old soldier," and Uriah Heep's machinations. A misunderstanding

develops but is cleared up with David Copperfield's help. From the novel, *David Copperfield*, by Charles Dickens. Produced by Desmond Davis in conjunction with the Dickensian Society of London.
Perspective 24½ min B&W 1962

1038 The Only Good Indian. Breaks the Hollywood stereotype of the barbarous Indian. A U.S. Cavalry scout assigns himself the peacemaker's mission and befriends an Apache, learning that Indians are human after all. Based on Elliott Arnold's novel, *Blood Brother*. Excerpted from the feature film *Broken Arrow* by 20th Century-Fox, with James Stewart, Jeff Chandler, and Debra Paget. Directed by Delmer Daves.
Films, Inc. 24 min Color 1975

1039 Philip and the White Colt. Photographed on the moors of England, this story stars Mark Lester (of *Oliver* fame) as a lonely boy whose speech is restored by an act of love for his pet horse. Specially edited for education from the Columbia Pictures feature *Run Wild, Run Free*, based on the book by David Rook.
Learning Corp. 23 min Color 1973

1040   P.J. and the President's Son. Two 15-year-old boys in Washington, D.C., discover they look so much alike they could pass for twins. One is from a middle-class family; the other, the son of the President. Both are somewhat envious of each other, and decide to exchange places for a few days. Neither expects the eventual chaos that results from their impersonations. This up-dated version of Twain's *Prince and the Pauper* uses its contemporary setting to prove that the grass is not always greener—even on the White House lawn! Produced by Daniel Wilson. Director: Larry Elikann.
Time-Life 47 min Color 1976

1041   Pride and Prejudice. Jane Austen's charming novel of 18th-century manners and witty conversation is portrayed by Greer Garson, Laurence Olivier, and Maureen O'Sullivan. Pictures the social world of provincial England. A condensation of the motion picture originally produced by Metro-Goldwyn-Mayer for theatrical release. Directed by Robert Leonard.
Films, Inc. 44 min B&W 1940

1042 The Prince and the Pauper. This is Twain's classic story about the young Prince of Wales who finds a look-alike in poor Tom Chantry and changes places with him. The king dies and Tom is about to be crowned when the Prince arrives just in time to claim his throne, then bestowing upon his friend the new title of King's Ward. This edited version of the feature production stars Guy Williams and Laurence Naismith.
Disney 28 min Color 1964

1043 Psst... Hammerman's After You! "Mouse," a timid 11-year-old, provokes the school bully by writing his name under a classroom picture of the Neanderthal man. He learns a lesson in honor and self-respect as he faces the consequences of his actions. Based on Betsy Byars' novel, *The 18th Emergency*. Produced by Martin Tahse. A television *After School Special*.
Disney 45 min Color 1977

1044 Ramona. This adaptation of Helen Hunt Jackson's novel represents the first time film royalties were paid for a literary work. Like other silents, only key segments of the original are retained. This story of marriage between a Spanish woman and Indian man was directed by D.W. Griffith.
Pyramid 10 min B&W 1910

1045 The Red Badge of Courage: A Film Prologue. The conflicting emotions of bravery and fear can be found in this film dissertation of Stephen Crane's classic war novel. One of three titles in the *Literary Prologues* film series.
Universal Ed. 17 min Color 1972

1046 The Resurrection. This silent production is a radical condensation of Tolstoy's lengthy and philosophical novel of the same name. It's about a housemaid who turns to prostitution after being raped, discovers Christ with the help of her seducer, then refuses his offer of marriage in favor of working for God among the prisoners in Siberia. Directed by D.W. Griffith.
Pyramid 10 min B&W 1909

1047 Robinson's Island. This puppet animation retells Daniel Defoe's classic *Robinson Crusoe*. We see Robinson, after the shipwreck, as he searches for fresh water. We follow him as he fells trees, builds a hut, and discovers the human tracks that lead to his companion, Friday. Robinson and Friday create utensils for a pleasant existence in difficult surroundings. When the two are finally rescued, they are sorry to leave. Produced by ACI Media.
Paramount 16 min Color 1969

1048 Romanticism: The Revolt of the Spirit. The mood of 19th-century Romanticism—escape from industrialization to nature—is revealed in dramatized excerpts from literature of the era. In a scene from *Les Misérables*, Victor Hugo shows society as the force that makes men evil. The attitude of Romantics toward dying is suggested in the death scene from Emily Brontë's *Wuthering Heights*. Their inclination toward heroic gesture is typified in Byron's grandiose pyre. Produced by John and Helen Jean Secondari.
Learning Corp. 24 min Color 1971

1049 Rookie of the Year. Should a capable 11-year-old girl be allowed to play on an all-male baseball team? When a regular is benched and an important game is at stake, Sharon (played by Jodie Foster) is invited to join the team. While her parents approve, other parents do not, nor do some of her teammates. Community tensions build. Despite intense pressure and many misgivings Sharon perseveres, gaining personal insight and strength. Based on the book, *Not Bad for a Girl*, by Isabella Taves. Produced by Daniel Wilson.
Time-Life 47 min Color 1976

1050 Roots (series of 12 episodes). These films are the same material (minus commercials) shown over national television, setting a record for viewing of serial programming. Characters and events originate from the historical novel by Alex Haley, author of *The Autobiography of Malcolm X*. Production by David Wolper for the American Broadcasting Company.
Films Inc. 581 min (series total) Color 1977

1051 Roots — Episode I: The African. The year is 1750, and in West Africa the villagers of Juffere rejoice at the birth of a baby to Omoro Kinte and his wife Binta — a baby named Kunta whose destiny lies in America. Fifteen years later, Kunta and his friends are inducted into manhood, learning the skills of the Mandinka warrior. And on the high seas, the slaveship *Lord Ligonier* is outfitted with wrist-shackles, neck-rings, and thumbscrews as it nears the African shore.
Films, Inc. 47 min Color 1977

1052 Roots — Episode II: The African (cont.). Kunta completes the rites of manhood, and once again the villagers rejoice. But their joy is short-lived. Seeking wood in the jungle to make a drum, Kunta is captured by white slavers, branded and chained in the hold of the *Lord Ligonier*, soon on its way with its human cargo to Annapolis, Md. Ravaged by dysentery, seasickness, and festering sores, the slaves have one flickering hope — mutiny.
Films, Inc. 50 min Color 1977

1053 Roots — Episode III: The Slave. Taken on deck, the slaves wait for a moment when the crew's attention is distracted. The signal is given. Kunta struggles for the key to the shackles, and the mutiny begins. The bloody confrontation ends; the slave rebellion is put down. On September 29, 1767, the *Lord Ligonier* anchors at Annapolis. Ninety-eight of the 140 captives have survived. At the slave auction, a defiant Kunta is bought by John Reynolds and given the name "Toby," a name Kunta refuses to accept.
Films, Inc. 53 min Color 1977

1054 Roots — Episode IV: The Slave (cont.). En route to his tobacco plantation in Virginia, "Massah" Reynolds places an older slave, Fiddler, in charge of the wild new African. Fiddler begins training Kunta, soon coming to admire his rebellious young pupil. Kunta contrives an escape but, hampered by leg chains, he is easily recaptured by overseer Ames. An almost fatal beating ends when Kunta surrenders to the inevitable, finally calling himself "Toby." Fiddler, caring for Kunta's wounds, reminds him that he will always be Kunta, no matter what the white man calls him.

Films, Inc. 44 min Color 1977

1055 Roots – Episode V: The Escape. Although resigned to the name "Toby," Kunta has not given up trying to escape. During a harvest celebration, he makes one more try for freedom, but is soon caught. His sadistic captors, professional slave catchers, lash him to a tree, beat him and chop off half a foot to prevent future escapes. For three weeks he lies unconscious in a cabin on Dr. William Reynolds' plantation where he had been taken, with Fiddler and young Genelva, as payment of John Reynolds' debt. Cared for by Belle, the plantation cook, Kunta recovers and vows that he will not only walk again, but will learn to run.

Films, Inc. 48 min Color 1977

1056 Roots – Episode VI: The Choice. At Belle's persuasion, Toby becomes Doctor Reynolds' driver. Grateful for all she has done for him, Kunta is drawn to Belle and, despite his penchant for solitude, marries her. A meeting with an African drummer rekindles his dreams of escape. The drummer is working out a plan and will beat a message when it is ready. Belle gives birth to a daughter to whom Kunta gives the Mandinka name of Kizzy. During the Mandinka ceremony with the newborn, the drummer signals. But Kunta, obligated now to his family, does not respond. Instead, as the drum beats in the distance, he recites the traditions of her heritage to his infant daughter.

Films, Inc. 49 min Color 1977

1057 Roots – Episode VII: The Uprooted. At sixteen, Kizzy is happy in her first love with handsome young Noah. Eagerly she awaits the return of Missy Anne, her white childhood playmate, after a four-year absence. Against all rules, Anne taught Kizzy to read and write, and now plans to ask Doctor Reynolds for Kizzy as her own personal slave. Noah puts an escape plan into action but, just when the terrified Kizzy believes he has succeeded, he is captured and tortured into admitting that Kizzy forged his travel pass. Despite the pleas of Belle and Kunta, Doctor Reynolds immediately sells Kizzy to sleazy Tom Moore. Kizzy hopes for Anne's last minute intervention, but Anne turns away. Kizzy is raped by Tom, and imbued with a lasting hatred, vows to have a son who will grow up and exact vengeance on her new owner.

Films, Inc. 49 min Color 1977

1058   Roots – Episode VIII: Chicken George. Kizzy in 1824 is a proud woman in her mid-thirties, and her son George is a promising game cocker, a special favorite of their debauched owner, Tom Moore. Kizzy falls in love with a flamboyant driver from another plantation. She persuades him to take her to the Reynolds plantation. At Kunta's grave, she renews her vow to live in the Mandinka tradition. George is elated to become Moore's principal cock trainer, and looks forward to buying his freedom and that of Tildy, the girl he intends to marry.
Films, Inc. 48 min Color 1977

1059   Roots – Episode IX: Chicken George (cont.). The aristocratic Squire James offers to buy Chicken George (so-called because of his prowess as a trainer of fighting cocks), together with his wife Tildy and sons, promising the family freedom after five years of service. In George's ensuing rage when Moore refuses to honor the promise, Kizzy confesses that Moore is George's natural father. At the next cock competition, Moore wages heavily and loses. George is sent to England as a trainer in lieu of payment of Moore's debt. Soon after George's departure, Moore sells Tildy and the children despite his promise to George to keep the family together.
Films, Inc. 48 min Color 1977

1060   Roots – Episode X: The War. Chicken George, now a free man, returns to Tildy and three grown sons: blacksmith Tom, Lewis, and Virgil. The redneck Brent brothers, Evan and Jemmy, sneeringly remind him that a freed slave may not remain in the state more than sixty days. George leaves, promising to return with enough money to free them all. The family befriends a white couple, Ol' George Johnson and Martha, who have lost their small farm to the ravages of the Civil War. Tom agrees to help an exhausted Jemmy desert the sinking Confederacy. But when Tom catches Jemmy trying to rape his wife, he strangles Jemmy and together they bury the body.
Films, Inc. 49 min Color 1977

1061   Roots – Episode XI: Freedom. The war is over but racists, like spiteful Evan Brent and wily Senator Justin, have no intention of tolerating the newly freed "uppity niggers." Ol' George and Martha join the family in sharecropping and are doing well until rampaging night riders destroy their crops. Tom, still a blacksmith, files a special mark on each horse shod to enable him to indentify future riders. The sheriff promises to act on proof, and Tom takes him evidence found after another raid. With Brent in charge, Justin assumes ownership of the plantation and announces that Tom cannot leave because of an outstanding debt.
Films, Inc. 52 min Color 1977

1062   Roots – Episode XII: Freedom (cont.). Brent hires Ol' George as overseer. Slavery, for all intents and purposes, is back in business.

Chicken George arrives and concocts a plan to extricate his family from under Brent's thumb and move them to the rich farmland he now owns in Tennessee. By putting on subservient attitudes in town, and with Ol' George's pretended brutality, they together pave the way for their exodus. Lured into an ambush at the plantation, the bully Brent is left beaten and broken while Chicken George and the others leave slavery behind forever. In Tennessee they start a prosperous new life, fulfilling Kunta Kinte's abiding dream of freedom. This is the final film in this series.
Films, Inc. 44 min Color 1977

1063 The Runaways. From the novel by Dickens, *The Holly Tree*. Mr. Wolmers, his fiancée, and a youngster of nine stop at the Holly tree Inn on their elopement. Mrs. Piff, Boots, and Lettie thwart their "honeymoon" plans but are, in turn, filled with the spirit of romance. Produced in London by Desmond Davis, in cooperation with the Dickensian Society of England.
Perspective 24½ min B&W 1962

1064 Sam Weller and His Father. In some of the most light-hearted moments in Dickens, two of his memorable characters, Sam Weller and his father, plot and scheme to release Mr. Pickwick from debtors' prison. From the novel, *The Pickwick Papers* by Charles Dickens. Produced by Desmond Davis, in association with the London Dickensian Society.
Perspective 24½ min B&W 1962

1065 Sara's Summer of the Swans. Sara, a 14-year-old stringbean with braces, is having a miserable summer. She is angry with the world and particularly with her family. Sara is really most angry with herself, unsure of who she is and what she wants to become. By rejecting friends and family, she isolates herself. But when her brother runs away and a teenage boy volunteers to help search for him, she realizes that her own attitudes are to blame for her unhappiness, and begins the painful emergence to young adulthood with a new sense of personal worth. Based on the Newbery Award-winning book of the same title by Betsy Byars. Produced by Martin Tahse.
Time-Life 57 min Color 1976

1066 1776: American Revolution on the Frontier. Gilbert Martin (played by Henry Fonda) and his bride faced incredible hardships establishing a farm in the colonial wilderness of upstate New York. A communal bond sustained the settlers, but they could not withstand an Indian attack. Home, crops, and hopes were destroyed. The Martins hired out to work, but the call to arms had to be answered. The German Flats "army" joined with the Continental troops and Gilbert marched off to war. A film extract from the old feature film *Drums Along the Mohawk*, based on the novel by Walter Edmonds.
Films, Inc. 22 min Color 1975

1067   1760: The New York Frontier. In the struggle for North America, only Rogers' Rangers, a rag-tag army in the area of Lake Champlain and Fort Ticonderoga, consistently won victories for the American colonists. Robert Young plays the part of Langdon Townes, who joined the Rangers to avoid any service with the Redcoats, personalizing a period when the Americans were on their way to becoming a new threat to the British Empire. A film extract from the early feature *Northwest Passage* also starring Spencer Tracy. Based on the novel by Kenneth Roberts.
Films, Inc.   24 min   Color   1975

1068   The Shot Heard 'Round the World. A dramatization of the historical role played by young members of the "Sons of Liberty" who supplied information about British troop movements. This surveillance allowed Paul Revere to alert the Minuteman. An excerpt from the feature film *Johnny Tremain*, based on the book by Esther Forbes.
Disney   32 min   Color   1966

1069   Snowbound. Popular teenager Tony offers a lift to plain and plumpish classmate Cindy simply to spite his girlfriend. When the car is wrecked in a snowstorm, they become lost in the wilderness. Encountering terrors that test personal courage to the breaking point, Cindy reveals unsuspected strength and resourcefulness and it is she who, in a final desperate effort, sets fire to the car and attracts the helicopter that rescues them. Directed by Robert M. Young; produced by Linda Gottlieb. Based on the novel by Harry Mazer.
Learning Corp.   33 min   Color   1978

1070   Spaces Between People. This is a specially edited excerpt from the movie starring Sidney Poitier, *To Sir, with Love*. He plays the part of a new teacher in England who, faced with a class of incorrigibles, abandons the traditional curriculum in his attempt to reach them on a human level. The original novel was written by E.R. Braithwaite.
Learning Corp.   18 min   Color   1972

1071   The Street. Through the technique of using watercolor washes, this animated production reflects the feelings of a boy toward his dying grandmother. Based on a segment from the book by Mordecai Richler. Produced by Caroline Leaf.
National Film Board   10 min   Color   1976

1072   Street of the Flower Boxes. An ethnically diverse neighborhood, where gangs, poverty, and drugs flourish, becomes a better place to live when young Carlos succeeds in beautifying the street and bringing people closer together. Based on the book by Peggy Mann. Directed by David Tapper. Released by Tapper Productions.
Films, Inc.   48 min   Color   1973

1073 A Tale of Two Cities. Dickens' novel of heroism and tragedy, capturing the intensity of its historical background, the French Revolution. Ronald Colman plays the part of Sydney Carlton; costarring Basil Rathbone and Elizabeth Allan. An abbreviated edition of the production by Metro-Goldwyn-Mayer. Directed by Jack Conway. Originally distributed by Teaching Film Custodians.
Films, Inc. 45 min B&W 1935

1074 Teach Me! Excerpt from the full-length feature film *Up the Down Staircase*, in which a new teacher discovers the satisfaction and rewards of working in a large inner-city high school. Directed by Robert Mulligan, with Sandy Dennis as the new teacher. Based on the novel by Bel Kaufman. Originally distributed by Teaching Film Custodians. A Warner Bros.-Seven Arts production.
Indiana U. 20½ min Color 1967

1075 Tell Me My Name. Some adopted children feel it is their right to know their natural parents. This is the drama of one such child. Sarah, given up at birth for adoption, tracks down and confronts her natural mother. Hoping for recognition and love, she is met instead with shock and shame. Her presence rocks the entire household, threatening the stability of all its members. First seen on TV as a *GE Theater* special on CBS, the teleplay is based on Mary Carter's book of the same name. Produced by David Susskind.
Time-Life 52 min Color 1978

1076 The Three Musketeers with Mr. Magoo. This is a cartoon version of the Alexandre Dumas tale, set in France during the reigns of Louis XIII and Louis XIV. Magoo, as d'Artagnan, joins the Musketeers to protect their queen against Cardinal Richelieu and his plots. Originally distributed by McGraw-Hill.
Macmillan 52 min Color 1965

1077 Tillie's Punctured Romance. Tillie is played by Marie Dressler in the silent movie that marked Chaplin's debut as a star. One of the earliest feature comedies, this Keystone contains much slapstick. Along with costars Mabel Normand and Mark Swain, six-year old Milton Berle made his acting debut as a newsboy here. Produced and directed by Mack Sennett. Based on the novel, *Tillie's Nightmare*, by Edgar Smith.
Macmillan 43 min B&W 1914

1078 "To Preserve the Constitution". In a constitutional crisis, the president and a general clash over a military takeover of the government in the name of patriotism. Based on the novel by Fletcher Knebel and Charles W. Baily II. Scenes are taken from Paramount's *Seven Days in May*, starring Burt Lancaster, Kirk Douglas, and Frederic March. Directed by John Frankenheimer.
Films, Inc. 26 min BW 1976

1079 Treasure Island. This is an abbreviated version of Robert Louis Stevenson's classic adventure story of gallant young Jim Hawkins against the sinister Long John Silver. Key roles are played by Wallace Beery, Jackie Cooper, Lionel Barrymore, and Otto Kruger. Directed for MGM Productions by Victor Fleming.
Films Inc, 40 min BW 1934

1080 Treasure Island with Mr. Magoo. Robert Louis Stevenson's classic is recreated in this cartoon of a boy's adventures amid a band of treasure-seeking priates. Magoo plays the role of the rascally Long John Silver. Originally released by McGraw-Hill.
Macmillan 52 min Color 1965

1081 The Trial of Billy Budd, Sailor. Based on *Billy Budd*, the novella by Herman Melville, this excerpt dramatizes the ethical considerations that impelled the ship's captain to execute a likeable seaman for the accidental death of the master-at-arms. This film clip provides an example of Melville's philosophy of the relationship between innocence and depravity, justice and law. Directed by Peter Ustinov. Edited by Teaching Film Custodians.
Indiana U. 20 min B&W 1962

1082 Two Years Before the Mast. This film, based on Richard Dana's novel, is an excerpt from a Paramount motion-picture. It visualizes the author's observations of cruelty aboard a merchant ship. Publication of this log influenced legislation to improve maritime working conditions. Originally distributed by Teaching Film Custodians.
Indiana U. 20 min B&W 1952

1083 Ulysses. Through the use of original graphics by Saul Field, James Joyce's difficult novel is interpreted for the benefit of the first-time reader. Narration by Nuala Fitzgerald.
Haida Films 20 min Color 1973

1084 Uncle Tom's Cabin. Harriet Beecher Stowe's novel, in the form of a stage play, was filmed in a fixed position from audience level. Despite these limitations, the silent storyline benefits from special effects that were relatively advanced for that era. Directed by Edwin (*Great Train Robbery*) Porter. Originally released by the Edison Company.
Film Images 14 min B&W 1903

1085 Uriah Heep. The 'umble Heep is one of Dickens' unforgettable villains. From his lowly position as Mr. Wickfield's clerk, he rises to become his business partner, and plans to marry his daughter. But eventually Micawber exposes Heep as a forger and a cheat. From the novel, *David Copperfield,* by Charles Dickens. Produced by Desmond Davis in

cooperation with the Dickensian Society of London, England.
Perspective 24½ min B&W 1963

1086 Very Good Friends. After seeing Martin Tahse's production of the film based on her novel, *Beat the Turtle Drum*, author Constance Greene decided to use his title on future publications of her book. The story is told from the point of view of 13-year-old Kate, whose sister dies in an accident just after she had coaxed her family into a dream present for her 11th birthday. The tragic storyline provides a way of learning to cope with personal loss.
Learning Corp. 29 min Color 1977

1087 Voltaire Presents Candide: An Introduction to the Age of Enlightenment. This dramatization of Voltaire's satiric novel provides a look at the history and culture of 18th-century Western civilization. The irascibly witty Voltaire acts as host, slyly challenging the optimism of the era by introducing the naive characters from his *Candide*, and commenting on their disastrous adventures. Adding to the spirit is an original song with lyrics by Clifton Fadiman and producer John Barnes. From the *Humanities* Program.
Encyc. Brit. 34 min Color 1975

1088 Washington Square. Excerpt from the Paramount feature film *The Heiress*, based on Henry James' novel, *Washington Square*. A shy young woman must decide whether to marry a charming fortune hunter. Open-ended and suitable for discussion. Directed by William Wyler, with Olivia de Havilland, Montgomery Clift, and Sir Ralph Richardson. Originally distributed for the National Council of Teachers of English by Teaching Film Custodians.
Indiana U. 20 min B&W 1949

1089 Wuthering Heights. This is a documentary-style portrayal of author Emily Brontë as if by her biographer-sister, Mary Robinson. It interweaves scenes from the novel, while contrasting the fictional characters of Heathcliff, Catherine, Isabella, and Emily herself. Produced by the Ontario (Canada) Educational Communications Authority. Director: Robert Gardner.
Films Inc. 29 min Color 1976

1090 You Can't Run Away. From the full-length production of William Faulkner's *Intruder in the Dust*. Selected scenes outline the arrest of a black on a murder charge, and his eventual release because of a white boy's belief in his innocence. Originally re-edited and distributed by Teaching Film Custodians. Produced by Metro-Goldwyn-Mayer.
Indiana U. 32 min B&W 1949

1091 Young Goodman Brown. Basically true to Nathaniel Hawthorne's plot, the only changes this adaptation makes are those dictated by the nature of film. The film ends on a note of ambiguity consistent with the original story. Did Young Goodman Brown only dream about the Devil's communion in the forest or did it actually occur? Film-maker: Donald Fox.

Pyramid 30 min Color 1972

Poetry

According to T.S. Eliot, "Shakespeare and Dante divide the world of poetry. There is no third." In so saying, Eliot—poet that he was—was exercising his artistic license to exaggerate. But those two giants—and Eliot, too—are represented in this section, along with greats and near-greats as "olde" as Chaucer and as "with it" as E.E. Cummings. But lesser works are important too. That's why, among these 151 films, you'll also find lighter poetry like "Casey at the Bat" (five versions) along with the playful verse of Ogden Nash and even Mother Goose. After all, if a taste for poetry is worth acquiring, then it's worth acquiring young.

1092 The American Dream. Henry Fonda and the First Poetry Quartet, in a small-town-American setting, present poems that express the dreams of a young nation — its beauty, hopes, frustrations, and achievements. Among the selections: Oliver Wendell Holmes' "The Deacon's Masterpiece," Frost's "The Gift Outright," Sandburg's "I Am the People, the Mob," and Langston Hughes' "I Dream a World." From the *Anyone for Tennyson?* series, coproduced by the Great Amwell Company and the Nebraska ETV Network.
Great Plains   30 min   Color   1976

1093 An American Original: e.e. cummings. Springtime in Greenwich Village is the setting for more than 20 poems by perhaps the most curious and innovative American poet of the 20th century. Among the Cummings verses performed by the First Poetry Quartet: "when faces called flowers float out of the ground," "who knows if the moon's a balloon," "Nobody loses all the time," and "you shall above all things be glad and young." From the *Anyone for Tennyson?* series, coproduced by the Great Amwell Company and the Nebraska ETV Network.
Great Plains   30 min   Color   1976

1094 The Ancient Voices of Children. This musical interpretation bases Pulitzer Prize-winning composer George Crumb's song cycle on five poems by Federico García Lorca performed with Arthur Weisberg and the Contemporary Chamber Ensemble. Sung in Spanish by mezzo-soprano Jan DeGaetani, the poems convey a confrontation between the images of life and death. Accompanied by a generative sound track of instruments, boy soprano, and choreography. Produced by Allan Miller.
Pyramid   28 min   Color   1975

1095 Animal Poems. This is a sign-language representation, with sound, of the poetry of Dorothy Miles. From the *Gestures* series of five films, named after Ms. Miles' volume of verse. Produced by John Joyce.
Joyce Media   10 min   Color   1976

1096 Animal Tales. This is a sign-language representation (with sound) of the poetry of Dorothy Miles. It is from the *Gestures* series of five films, named after Ms. Miles' volume of verse. Produced by John Joyce.
Joyce Media   10 min   Color   1976

1097 Annabel Lee. Television actor Lorne Greene recites this Edgar Allan Poe poem written in memory of his young wife. This dramatic reading is complemented by live-action photography and the music of Les Baxter. Produced by Art Evans.
Paramount   10 min   Color   1971

1098 Annabel Lee. This treatment of Poe's love poem contrasts color photography with special black and white cinematic effects. Vincent Price narrates, and an original score accompanies the combination of

live-action and still-picture scenes.
Prod. Unltd. 14 min Color 1973

1099 Annabel Lee. This is Edgar Allan Poe's classic work beginning, "Many and many a year ago in a kingdom by the sea...." In it, the young couple's tragic situation, climaxed by the woman's untimely death, is given verisimilitude by the live-action photography of the natural background. Narrator is Vincent Price.
Warner Bros. 10 min Color

1100 Autumn: Frost Country. The title is a play on words describing the setting for Robert Frost's reading of two of his poems. Both are delivered in an appropriately seasonal New England setting; they are "The Road Not Taken" and "Reluctance." Produced by naturalist-photographer Fred Hudson.
Pyramid 9 min Color 1969

1101 A Bronze Mask. The great Welsh poet, Dylan Thomas, reads six of his works, which are simultaneously pictured in related photographic segments. Produced by BBC-TV. (Purchase prints are available only on special order.)
Time-Life 30 min Color 1971

1102 The Brooms of Mexico. The everyday occupation of sweeping is used as the central image to symbolize the people of a town in Mexico. The poetry of Alvin Gordon combines with the drawings of Ted DeGrazia and live photography to represent the hopes and memories of six Mexicans for whom a broom becomes an important part of life. Music by Robert McBride. Producers: Ray Manley and Bill Briggs.
Int. Film Bureau 26 min Color 1971

1103 Captain Busby. "Captain Busby put his beard to his mouth and sucked it, then took it out and spat on it..." The opening of Philip O'Connor's poem conjures up bizarre imagery, and director Ann Wolff translates it into film. The poem itself is an Edwardian spoof, infected with the contemporary surrealism of Lewis Carroll. A British Film Institute production.
Films Inc. 15 min B&W 1968

1104 Casey at the Bat. Here is John Wilson's animated version of the poem that has been called an authentic American masterpiece. Written by E.L. Thayer, as a young Harvard philosophy graduate, the verse first appeared in the San Francisco *Examiner* in 1888. Admired by such lights as T.S. Eliot, the poem was said by William Lyon Phelps to represent "a tragedy of destiny."
AIMS 7 min Color 1977

1105 Casey at the Bat. This is the poetic saga of Casey, the star of the Mudville Nine, who stepped up to the plate with two out, three men on base, and a chance to win the game. What follows has appalled and delighted generations of baseball fans and readers of verse. Animated.
Disney 9 min Color 1971

1106 Casey at the Bat. This version of Ernest L. Thayer's masterpiece is part of the *Living Poetry* series. Animation is based on original illustrations made specifically for this production.
McGraw-Hill 8 min Color 1967

1107 Casey at the Bat. The visual treatment of the Ernest Lawrence Thayer poem is two-fold. A first reading is done over a scene showing boys playing baseball. The juxtaposition of "Mighty Casey," portrayed by a young player, adds to the humor. The poem is read again with the words superimposed over a slow-motion sequence from a major league game. Television star George Maharis narrates. Produced by Art Evans.
Paramount 12 min Color 1970

1108 Casey at the Bat. The classic baseball verse, by E.L. Thayer, about the mighty batter Casey. What happened in Mudville, long ago, is illustrated by a recitation of the poem, plus drawings that recapture the flavor of the era.
Sterling Educ. 6 min Color 1967

1109 A Child's Garden of Verses. Robert Louis Stevenson's poetry is delineated by cinematographers Mary Louise Love and Robert Blaisdell, who inter-weave the storybook art of Carolyn Tyson with performances by four children. Accompaniment is provided by guitarist Larry Varga. Produced by Black Lion-Moongate.
Extension Media 9 min Color 1974

1110 A Child's Garden of Verses. A filmed recitation of Robert Louis Stevenson's collection of poems about his childhood — its happiness, sadness, adventures, and dreams. Read by Robert Goulet. From the "Reading Incentive Films" series. Produced by the Bank Street College of Education (New York).
McGraw-Hill 11 min Color 1968

1111 A Child's Garden of Verses. Seven poems from the Robert Louis Stevenson classic are woven into a day in the life of a small-town boy. Through visuals, sound effects, music, and recitation, the film creates a background for reading poetry. The setting is contemporary.
Sterling Educ. 10 min Color 1062

1112 The Christmas Visitor. Also known as " 'Twas the Night Before Christmas," Clement Moore's "A Visit from St. Nicholas" is re-told with

animation by John Halas and Joy Batchelor, husband-and-wife production team from London, England.
Phoenix 7 min Color 1961

1113 Collage. This is about the work of John Sennhauser, an artist and craftsman who is dedicated to interpreting Dante's *Divine Comedy*. He is seen here creating a collage for each of the hundred cantos. The collages are large (some six feet square) and are made up of pieces pasted to linen. The technique for making a collage is shown in the film.
Sterling Educ. 14 min Color 1966

1114 A Cortege of Eagles. Loosely suggested by tales from Homer's *Iliad*, Martha Graham interprets in dance Hecuba's grief at the successive loss of her loved ones. Because of the abstract nature of ballet, this film is suitable only for more sophisticated viewers. Produced by John Houseman.
Pyramid 38 min Color 1970

1115 The Creation. The story of Genesis told poetically in the language of black culture. It is one of seven verse-sermons in the volume *God's Trombones* by James Weldon Johnson. The poem is recited off-screen by black actor Raymond St. Jacques. It is then re-read (with words superimposed on the screen) by Margaret O'Brien, also off-screen. Produced by Art Evans.
Paramount 12 min Color 1970

1116 Daffodils. While a black student's teacher reads Wordsworth's poem, "Daffodils," the boy daydreams about a beautiful springtime world of his own. The school bell shatters his reverie, and he is again engulfed by the harsh realities of city life. Includes an original score. Produced by Communico Films for ACI Media.
Paramount 11 min Color 1972

1117 Daybreak. "Daybreak comes first/ In thin splinters shimmering...." These words from Carl Sandburg's poem set the stage for a camera view of a sunrise over the southwestern desert of Monument Valley. Broad plains, winding canyons, and gigantic rock formations gradually reveal the coming of dawn. Orchestral accompaniment and Indian poetry add to the awe of this daily miracle.
Encyc. Brit. 9 min Color 1975

1118 The Decision. Should a person "buck the establishment?" Or should one leave the status quo alone and hope things work out? In this film, a wife helps her husband make a decision that remains a mystery until it is revealed that the time is 1775 and the place is Colonial America. The husband's "small" decision to join the Minutemen then takes on a larger meaning. Accompaniment consists of background

music, sound effects, and poetry from Ralph Waldo Emerson's "Concord Hymn." Produced by Fred Niles.
Xerox Films   5½ min   Color   1975

1119 The Deserted Village. Oliver Goldsmith's poem, with its depth of understanding for the desolation caused by England's various enclosure acts, is visualized here by the expressionistic graphics of C. Walter Hodges, the British filmstrip artist. Subject specialist: Clarence W. Hach, Evanston (Ill.) High School.
Encyc. Brit.   17 min   Color   1970

1120 The Devil and Daniel Mouse. An up-dated, youth-oriented version of the person who, seeking instant gratification, sells out to the Devil. In the story, the seeker is a folksinger in pursuit of success as a "rock" star. Based on Stephen Vincent Benét's *Devil and Daniel Webster*. Music and lyrics were specifically composed for this film. Four-page less on guide available. Cel animation by Robert Vale.
Beacon Films   24 min   Color   1978

1121 Espolio. The title is from Earl Birney's poem, "El Greco: Espolio," which provides the narration for this series of animated photographs. It's about the carpenter who made the crucifix for Christ's execution ... without regard to the moral consequences. As such, the theme is a possible starting point for discussion of responsibility for personal actions. Produced by the National Film Board of Canada.
National Film Board   6½ min   Color   1970

1122 The Excuse. "The Excuse" is the finest poem Ruth Stone wrote after her husband died. In it she retraces the childhood origins of her poetry but, throughout the film — as in her poem — her recollections keep returning to her husband and his suicide. The film footage includes scenes from their home movies. Produced by Sidney Wolinsky.
Extension Media   16 min   Color   1976

1123 The Fish and the Fisherman. Alexander Pushkin's poem supplies the storyline for this Russian folktale of an aged angler who catches a golden fish in his net. English narration. Directed by Alexander Ptushko.
Macmillan   30 min   Color   1950

1124 Fog. Visualizes the poetic and artistic mood of fog while exploring the phenomena of its textures, patterns, and motion. Carl Sandburg's poem "Fog," was the inspiration for this nonnarrated film, produced in live-action photography.
Encyc. Brit.   9 min   Color   1971

1125 The Foolish Frog. Pete Seeger sings and plays the nursery-rhyme

folksong about the amphibian whose vanity led to his own destruction when carried away by a song of praise that he heard a farmer singing. Based on the storybook by Charles Seeger. Iconographic animation originates from the illustrations by Miloslav Jagr of Czechoslovakia.
Weston Woods 8 min Color 1971

1126 Frog Went A-Courtin'. John Langstaff sings and narrates this 400-year-old Scottish ballad of the courtship and wedding of Mr. Frog and Miss Mouse. Piano accompaniment reflects the personalities of each of the characters. Author of the picturebook is John Langstaff. Illustrated by Feodor Rojankovsky. Produced by Morton Schindel. Animated.
Weston Woods 12 min Color 1961

1127 From the Tower. Robinson Jeffers celebrated his love of beauty, nature, and youth in his poem, "Granddaughter," written in 1960 to his granddaughter Una Jeffers. In her 18th year, Una (who lives at the ocean-side home Jeffers built in Carmel, Calif.) is shown climbing past his workroom to his favorite lookout over the Pacific, and roaming the countryside he memorialized in his poetry. Produced by Mary Louise Love and Robert Blaisdell.
Extension Media 10 min Color 1974

1128 Frontier Poetry. Recreates Western settings in a program that features Cameron Mitchell and the First Poetry Quartet. Concludes with a happy Western social occasion—the square dance. Among the selections: Arthur Chapman's "Out Where the West Begins," Robert Service's "The Shooting of Dan McGrew," Joaquin Miller's "The Heroes of Oregon,"Vachel Lindsay's "The Flower-Fed Buffaloes." From the *Anyone for Tennyson?* series, coproduced by the Great Amwell Company and the Nebraska ETV Network.
Great Plains 30 min Color 1976

1129 G.C. Oden. One of two films (the other is *May Swenson*) from the series *Poetry is Alive and Well and Living in America*." While author Oden recites his poetry, the camera produces appropriate visualization of subject or mood. This film is also available as part of a multimedia program.
Media Plus 8 min Color

1130 God's Grandeur. This is a visual interpretation of Gerard Manley Hopkins' poem. In it, photography of earth, sea, sky, still life, and city scenes all suggest the poem's message. Produced by the Franciscan Communications Center.
TeleKETICS 3½ min Color 1976

1131 Greek Lyric Poetry. University of Chicago scholar and poet-in-residence David Grene explains an important aspect of Greek letters, lyric poetry. His examples include segments by Sappho, Simonides, and

Pindar, with scenes filmed "on location" at the temple of Zeus in Olympia. Dramatization of a lyric chorus is led by British actor John Neville. From the *Humanities* Program. Directed by John Barnes.
Encyc. Brit. 31 min Color 1963

1132 The Growth of a Poet: Sylvia Plath. Focuses on the urgency that moved Ms. Plath as a writer. Through 13 poems and excerpts from letters, the First Poetry Quartet follows the development of this young American poet. Among the selections: "If You Ask Me Why I Spend My Life Writing," "Morning Song," "Lesbos," "Ariel," and "Edge." From the *Anyone for Tennyson?* series, coproduced by the Great Amwell Company and the Nebraska ETV Network.
Great Plains 30 min Color 1976

1133 Gunga Din. In this animated version of Rudyard Kipling's famous poem, Mr. Magoo is the fearless Hindu water-boy who braves the din of battle to serve Her Majesty's troops. During one attack, he rushes to aid a wounded soldier, then falls mortally injured. Animated by United Productions of America (UPA).
Macmillan 26 min Color 1965

1134 Haiku. Haiku is Japanese poetry written in three lines totalling 17 syllables, broken into three lines of five, seven, and five syllables. It is about nature, almost always referring to one of the seasons of the year. This film is photographed in muted tones, expressing the quiet simplicity of the Japanese. The score, although modern, is in an Oriental idiom. Produced by Art Evans.
Paramount 7½ min Color 1971

1135 Haiku. The attitude of the Japanese toward nature is revealed in this brief but disciplined poetic form. This film essay helps to create an understanding, not only of the art, but of the people who created it. Utilizes live-action photography and original music.
Stanton 14 min Color 1969

1136 Haiku: Introduction to Poetry. To convey the impression of this Japanese form as the briefest and purest of poetry, this production creates visual impressions of nature and life, supplemented by music. Filmed by the Institute of Design at the Illinois Institute of Technology.
Coronet 12 min color 1970

1137 Hailstones and Halibut Bones: Part I. From the poem of the same name by Mary O'Neill. The film shows how colors can convey "ways of feeling." The animated drawings and verse describe white, gold, red, green, and black. Produced for the National Broadcasting Company by John Wilson.
Sterling Educ. 6 min Color 1963

1138 Hailstones and Halibut Bones: Part II. The colors described in this sequel to Part I are blue, gray, orange, purple, and brown. Also animated, and based on the poetry of Mary O'Neill.
Sterling Educ. 7 min Color 1968

1139 The Hangman. Maurice Ogden's allegorical poem won the Award of the National Poetry Society in 1961. Mood is accentuated by the simple ballad narrated by Herschel Bernardi. In this allegory, the coward, who has let others die to protect himself, becomes the hangman's final victim. Produced by Les Goldman. Animated. A Contemporary/McGraw-Hill release.
Nat. Educ. Film 12 min Color 1963

1140 Harlem Renaissance: The Black Poets. This is a film record of the black experience of the 1920's and 1930's. Even then, writers were thinking "black is beautiful," as dramatized here in vignettes of poetry by Countee Cullen and Waring Cuney. Also included are works of Georgia Douglas Johnson. Fenton Johnson, and W.E.B. DuBois, with segments from "Dream Variations" and "The Weary Blues" by Langston Hughes. Produced by WCAU-TV, Philadelphia.
Carousel 20 min Color 1970

1141 The Heroic Tradition. Presents renditions by the First Poetry Quartet of Sir Walter Scott, Alfred Lord Tennyson, and Rudyard Kipling. Their lives and works embraced the 19th century when British customs and culture were carried to the corners of the world. Included are: "Lochinvar," "The Charge of the Light Brigade," "Gentlemen-Rankers," and "Gunga Din." From the *Anyone for Tennyson?* series, coproduced by the Great Amwell Company and the Nebraska ETV Network.
Great Plains 30 min Color 1976

1142 Holy Thursday. An open-ended nonnarrated film whose imagery parallels the themes implicit in poet William Blake's two versions of "Holy Thursday": the innocence of children as reflected in nature, and the state of experience as symbolized by institutions. From his collection entitled *Songs of Experience*.
American Educ. 17 min Color 1970

1143 The House That Jack Built. Used primarily in the first grade, this animated version of the children's nursery rhyme can help create a background for reading, memorizing, and art activities. Produced by Jack Kuper.
Sterling Educ. 6 min Color 1965

1144 How to Kill: A Solider-Poet's Premonition of Death. These six poems are, in effect, a diary of poet Keith Douglas. They take us from his Oxford student days in 1941, through the carnage in North Africa during World War II, to a premonition of his own death in 1944. The

visuals consist of 120 original watercolors painted expressly for the film by Robert Andrew Parker, a Guggenheim Fellow. Original music is by Hal McKusick. Produced by Walter Goodman.
Benchmark   11 min   Color   1971

1145   Impressions of Prejudice. This examination of bias in modern America shows its many victims: the old, the young, women, and ethnic minorities. It includes selections from Conrad Kent Rivers, Shakespeare, Countee Cullen, Carl Sandburg, Langston Hughes, Lord Chesterfield, Margaret Danner, and Lorraine Hansberry. Originally distributed by Guidance Associates.
Xerox Films   18½   Color   1974

1146   In a Dark Time. This film makes use of the relation between spoken word and visual image, as it presents the range and variety of the works of poet Theodore Roethke. Produced by the Poetry Center in cooperation with the Associated Students of San Francisco State College. Directed by David Myers.
McGraw-Hill   27 min   B&W   1963

1147   In a Spring Garden. This film follows a day of spring, from the red morning to the glowing good-night of a firefly. Its structure is based on haiku written by Richard Lewis. Illustrated by Ezra Jack Keats. Produced by Morton Schindel.
Weston Woods   6 min   Color   1968

1148   In India. A work of animation about a harsh ruler who built a city in the jungle and amassed great treasure there. Still discontented, he tried to acquire the sun. The sun took its revenge and burnt the city; the jungle reclaimed its own. Inspired by "Indiaban," by Hungary's 20th-century poet, Attila József. It has a parallel in Shelley's "Ozymandias." Directed by Zsolt Richly.
Macmillan   5 min   Color   1966

1149   Invitation to Romance. The First Poetry Quartet, in a swank supper club setting, express to each other the many moods of love through 20 poems, from Shakespeare's "If Music Be the Food of Love" to Richard Armour's "What You Don't Know Won't Hurt You till Later." Works of Edmund Waller, Lord Byron, Elizabeth Barrett Browning, and Noel Coward are also included. From the *Anyone for Tennyson?* series, coproduced by the Great Amwell Company and the Nebraska ETV Network.
Great Plains   30 min   Color   1976

1150   Jabberwocky. This is a costumed enactment, in sign language and sound, of the nonsense poem from Lewis Carroll's *Alice in Wonderland*. Manual communication is performed by Lou Fant, Jr., exponent

and practitioner of "Ameslan," American Sign Language. Cleared for TV.
Joyce Media 10 min Color 1974

1151 A Journey Through Life: Edna St. Vincent Millay. Valerie Harper and the First Poetry Quartet perform the poetry of America's first female Pulitzer Prize winner. The selections show the poet's understanding of different life stages, and alienation, especially through death of loved ones. Some of the pieces are: "First Fig," "Departure," "Sonnet cxxvii," "Recuerdo," and "The Buck in the Snow." From the *Anyone for Tennyson?* series, coproduced by the Great Amwell Company and the Nebraska ETV Network.
Great Plains 30 min Color 1976

1152 Karl Shapiro's America. The Pulitzer Prize winning poet weaves his personal free verse statements about the United States into a visualization of everyday objects and occurrences. Uses a combination of collage animation and live-action scenes. Some of the poems rendered are "August Saturday Night," "The Living Room of My Neighbors" and "I'm Writing This Poem." Film-maker: Arthur Hoyle.
Pyramid 13 min Color 1976

1153 The Lady of Shalott This poem, as the forerunner of Tennyson's *Idylls of the King*, was a turning point in the poet's career. This important work of his is visualized by C. Walter Hodges, British actor who has designed many literature-oriented filmstrips, upon whose still pictures this film content is based.
Encyc. Brit. 10 min Color 1970

1154 Limericks, Epigrams, and Occasional Verse. Features writer George Plimpton and the First Poetry Quartet in a romp through the world of humorous rhyme. Included are the high-spirited verses of Dorothy Parker, Hilaire Belloc, Edward Lear, John Betjeman, and the renowned Anonymous. The program ends with a rapid-fire rendering of "familiar lines." From the *Anyone for Tennyson?* series, coproduced by the Great Amwell Co. and the Nebraska ETV Network.
Great Plains 30 min Color 1976

1155 London Bridge Is Falling Down! London Bridge, as it was in the 18th century when shops and houses lined both sides, is explored in this modern treatment of the nursery rhyme, arranged by Frank Lewin and sung by the Colmbus Boychoir. The artwork is from Peter Spier's picture book.
Conn. Films 9 min Color 1969

1156 Longfellow: A Rediscovery. Guest star Will Geer is landlord of the Wayside Inn, of Sudbury (Mass.), made famous by Longfellow's narrative poem, "Tales of the Wayside Inn." By the inn's fireside, over

cups of mulled wine, Geer and his guests, the First Poetry Quartet, share their enjoyment of such Longfellow poems as "The Arrow and the Song," "The Castle-Builder," "The Village Blacksmith," "The Slave in the Dismal Swamp," and "Excelsior." From the *Anyone for Tennyson?* series, coproduced by the Great Amwell Company and the Nebraska ETV Network.
Great Plains   30 min   Color   1976

1157   Lullaby (Altató). In this animated film, everything moves and changes to the lazy melody of a lullaby. Pinwheels spin into wagon wheels, and wagon wheels into clocks, with hands sweeping away the time. Butterflies become bows, and bows become bugles as a balloon drifts across the sky. It is the world within a child's eye. As the eyelid drops, a paper airplane drifts peacefully to the ground, and the child is asleep. Based on a poem by Attila József who lived and wrote in Hungary during the difficult 1930's. Produced by Csonka Cyorgy for Pannonia Films (Romania). Translated by Vernon Watkins.
Int. Film Bureau   3½ min   Color   1977

1158   Lycidas. Faithful to the lyrical tone of Milton's elegaic poem, the film's visual content consists of watercolors by Jasper Rose. The painter also provides a dramatic reading of the text, with piano and flute accompaniment. Produced by the University of California at Berkeley.
Extension Media   18 min   Color   1977

1159   Magic Prison (A Dialogue Set to Music). This dramatized "dialogue" of letters between Emily Dickinson and a stranger, Colonel T.W. Higginson, reveals the romantic mind and character of the American poet. Archibald MacLeish selected the poems and introduces the film. From the EBE *Humanities* series.
Encyc. Brit.   36 min   Color   1968

1160   Making Haiku. Children's drawings, coupled with spontaneous readings of their own poems, demonstrate the principles of this concise Japanese poetic form. Projector stopping-points allow young viewers to compose their own haiku, based on scenes and sounds from nature, the usual source of inspiration for haiku.
Encyc. Brit.   9 min   Color   1972

1161   Man of Rope. Inspired by Oscar Wilde's *Ballad of Reading Gaol*, this film traces the last hours of a man condemned to be hanged. Opening as a documentary, the viewpoint slowly shifts to the fantasy world of a man about to be strangled by "the system." Builds to a gruesome climax, so preview for young or sensitive viewers. A British Film Institute production in live-action photography.
Films Inc.   10 min   B&W   1970

1162 Mary Had a Little Lamb. Explores the nursery rhyme, first through a reading, then via live-action dramatization. Illustrates each couplet of the verse, with the girl and her pet en route to her school. The format then encourages sing-along participation, ending with questions designed to motivate in drawing, reading, writing, and play-acting.
Coronet 10½ min Color 1952

1163 Maurice Sendak's *Really Rosie* Starring the Nutshell Kids. The characters from *The Nutshell Library* and *The Sign on Rosie's Door* have been animated here, and the poems of Maurice Sendak are set to music and sung by Carole King. Rosie is a larger-than-life personality who's determined to prove that make-believe is not just a game but a way of life. Produced for television by Sheldon Riss.
Weston Woods 26 min Color 1975

1164 May Swenson. One of two films (the other is **G.C. Oden**) from the series *Poetry Is Alive and Well and Living in America*. While author Swenson recites from her poetry, the camera produces appropriate imagery of mood or subject. This film is available separately or as part of a multi-media program.
Media Plus 9 min Color

1165 Mending Wall. This poem by Robert Frost is essentially one that questions the barriers people erect between themselves. For privacy? For protection? There is one man who asks why the wall is necessary at all. And there is another who says, "Good fences make good neighbors." Leonard Nimoy, star of *Mission: Impossible* and *Star Trek*, supplies the narration. Produced by Art Evans.
Paramount 10 min Color 1973

1166 The Midnight Ride of Paul Revere. From the belfry steps of the Old North Church to the battle of Concord, the film recreates in authentic settings the events of Longfellow's poem, "Paul Revere's Ride."
Coronet 10½ min Color 1957

1167 The Midnight Ride of Paul Revere. Reviews the explosive situation in the colonies during the spring of 1775, and recreates the events that occurred on the night of April 18th. Illustrates the significance of Revere's ride, while correcting several historical inaccuracies of Longfellow's poem. Filmed in live-action photography.
Encyc. Brit. 11 min Color 1957

1168 Minnie Remembers. The fundamental human need for physical and emotional affection is expressed in this visualization of Donna Swanson's poem. An elderly widow, Minnie recalls the tenderness of her childhood, youth, and marriage. Searching beyond roles and functions,

she voices the desperate longing for affirmation as a person. Production by Kay Henderson, Phil Arnold, and Wayne Smith for the United Methodist Church.
Mass Media   5 min   Color   1976

1169   Morning on the Lièvre. Explores the places and scenes described in a 19th-century lyric poem by Archibald Lampman. In his poem, "Morning on the Lièvre," he describes the effects of sunlight, shadows, and mist on the river at dawn and recalls his reactions to the changing light and colors. A cameraman was able to record each scene on film, matching pictues to words, line by line. Previously available through *Encyclopaedia Britannica*.
Nat. Film Board   13 min   Color   1961

1170   Mother Goose. This filmed reading by actress Betsy Palmer is designed to introduce children to the characters and rhymes of this collection of stories. Illustrated by Brian Wildsmith. Produced by the Bank Street College of Education (New York).
McGraw-Hill   11 min   Color   1968

1171   Mother Goose Stories. Mother Goose steps out of her nursery book and, waving her magic wand, brings to life several of her best-loved characters: Little Miss Muffet, Old Mother Hubbard, the Queen of Hearts, and Humpty Dumpty. A Ray Harryhausen production.
BFA Educ. Media   11 min   Color   1969

1172   My Last Duchess: A Film Prologue. Paintings of the period described in the poem complement a dramatic rendering of Robert Browning's classic by a member of the Old Vic Acting Company of England.
Universal Education   11 min   Color

1173   The Naming of Parts. The words of this poem by Henry Reed are paralleled by scenes of "boot camp" trainees receiving instruction in the nomenclature of the M-14 rifle. The starkness of the military assembly room sporadically clashes with images of flowers, bees, and open fields. Produced by R. Bloomberg.
McGraw-Hill   5 min   B&W   1972

1174   Nature Poetry. This is a sign-language representation, with sound, of the poetry of Dorothy Miles. From the *Gestures* series of five films. Produced by John Joyce.
Joyce Media   10 min   Color   1976

1175 The Neighboring Shore. America is visually interpreted through more than 100 woodcuts by Antonio Frasconi, with selections from Walt Whitman. The result is an overview of our country, suggesting that each of us has a role in determining the future. Narrated by Pat Hingle.

Produced by Meyers, Frasconi, Feinman, and Graff.
Macmillan 15 min Color 1959

1176 The Night Before Christmas. Using original materials as sung and spoken by Jerry Styner, the film utilizes a three-dimensional animation technique to illustrate Clement C. Moore's seasonal poem. A Cahill Production.
AIMS 10 min Color 1968

1177 The Night Before Christmas. Presents, in animation, not only the holiday verse itself but also the true story of how Clement C. Moore happened to write it. Features the Norman Luboff Choir and Orchestra in a series of related songs about the Yuletide season.
Prod. Unltd. 27 min Color

1178 The Night Before Christmas. A live reenactment of Clement Moore's holiday poem, "A Visit from St. Nicholas," with an original musical score, a 19th-century setting, and authentic costumes.
Encyc. Brit. 11 min Color 1955

1179 No Deposit — No Return. The poetry of Mark Van Doren is featured in this environment centered motion picture. All of the poems and song lyrics from the sound track are reprinted in the leader's guide. Both the lyrics and poems can enhance discussion of American poetry as well as ecology. An ABC Television News production.
Centron 10 min Color 1971

1180 No Man Is an Island. John Donne's 17th-century poem is interpreted orally by Orson Welles, musically by Andrea, and visually by Virginia Hughes' language superimposed over related live-action scenes. Produced by Al Saparoff.
Dana Prod. 11 min Color 1972

1181 Nursery Rhymes. "Hickory Dickory Dock" is visualized in this animated picture, along with the lullaby "Hush, Little Baby." Based on paintings by Gary Lund, who created the character of little Oblio in "The Point." Produced by Motorola Teleprograms, Inc.
MTI Teleprograms 3 min Color 1974

1182 O Captain! My Captain! This elegy was written to express Walt Whitman's grief over Lincoln's death. The poem lends itself to involvement now, for this film is designed to relate the poem not only to Lincoln, but to heroes of modern times who died by assassination. Narrator: Efrem Zimbalist, Jr. Produced by Art Evans.
Paramount 12 min Color 1970

1183 The Odyssey: Part I — The Central Themes. First in the series

of three films, with professional dramatizations interpreted by Columbia University scholar Gilbert Highet. From the *Humanities* series. Based on Homer's epic poem. Directed by John Barnes.
Encyc. Brit. 28 min Color 1965

1184 The Odyssey: Part II—The Return of Odysseus. This film focuses upon Odysseus' activities after his return to Ithaca, and the manner in which these actions reveal his true character. This is the second lesson in the series of three films, each professionally enacted along with interpretation by Gilbert Highet. Based on Homer's epic. Part of the *Humanities* series, directed by John Barnes.
Encyc. Brit. 26 min Color 1965

1185 The Odyssey: Part III—The Structure of the Epic. Gilbert Highet unravels the three interlocking tales of Homer's epic: first Odysseus' escape from the lonely island and return to Ithaca; second, the story of Telemachus' growth to manhood; and third, a long flashback that recounts Odysseus' adventures. This is the last of three lessons, theatrically performed, with related matter introduced by Gilbert Highet. From the *Humanities* series. Director: John Barnes.
Encyc. Brit. 27 min Color 1965

1186 Over in the Meadow. This sing-along film presents an old counting song and nursery rhyme. From the John Langstaff book, illustrated by Feodor Rojankovsky whose pictures provided the iconographic animation. Producer: Mort Schindel.
Weston Woods 9 min Color 1969

1187 The Owl and the Pussy-Cat. This tale of the amorous voyage of a seemingly ill-suited pair is perhaps the best loved of all the verses by the master of nonsense, Edward Lear. Produced by Morton Schindel.
Weston Woods 3 min Color 1972

1188 Paul Revere. The famous midnight ride of Paul Revere took place on the 18th of April, 1775, as the Americans began their battle to overthrow the British. As in Longfellow's poem, Mr. Magoo rides from Concord to Lexington to warn the populace, "the British are coming." Cartoon animation by UPA (United Productions of America).
Macmillan 26 min Color 1965

1189 Paul Revere's Ride. This film offers a reading and visualization of Henry Wadsworth Longfellow's poem, "Paul Revere's Ride." As an introduction, the British march and Revere's ride are described, to clarify the action outlined in the poem.
BFA Educ. Media 10 min Color 1964

1190 Pippa Passes. Robert Browning's poem, about the once-a-year

holiday of Pippa, is seen in selected segments only. By the director of *Birth of a Nation*, D.W. Griffith. A silent film production.
Pyramid   10 min   B&W   1909

1191 The Poem as Allegory: The Ebb Begins from Dream. Depicts the allegory contained in the words of the Earl Birney poem, using the daily ebb and flow of the tides of the ocean to parallel the cycles of everyday life in the city. Teacher's manual is available. Produced by Canadian film-maker Paul Quigley.
Learning Corp.   7 min   Color   1975

1192 The Poem As a Personal Statement: To a Very Old Woman. The camera becomes an observer, following an elderly woman as she occupies herself in the simple fulfillment of her life, and suggesting her attitude in greeting death as a natural completion of that life. Based on the poem by Canadian Irving Layton. Produced by Paul Quigley.
Learning Corp.   10 min   Color   1975

1193   The Poem as Evocation: Roblin's Mills. From the *Sense of Poetry* series of seven films, each devoted to the contemporary work of different authors. An off-screen reading of Al Purdy's poem is the only narration provided. A printed copy of the poem is available with the film. The live-action photography is by Canadian film-maker Paul Quigley.
Learning Corp.   9 min   Color   1975

1194 The Poem As Imagery: Progressive Insanities of a Pioneer. Photography captures a lone man's frustration in struggling to cultivate the land around him against the forces of nature, while the poem makes us aware that in reality his conflict is with himself. Discussion-guide available. Poem by Margret Atwood Striking. Film-maker is Canadian Paul Quigley.
Learning Corp.   5 min   Color   1975

1195 The Poem As Irony: The Beggars of Dublin. From the *Sense of Poetry* series of seven films, each devoted to a contemporary work by a different author. An off-screen reading of Alden Nowlan's poem is the only narration provided. A printed copy of the poem is available with the film. The live-action photography is by Canadian film-maker Paul Quigley.
Learning Corp.   11 min   Color   1975

1196   The Poem As Social Comment: The Examiner. A satirical visual treatment underlines the social comment in poet F.R. Scott's words as a class examination takes place with students and examiners wearing masks of conformity. Teacher's manual is available. Producer: Paul Quigley, Canadian film-maker.
Learning Corp.   13 min   Color   1975

1197 The Poem As Symbolism. From the *Sense of Poetry* series of seven films, each devoted to contemporary works by a different author. The poems included here are "The Wreckers," "Wrecking Ball," and "John Street" by Raymond Souster. An off-screen reading of Souster's poems is the only narration provided. A printed copy of the poems is available with the film. The live-action photography is by Canadian film-maker Paul Quigley.
Learning Corp. 7 min Color 1975

1198 Poems of Experience. This is one of five films from the *Gestures* series of signlanguage poetry by Dorothy Miles. The words are also presented on the soundtrack. Produced by John Joyce.
Joyce Media 10 min Color 1976

1199 Poems of Love and Womanhood. This is a sign-language representation, with sound, of the poetry of Dorothy Miles. From the *Gestures* series of five films, named after Ms. Miles' volume. Produced by John Joyce.
Joyce Media 10 min Color 1976

1200 Poems of the Sea. The First Poetry Quartet visits Mystic Seaport—the outdoor Maritime Museum in Connecticut. There they are joined by chanty singer Stuart Gillespie in representation of the feelings that 16 poets have expressed about the sea. Among the selections: Masefield's "Sea Fever," Coleridge's "The Rime of the Ancient Mariner," Southey's "The Inchcape Rock," and Kingsley's "The Three Fishes." From the *Anyone for Tennyson?* series, coproduced by the Great Amwell Company and the Nebraska ETV Network.
Great Plains 30 min Color 1976

1201 Poet at Lobos. Eric Barker strolls along the shore of Point Lobos, Calif. reciting poems from his volumes *Looking for Water* and *Directions in the Sun*. Segments, combining only music and the beauty of the surroundings, suggest the inspiration of this Englishborn poet, described as one who lived as an artist should—simply and with nature. Chosen as California's poet laureate, Barker declined the honor because he believed that a poet should not be publicized. Produced by Mary Louise Love and Robert Blaisdell.
Extension Media 13 min Color 1974

1202 A Poetic Feast. Vincent Price and the First Poetry Quartet, in kitchen and dining room, whip up poetry that celebrates the joys of wining and dining. Among the selections: Justin Richardson's "Shelling Peas," "A Song of Gluttony" by E.O. Parrott, Ogden Nash's "A Drink with Something in It," "Turtle Soup" by Lewis Carroll, and "Shakespeare Stew" from *Macbeth*. From the *Anyone for Tennyson?* series, coproduced by the Great Amwell Company and the Nebraska ETV Network.
Great Plains 30 min Color 1976

1203 Poetry for Fun: Dares and Dreams. A companion piece to *Poetry for Fun: Poems about Animals*. This is a melange of humor, solemnity, fantasy, and reality captured in a variety of film techniques. The poems include "The Cave Boy," "The Pirate Don Durk of Dowdee," "The Fairies," "Strange Tree," "Foul Shot," and "Behind the Waterfall." Targeted for grades 4-6. Adviser: Nita Wyatt Sundbye, Ed.D., professor of education, University of Kansas.
Centron 12½ min Color 1974

1204 Poetry for Fun: Poems about Animals. The eight poems in this film are presented for fun and appreciation. Each was selected after testing with intermediate students representing a variety of ethnic and economic backgrounds. Selections include: "Camel's Lament," "Night with a Wolf," "The Spangled Pandemonium," "Lone Dog," and Odgen Nash's "Introduction to Dogs." Both cartoon animation and live-action photography are used.
Centron 13 min Color 1972

1205 Poetry to Grow On. Most of the poems quoted in this film are included, in whole or in part, in *The First Book of Poetry* by Isabel J. Peterson. Some authors represented are: Rachel Field, Edna St. Vincent Millay, Emily Dickinson, Walter de la Mare, Vachel Lindsay, and John Masefield. A Grover Production.
Screenscope 18½ min Color 1966

1206 The Poet's Eye: Shakespeare's Imagery. This is a filmic introduction to the language and poetry of Shakespeare. It presents graphic examples of Shakespeare's imagery or "visual quotations," including an excerpt from *Henry V* with Laurence Olivier. Released by COI Productions. Narrated by Stephen Murray.
Films/Human. 16 min Color 1976

1207 The Prisoner of Chillon. This visual rendering of Lord Byron's elegaic poem is an adaptation of the filmstrip art of C. Walter Hodges. The poem itself, abridged here, is a tribute to the freedom of the human spirit. Production collaborator: Clarence W. Hach, Evanston (Ill.) High School.
Encyc Brit. 15 min Color 1970

1208 A Program of Satire. Features the First Poetry Quartet in readings from a dozen poets who have trained their wits against a variety of targets—from postmasters and politicans to war and religion. Among the selections: Richard Armour's "The Discriminating Reader," Jonathan Swift's "Verses on the Death of Dr. Swift," Odgen Nash's "Everything's Haggis in Hoboken or Scots Wha' Hae Ye," and Edith Sitwell's "Tarantella." From the *Anyone for Tennyson?* series, coproduced by the Great Amwell Co. and the Nebraska ETV Network.
Great Plains 30 min Color 1976

1209 Pulitzer Prize Poets — Part I. This is the first of two programs dealing with those distinguished by Pulitzer recognition since inauguration of the award in 1922. Among the 1922-1950 selections by the First Poetry Quartet: E.A. Robinson's "Miniver Cheevy," Frost's "The Vantage Point," "The Preacher Ruminates Behind the Sermon" by Gwendolyn Brooks, Karl Shapiro's "The Progress of Faust," and Stephen Vincent Benét's "American Names." From the *Anyone for Tennyson?* series, coproduced by the Great Amwell Company and the Nebraska ETV Network.
Great Plains 30 min Color 1976

1210 Pulitzer Prize Poets — Part II. The First Poetry Quartet presents the works of Pulitzer winners from 1951 through 1975. Among the selections: "Mourning's at Eight-Thirty" by Phyllis McGinley, Gary Snyder's "Front Lines," Sandburg's "Chicago," "Silence" by Marianne Moore, and Archibald MacLeish's "Ars Poetica." From the *Anyone for Tennyson?* series, coproduced by the Great Amwell Company and the Nebraska ETV Network.
Great Plains 30 min Color 1976

1211 A Quiet Evening with Mother Goose. Includes traditional nursery rhymes along with the children's poetry of Robert Louis Stevenson, A.A. Milne, and John Ciardi. Recitations are performed by the First Poetry Quartet, a professional theatrical group. From the *Anyone for Tennyson?* series, coproduced by the Great Amwell Company and the Nebraska ETV Network. Executive Producer: William Perry.
Great Plains 30 min Color 1976

1212 Rainbow Black. Photography plus her own words reveal the many facets of Sarah Webster Fabio, one of America's foremost black poets. She and her ex-husband discuss the black power movement of the 60's and the humorous side of teaching at white universities. She recites her "Juju for Grandma" and "Evil Is No Black Thing". Filmed by Cheryl Fabio.
Extension Media 31 min Color 1976

1213 The Raven. This interpretation of Poe's classic work draws on the famous engravings by Gustave Doré, lugubriously suggesting the poet's tormented imagination. The soundtrack combines a reading by actor Gregg Morton and the music of Maurice Ravel. Produced by Lewis Jacobs.
Texture Films 11 min Color 1976

1214 The Renascent. This film is based on Edna St. Vincent Millay's poem of a young woman's wish to die. Her gratitude for rebirth is portrayed through dance by Donald Redlich against natural backdrops. Accompanied by selections from Harry Partch's score, "Dance Percussions,"

Produced by Madeleine Tourtelot.
Grove Press 14 min Color

1215 The Restoration Wits. Cyril Ritchard plays the Earl of Rochester in a dramatization of 17th-century light verse and poetry. In a Restoration coffee house setting, Ritchard and the First Poetry Quartet bring alive the poetry of Dryden, Thomas D'Urfey, and the merry gang of aristocrats who made up Charles II's circle of court wits. From the *Anyone for Tennyson?* series, coproduced by the Great Amwell Company and the Nebraska ETV Network.
Great Plains 30 min Color 1976

1216 The Rime of the Ancient Mariner. Samuel Taylor Coleridge's narrative poem, illustrated by the 19th-century wood engraver and illustrator, Gustave Doré. Combines the entire poem and the collection of Doré engravings. Produced by the University of California (Berkeley).
Extension Media 28 min B&W 1953

1217 The Rime of the Ancient Mariner. The animated engravings of Gustave Doré supply the pictorial content for the Coleridge masterpiece. The narration by Orson Welles is separately available on audio-tape. Produced by Studio Films.
Studio Films 42 min Color 1978

1218 Robert Frost's New England. A selection of Frost's poetry about New England and its seasons. Although the poems find their source in the rocks, leaves, and snows of Vermont, Frost uses them as metaphors to lead us into deeper reaches of the mind. The nature photography adds emphasis. Some poems included are "The Road Not Taken," "Reluctance," and "October." Film-maker: Dewitt Jones, writer-lecturer-naturalist.
Churchill 22 min Color 1975

1219 Robert Frost's The Death of the Hired Man. Frost here writes of country people, a rhythm of another time and place. His simple yet powerful blank verse lends itself well to the characters and the setting, as the film converts the mood of this poem into visual and dramatic form. Produced by Jeanne Collachia.
Encyc. Brit. 22 min Color 1979

1220 The Rose and the Mignonette. This film is based on a French poem by Louis Aragon, translated by Stephen Spender. Its subject concerns an actual incident in a French town occupied by the Germans in World War II. The music, by George Auric, is from a Bach chorale. The recitation is by Emlyn Williams. Produced in France by André Michel.
Film Images 9 min B&W

1221 Runner. The poet W.H. Auden analyzes the essence of running,

by pairing his verse with the poetry of human movement as shown in live-action photography. Produced by the National Film Board of Canada.
Pyramid 12 min B&W 1962

1222 Sea Fever. Based upon John Masefield's poem, the narrative from the poet laureate of England is set against scenes of a square-rigged clipper at sea, in fair weather and foul. Lorne Greene is narrator.
AIMS 6 min Color 1966

1223 The Search for Ulysses. Ernie Bradford, British sailor and scholar whose book, *Ulysses Found,* inspired this film, goes on a journey and finds that Ulysses really lived, and that his adventures took place on existing islands. Following the words of Homer, we see the land of the lotus eaters, the Siren's rocks, the cave of Cyclops, Charybdis, and the islands of Circe and Calypso. Narrated by James Mason. Produced by CBS-TV.
Carousel 53 min Color 1966

1224 Song of a Nation. Produced by Warner Bros., this film is a dramatization of the writing of "The Star Spangled Banner" by Francis Scott Key on board a British ship opposite Fort McHenry. Originally distributed by Teaching Film Custodians in conjunction with the National Council of Teachers of English.
Indiana U. 19 min Color 1936

1225 The Sonnets: Shakespeare's Moods of Love. As we hear the words of the poet off-screen, they become a counterpart to the emotions silently depicted. Three people, in a modern setting (a man, a woman he loves, and his young friend), are involved in passsionate exchanges of anger, jealousy, tenderness, and joy—all reflecting the many aspects of love expressed in the ten sonnets. Photographed in the English countryside. Played by members of the Royal Shakespeare Company.
Learning Corp. 21 min Color 1972

1226 Spoon River Anthology. The poetry of Edgar Lee Masters, along with photos and artifacts of the period, compares the moods of mid-America in 1960, 1940, and 1900. Narrator: Gene Barry. Produced by Thomas G. Smith.
BFA Educ. Media 20 min Color 1976

1227 The Star-Spangled Banner. The words of lawyer-poet Francis Scott Key's patriotic verse are visualized by artist Peter Spier. Choral background is provided by the cadet glee club of the U.S. Military Academy at West Point. Producer: Morton Schindel.
Weston Woods 7 min Color 1975

1228 The Story of the Star-Spangled Banner. Lou Fant, Jr., uses

"Ameslan" (American Sign Language) to tell the story of the poetic origin of our national anthem. Filmed where Francis Scott Key wrote it, in Fort McHenry and Baltimore harbor. Cleared for TV.
Joyce Media 15 min Color 1977

1229 The Strangest Voyage. The opening live-action segment of this motion picture examines the troubled life of the 18th-century poet, Samuel Taylor Coleridge. Then the newly animated and colored engravings of Gustave Doré, plus a British cast of voices (led by Sir Michael Redgrave), dramatize all seven parts of *The Rime of the Ancient Mariner*. Producer: Raul da Silva for Lumière Ciné. Winner of six film festival awards.
Mariner Productions 55 min Color 1974

1230 Tales of Hiawatha. Adapted from Henry Wadsworth Longfellow's poem, "The Song of Hiawatha," this animated puppet film combines sections of the work with narration to relate the Indian legend. Episodes tell how Hiawatha was sent as a prophet to bring peace to his people, how his exploits as a hunter brought them wealth, and how his marriage to Minnehaha united enemy tribes.
Sterling Educ. 19 min Color 1967

1231 The Thirteen Cantos of Hell. Using an animation style of stark silhouettes, director Peter King conjures up the terrifying horror of Dante's *Inferno*. The complexity and impact of the first 13 cantos are conveyed in a series of symbolic images accompanied by a cacophonous electronic soundtrack. Should be seen in connection with a reading of the *Divine Comedy*. A British Film Institute production.
Films Inc. 21 min B&W 1968

1232 Trees. This film is a blending of the poem by Joyce Kilmer, music by Oscar Rasbach, singing by Fred Waring's Pennsylvanians, and depiction by Walt Disney's animators.
Disney 5 min Color 1971

1233 The Tuft of Flowers. This film matches the reading of Robert Frost's "Tuft of Flowers" with scenes of the Grand Canyon and its natural wonders. The original setting of the poem was New England. Produced for the Haboush Company by David and Ivan Dryer.
Creative Films 7 min Color 1972

1234 Tyger, Tyger. An inquiry into the meanings of William Blake's poem. This film interviews people from all walks of life, old and young, as they come to terms with the mystery and meaning of the verse. Robert Graves, who himself has written a simplified version of "the Tyger," is among the interpreters. Poets Kathleen Raine, Adrian Mitchell, schoolchildren, a housewife, a taxidermist, and a zoo keeper also con-

tribute their insights. From BBC-TV.
Time-Life 30 min Color 1969

1235 Tyrannus Nix? Lawrence Ferlinghetti, the antiestablishment American poet, narrates his diatribe against Nixon. He sees Nixon's face as the mask of a tyrant, of an actor, of an ad, of TV itself. The face disguises the computerized man, the war machine, the betrayal of the American dream. Recited against a collage of American scenes, symbols, historical moments, and newsclips. Directed by Irving Saraf.
New Yorker 12 min Color

1236 A View of Four Centuries. Presents the First Poetry Quartet as fictional characters from four time spans who share their love of poetry. Among the selections: John Donne's "Death, Be Not Proud," Milton's "Song on May Morning," Gray's "Elegy Written in a Country Churchyard," Robert Browning's "Home-Thoughts from Abroad," and "Do Not Go Gentle into that Good Night" by Dylan Thomas. From the *Anyone for Tennyson?* series, coproduced by the Great Amwell Company and the Nebraska ETV Network.
Great Plains 30 min Color 1976

1237 A Visit from St. Nicholas. This seasonal verse by Clement Moore retells, in animation, the story of Santa's midnight visit. This version is the shortest of several films of the same poem.
Coronet 4 min Color 1949

1238 Voices from the South. Explores the works of native Southern poets and poets who have moved to the South. Ruby Dee joins the First Poetry Quartet in presenting such works as "The Celebration" by James Dickey, "Jazz Poem" by Carl W. Hines, Jr., "Crepe De Chine" by Tennessee Williams, and as a finale, "The Judgment Day"—a spirited evocation of a revival meeting—by James Weldon Johnson. From the *Anyone for Tennyson?* series, coproduced by the Great Amwell Company and the Nebraska ETV Network.
Great Plains 30 min Color 1976

1239 Walt Whitman and the Civil War. Takes guest star Richard Kiley and the First Poetry Quartet to the site of the battle of Gettysburg. There they present the Whitman works that reflected his concern and love for country. Among the selections: "Beat! Beat! Drums!" "O Captain! My Captain!" "When Lilacs Last in the Dooryard Bloom'd," and "I Hear American Singing." From the *Anyone for Tennyson?* series, coproduced by the Great Amwell Company and the Nebraska ETV Network.
Great Plains 30 min Color 1976

1240 What Is Poetry? Contrasts a news report about an auto accident with the poem, "Auto Wreck," by Karl Shapiro. By selection of elements

and the use of descriptive words, the poet makes this message an emotional experience.
BFA Educ. Media 9½ min Color 1963

1241 The World of Emily Dickinson. Features actress Claire Bloom as the shy 19th-century poet who seldom left her room in her father's house in Amherst, Mass. She did, however, send out "letters to the world' in the form of more than 1,700 poems. Among the selections: "I'll Tell You How the Sun Rose," "A Narrow Fellow in the Grass," "Faith Is a Fine Invention," and "I Never Saw a Moor." From the *Anyone for Tennyson?* series, coproduced by the Great Amwell Company and the Nebraska ETV Network.
Great Plains 30 min Color 1976

1242 Wynken, Blynken, and Nod. Barbara Cooney's illustrations complement the camera movement and reading behind the cinematic rendition of this verse. Animated by Cochran. Producer: Morton Schindel.
Weston Woods 4 min Color 1972

Short Stories

Fred Marcus, in *Short Stories/Short Films*, makes this observation: "For many years the motion-picture industry has ransacked literary storehouses, seeking sources for feature films. Only during the last ten years have short films, adapted from short stories, become numerous enough and attained the quality necessary to merit serious academic study."

Dr. Marcus goes on, in his own book, to give ample evidence of this trend towards "scriptogenic" films. The following 168 titles provide even more proof of his statement.

1243 All Gold Canyon. This adventure, freely adapted from the Jack London story, deals with the effect of gold on man's character. As a lone prospector discovers gold in a deserted canyon and begins laboriously extracting it from the ground, his former partner ambushes him. Dramatized in live-action photography, without narration or dialogue. Background music by Lubos Fiser. Produced by Shortfilm Studio (Prague).
Weston Woods 21 min Color 1970

1244 All the Troubles of the World. This story by Isaac Asimov takes viewers into a civilization run by Multivac, an all-powerful computer system. Ben Manners' father is suspected of plotting to sabotage this system. In trying to help his father, Ben involves himself in a scheme to destroy Multivac. In a climactic revelation, viewers learn that Multivac is its own saboteur; the ultimate machine seeks self-destruction as an alternative to managing mankind's endless problems. A Bernard Wilets production.
BFA Educ. Media 22½ min Color 1978

1245 Almos' a Man. LeVar Burton, who played young Kunta Kinte in *Roots*, portrays Richard Wright's character: the adolescent who thought he could find manhood in the possession of a pistol. The accidental killing of a work-mule teaches him he's wrong. Production funded by the National Endowment for the Humanities. Directed by Stan Lathan.
Perspective 38 min Color 1977

1246 The Assignation. Amidst the mysterious beauty of Venice, this production tells Poe's story in which a figure, suggesting Death, meets a Maiden during a traditional costume carnival. Produced by Curtis Harrington.
Macmillan 8 min Color 1963

1247 Ballet of Central Park. A pretty ballerina meets up with some street-wise Puerto Rican boys in New York. For a while they seem to bridge the gaps of class and race, as the girl creates a dance about the boys for a school assignment. But, in so doing, she becomes disillusioned by her own idealism. Based on the story by Kay Boyle. Produced by Witty-Siris.
Macmillan 15 min Color 1972

1248 Bartleby. Herman Melville's enigmatic, haunting story of the man who "preferred not to" has been translated onto film, with authentic locales, period sets, and professional acting performances. From the *Humanities* series ("Short Story Showcase."). Produced by Larry Yust.
Encyc. Brit. 28 min Color 1970

1249 Bernice Bobs Her Hair. This is F. Scott Fitzgerald's pre-flapper-

era story of the wall flower-turned-flirt whose nonconformity pleases but shocks her college-age peers—especially the girl-cousin who coached her in her new and daring ways. Shelly Duval stars in the leading role as Bernice. Executive producer: Robery Geller, Director: Joan Macklin Silver.
Perspective 47½ min Color 1977

1250 The Bespoke Overcoat. This is Gogol's story of friendship between Morry, a poor tailor, and Fender, a frail old clerk. For forty years, Fender has stacked sheepskin coats in a warehouse. He is too poor to buy one for himself, and his boss won't give him one. Fender and Morry conspire to obtain a coat ... even after death. Winner of several awards, including an "Oscar." Alfie Bass and David Kossoff enact the main roles. Director: Jack Clayton.
Janus Films 38 min BW 1955

1251 The Bet. This up-dated version of the Chekhov story captures the boredom, panic, hysteria, and near-madness experienced by a young man who bets a wealthy friend that he can isolate himself in a single room for five years. Filmed mostly in black and white; color is used at symbolic points. Produced by Ronald Waller.
Pyramid 24 min BW 1969

1252 Bezhin Meadow. This story by Ivan Turgenev concerns the gallant work of Russian youths on a collective farm. The leading figure is killed in the climactic scene while guarding the harvest at night. His assassin is his own father, a mad saboteur. Though most of the Eisenstein footage for this film was destroyed in the bombing of Moscow, his colleagues used still photos to salvage the production. Music by Sergei Prokofiev.
Macmillan 30 min B&W 1935

1253 The Big Red Barn. Based on the book by Margaret Wise Brown, this film brings to life the atmosphere of rural living. It transports young viewers into a country setting, acquainting them with the animals most often found on farms, and encourages oral and written stories, poems, and art work. One of five films from the *Reading Short Stories* Series.
Paramount 8 min Color 1972

1254 The Blue Hotel. The time is the 1880's; place, a frontier Nebraska town. A stranger checks in at the local hotel; he's an erratic Swede whose strange forebodings and behavior unsettle the townspeople. Especially disturbing is his announcement that he'll be killed in the very room he's occupying. An evening of card-playing leads to his death as he predicted. Was it fate? Coincidence? Self-will? Or the unwitting involvement of all concerned? Story by Stephen Crane. Director: Jan Kadar.
Perspective 54½ min Color 1977

1255 The Boarded Window. Based on a horror story by Ambrose Bierce, this live-action production seeks to explain the circumstances behind the apparent death of a hunter's wife and the wildcat he stalked. The open-ended format is suited for discussion but semi-violent scenes dictate discretion in choice of audiences. PREVIEW. No narration or dialogue except for brief introduction. Produced by Alan W. Beattie.
Perspective 17½ min Color 1974

1256 The Boarding House. A young and penniless painter answers an ad for a room. His landlady turns out to be a pretty widow whose rent is surprisingly low. Infatuated, he "seduces" her ... only to receive a stiff bill for her favors. Financially strapped, he's forced to go into debt to repay. From the story by Chekhov.
Macmillan 27 min BW

1257 The Bold Dragoon. This is Washington Irving's folk story of the Hudson River innkeeper who rids himself of a troublesome guest by giving him a haunted room. One of 13 films from the *On Stage* series, with character actor Monty Wooley. Produced by Dynamic Films.
Macmillan 15 min B&W 1954

1258 The Boor. Anton Chekhov's merry tale of the tenant farmer who comes to collect a debt and matches wits with an attractive widow. Features actor Monty Wooley. From the series of 13 *On Stage* productions by Dynamic Films.
Macmillan 15 min B&W 1954

1259 A Boring Afternoon. Takes place in a tavern on a typical afternoon, as a man tries to read a book while others fanatically discuss soccer or play cards. Satirizes the generation gap and the average man's contempt for the nonconformists who would rather read than play cards or talk sports. Its surprise ending makes a point about how little any of us see in others. Directed by Ivan Passer. Based on the story of Bohumil Hrabal. Czech dialogue with English subtitles.
Macmillan 14 min B&W 1965

1260 Brown Wolf. Photographed in the natural surroundings of the Klondike, this adaptation of Jack London's story of a spirited dog and the people whose lives he crosses spotlights the conflicts between the call of the wild and civilization.
Learning Corp. 26 min Color 1971

1261 The Canterville Ghost. A modern adaptation of Oscar Wilde's satirical short story about a tired old ghost, two children who torment him, and a young lady who befriends him and finally releases him from his indeterminate state. Monty Wooley plays the lead. Produced by Dynamic Films. Originally distributed by AIMS.
Macmillan 15 min B&W 1953

1262　The Cask of Amontillado. This is an enactment of Edgar Allan Poe's classic tale of suspense and revenge, in which Montresor lures Fortunato to his death in a walled-in wine cellar. From the *On Stage* series, with actor Monty Wooley. Produced by Dynamic Films.
Macmillan　15 min　B&W　1954

1263　Chaucer's England. After a brief segment of original Chaucerian language, this film presents a dramatization of the complete "Pardoner's Tale" as translated into verse by Theodore Morrison. Produced in England, with British actors directed by John Barnes.
Encyc. Brit.　34 min　Color　1958

1264　Chickamauga. This nonverbal adaptation of Ambrose Bierce's short story creates a symbolic world of the horror of war. A boy wanders away from home, reaches a battlefield, plays a soldier among the dead and dying, then returns home to find his home burned and his family slain. A Contemporary Films release. Produced by Robert Enrico.
McGraw-Hill　33 min　B&W　1963

1265　A Christmas Carol. This is a musical version of the Dickens short story. Its libretto was written by playwright Maxwell Anderson, with the score by Bernard Hermann. The lead actors are veterans Fredric March and Basil Rathbone. Produced by CBS Television.
Carousel　54 min　B&W　1956

1266　A Christmas Carol. Basil Rathbone heads the British cast of this classic Christmas tale of the moral regeneration of the miserly Scrooge. A Perspective Film. Produced by Desmond Davis in association with the Dickensian Society (London).
Coronet　24½ min　B&W　1962

1267　A Christmas Carol. A retelling of the ageless Dickens favorite about the miser who had no room in his heart for his fellow man until Christmas taught him the value of love and friendship. Reginald Owen plays Scrooge. Produced by Metro-Goldwyn-Mayer. Directed by Edwin L. Marin.
Films Inc.　42 min　B&W　1938

1268　A Christmas Carol. Dickens' poignant Victorian tale comes alive in this animated film, with Sir Michael Redgrave as narrator, and with Alistair Sim providing the voice of Scrooge—the role with which that actor is most closely associated. (Note: This is not a live-action production.)
Xerox Films　26 min　Color　1971

1269　A Christmas Carol with Mr. Magoo. The cartoon character, with Jim Backus providing the voice, plays the role of Scrooge in this version of Dickens' seasonal story. Original music is by Julie Stein and Bob

Merrill, with other vocal characterizations by Jack Cassidy and Morey Amsterdam. Produced by Lee Orgel. Director: Abe Levitow.
Macmillan 60 min Color

1270 Christmas Slippers. Excerpts from the operetta *Cherevichki* (by Tchaikovsky) musically recount a Russian folktale. Vakula, the blacksmith, is told by Oxana that she will marry him if he brings her the most beautiful slippers in the world. Based on the story by Nikolai Gogol. Featuring the chorus and orchestra of the Bolshoi Theatre. Songs in Russian, with English subtitles.
Macmillan 32 min B&W 1946

1271 A Circle in the Fire. The security of a farm is shattered by a visit from three vaguely unsettling teenaged boys. Jealous of the farm's tranquility and challenged by the smugness, they set about destroying what they cannot possess, first through petty vandalism, finally through downright maliciousness. A young daughter starts out as mere witness to events, but is finally engulfed into them — along with her mother and the hired woman. Based on the short story by Flannery O'Connor. Filmmaker: Victor Nunez.
Perspective 49½ min Color 1976

1272 The Colt. This film is based on a story by Mikhail Sholokov, author of *And Quiet Flows the Don*. At the height of the Russian Civil War, Trofim, a cavalryman, is ordered to destroy a colt. He cannot bring himself to do this. When the squadron goes into action again, the colt trails along, and finds itself in enemy territory. Trofim gives up his life to save the colt. Before he dies, he sees the colt running to its mother. Directed by Vladimir Fetin. Russian dialogue with English subtitles.
Macmillan 42 min B&W 1960

1273 The Comforts of Home. This enactment, adapted from Flannery O'Connor's short story, is a psychological drama of three family members doomed by their own perversions. Nudity, strong language, and the theme itself call for relatively mature audiences. Produced by Leonard Lipson and Jerome Shore.
Phoenix 40 min Color 1974

1274 The Coup de Grace. This story by Ambrose Bierce gives insights into the Civil War but, more than that, it raises questions about friendship and the frustration experienced by individuals caught in the midst of combat. Produced by Zack and Karen Taylor.
Barr Films 19 min Color 1978

1275 The Cricket on the Hearth. Animated film based on the Christmas story by Charles Dickens. A poor toymaker and his beautiful daughter Bertha are rescued from the evil Gruff Tackleton by an unusual

cricket. The cricket foils Gruff's scheme to marry Bertha. At considerable risk to its own life, it reunites Bertha with her fiancé, whom she had believed to be lost at sea. Narrated by Danny Thomas.
Macmillan 57 min Color 1969

1276 The Cricket on the Hearth. This segment from Dickens' "other" Christmas story is one of the early narrative productions of a serious nature. Directed by silent-movie innovator D.W. Griffith of *Birth of a Nation* fame.
Pyramid 10 min B&W 1909

1277 The Crocodile. Green and slimy, the crocodile stretches its jaws and swallows Ivan Matveyevitch. What's more, Ivan refuses to come out. "This is utopia!", he cries from within the creature's belly. "I always thought this would happen to him," remarks Ivan's superior. An absurd fantasy? A satire on 19th-century Russia? A pessimistic statement on progress? Viewers can draw their own conclusions from this dramatization of the short story by Dostoyevsky. Producer: Larry Yust.
Encyc. Brit. 29 min Color 1973

1278 The Crocodile (A Discussion). A companion film to the Dostoyesky story, with commentary written and presented by Clifton Fadiman, noted literary scholar. Fadiman reviews the author's characterizations, the acting techniques, and some production decisions. Part of the *Short Story Showcase* series from the *Humanities* program.
Encyc. Brit. 11 min Color 1973

1279 David Swan. This is the story of the "non-events" in a young man's journey in late 18th-century America. While awaiting the stagecoach to Boston, David falls asleep by the road and has three encounters which, had he been awake, would have changed his life. A wealthy merchant couple would have adopted him, a beautiful young woman would have given him her love, and two robbers would have killed him. He finally awakes to the sound of the approaching stage and completes his journey—none the wiser for his threefold brush with fate. Based on the short story by Nathaniel Hawthorne. Produced by Galen Films.
Perspective 23 min Color 1977

1280 Day Dreams. Charles Laughton and Elsa Lanchester star in this pre-sound satire about a servant woman's visions of grandeur. It is based on a story by H.G. Wells. Director: Ivor Montagu. (This is a silent film production.)
Macmillan 23 min B&W 1928

1281 The Dead Bird. From the short story of the same name, by Margaret Wise Brown. The theme of the film lends itself to a discussion about the naturalness of death, leading to appraisal of the essential values

in living. Produced by Moreland-Latchford, Ltd. (Canada).
Paramount 13 min Color 1973

1282 The Death of Ivan Ilych. This dramatization of Leo Tolstoy's short story is told in the person of the sufferer. Examining his life for "reasons" for his agony, the dying man is devastated by the possibility that his entire existence may lack meaning. Clinging desperately to each new medicine, and each brief respite from pain, Ivan grows paranoid and wildly accuses his doctor and his own family of lying to him. The dramatization, performed for a group of seriously ill patients, evokes in discussion important echoes of its protagonist's experience. Produced by Jeffrey Weber for United Methodist Communications in cooperation with KERA-TV.
Mass Media 28 min Color

1283 Desire to Sleep. A young woman, working as a servant and governess, is driven to sleeplessness by her mistress's demands and the crying of the baby. As insomnia pushes her to the breaking point, she begins to hallucinate, then strangles the child in her desperate attempt at relief. From the story by Chekhov.
Macmillan 14 min BW

1284 The Displaced Person. The subject refers to a World War II Polish refugee whom a Georgia priest brings in as a worker for a local farm. The Pole's efficiency, hard work, and high intelligence pose a threat to his coworkers. His life and death makes everyone, in different ways, a "displaced person" too. Story by Flannery O'Connor. Director: Glenn Jordan.
Perspective 57½ min Color 1977

1285 Dr. Heidegger's Experiment. This dramatization is based on the short story about the scientist who sought to discover a formula to achieve perpetual youth. It correlates with other works by Nathaniel Hawthorne because this short story deals with two of his favorite themes: the consequences of tampering with nature, and the perils of rejecting conventional morality. From the *Humanities* series. Producer: Larry Yust.
Encyc. Brit. 22 min Color 1969

1286 Dr. Heidegger's Experiment. Nathaniel Hawthorne's symbolic story of the search for the elixir of youth, set in a doctor's study in 19th-century New England. With actor Monty Wooley playing the lead role, this is one of 13 productions in the *On Stage* series. Produced by Dynamic Films.
Macmillan 15 min B&W 1954

1287 The Dot and the Line. This animation is a fantasy fable about love among geometric figures. It can also, on another level, serve as a

discussion-starter on questions of personal relationships and conformity. Recipient of an Academy Award. Produced by MGM. From the line-drawing story by Norton Juster.
Films Inc. 9 min Color 1965

1288 Dylan Thomas' A Child's Christmas in Wales. Still photographs of the people of Wales create a visual treatment of this Christmas story written and recited by Dylan Thomas. Directed by Marvin Lichtner. A Contemporary Films release.
McGraw-Hill 26 min B&W 1962

1289 An Energy Carol. This is an animated rendition of the Dickens classic, *A Christmas Carol*. In it, Ebenezer Scrooge is not a self-employed merchant but president of the Zeus Energy Co. corporation and is conducted by the Spirit of Future Energy on a tour of tomorrow's world.
Nat. Film Bd. 11 min Color 1975

1290 Exit 10. This is a romance adapted from Katherine Mansfield's short story, *Bliss*. In it, a young lawyer who had traded the pleasures of bachelorhood for those of marriage, begins to discover his deeper emotions. His attempts at expressing these feelings to his wife and a mysterious friend lead him into an unexpected situation. Produced by Terry Kemper. Directed by Stephen Gyllenhaal.
Phoenix Films 35 min Color 1978

1291 The Fall of the House of Usher. This American avant-garde silent film was influenced by *The Cabinet of Dr. Caligari*. It features expressionistic settings, combined with imaginative trick photography. Analyzed in detail by Lewis Jacobs in his book, *Experiment in the Film*. Based on Edgar Allan Poe's classic story. Produced by James Sibley Watson and Melville Webber with music by Alec Wilder.
Creative Film 12 min B&W 1928

1292 The Fall of the House of Usher. Shadows of blue, green, and violet permeate this dramatization of Poe's gothic tale of horror. Music creates a sense of suspense as events surrounding the mysterious Usher twins—the last survivors of an ancient family—build to a violent climax. From the *Short Story Showcase* series of the *Humanities* program. Producer: Guerdon Trueblood.
Encyc. Brit. 30 min Color 1975

1293 The Family That Dwelt Apart. This tall and salty Yankee story about a family done in by do-gooders is narrated by the author, E.B. White. Yvon Mallette's animation matches the humor of this black comedy from the National Film Board of Canada.
Learning Corp. 8 min Color 1974

1294 The Father. This adaptation of Chekhov's short story, *Grief*, dramatizes the lot of an old man who, so alienated by his miserable life in a big city, is not even able to share his sorrow over the death of his son. A live-action production, featuring Burgess Meredith.
New Line Cinema 28 min B&W 1970

1295 The Forgotten Village. In this John Steinbeck story, Juan, a young Mexican peasant, faces superstitious resistance to medical treatment for his brother's colitis. Even his own father joins the rest of the townspeople in condemning Juan's belief in modern cures. This leads to the youth's determination to become a doctor. Narration by Burgess Meredith. Also available in Spanish. Directed by Herbert Kline and Alexander Hammid.
Macmillan 60 min B&W 1941

1296 For the Love of Gold. Based on Jack London's story, "Just Meat," this vintage silent movie is about two thieves who poison each other over stolen money. Filmed without sub-titles, and directed by D.W. Griffith.
Pyramid 10 min B&W 1908

1297 From Every Shires Ende: The World of Chaucer's Pilgrims. This is a re-enactment of a 14th-century pilgrimage to Canterbury Cathedral and the shrine of Thomas Becket. References to characters of Chaucer are paralled by authentic medieval music. A detailed study-guide itemizes locations, related artwork, and bibliography. Produced by Mary Kirby and Naomi Diamond.
Int. Film Bureau 38 min Color 1968

1298 The Fugitive. A boy of seven, living in a remote village, becomes sick. He is brought to a hospital where, for the first time, he meets elderly and terminally ill people. Frightened by these faces of death, he runs away. After a night of terror in the woods, he's found and returned to the hospital where a kindly doctor reverses his attitudes toward the institution and its occupants. Story by Anton Chekhov.
Macmillan 15 min BW

1299 A Fuzzy Tale. Adapted from the original story by Claude Steiner, this animation is about the basic human need for warm relationships, and what happens when they are missing. The film shows that superficial relationships and "things" are poor substitutes for unselfish sharing in everyday life. Artwork is by Howard Beckerman. Music is composed by Jay Lee and Bert Alcantara. Vocalist: Emme Kemp. Produced by United Methodist Communications.
Mass Media 12 min Color 1976

1300 A Game of Catch. This film enactment depicts Richard Wilbur's story of a boy who wants to join in a game of catch but is not accepted.

Sulking, he tries to gain advantages by claiming that he "made" the other two do what they did. He is shaken down from his perch in a tree by one of the angered pair and, as he lies wounded on the ground, he calls to the parting boys, "I want you to do whatever you're going to do for the rest of your life." Produced by Witty-Siris.
Macmillan 7 min Color 1972

1301 The Garden Party. Katherine Mansfield's short story is here dramatized and re-set in post-World War II New England. The reactions of a young woman's first exposure to death can provide a springboard for discussion of that sensitive subject. A Gurian/Sholder production for ACI Media.
Paramount 24 min Color 1974

1302 The Gift. This is the story of a 12-year-old boy who, in the Depression of the 1930's, has only 39 cents to buy a Christmas present for his dad. Disappointed in being able to afford only a tie, he decides to get up early Christmas morning and do all the farm chores before his father awakens. His simple act of service provides his father with a gift never to be forgotten. Based on the story by Pearl Buck.
Brigham Young 18 min Color 1978

1303 The Gift of the Magi. This excerpt from the Hollywood feature film, *O. Henry's Full House*, dramatizes the story of the improverished husband and wife who sacrifice their most prized possessions to buy Chiristmas gifts for each other. Directed by Henry King. Originally distributed by Teaching Film Custodians, in cooperation with the National Council of Teachers of English.
Indiana U. 20 min B&W 1952

1304 The Happy Failure. Herman Melville's story about the old man who learns from his nephew that material success is less important than happiness. From the *On Stage* series, with Monty ("The Man Who Came to Dinner") Wooley. Produced by Dynamic Films.
Macmillan 15 min B&W 1954

1305 Her One True Love. Performances by Kate Reid and John Horton enliven this Maxim Gorky story. Aging, illiterate Mae tries to fill the void in her life by entertaining gentlemen callers. Her rooming-house neighbor, John, lives in equally desperate ways. When she seeks his help in writing a letter to an imaginary lover, a tragically brief moment of understanding and happiness emerges. Director: Henry Comor. Producer: Bruce Raymond. Music by Franz Schubert.
Learning Corp. 24 min Color 1977

1306 The Hunt. Two men on a hunting trip find their weekend going sour when one of them discovers that he doesn't enjoy shooting at

animals. His companion leaves him in disgust. He meets an older hunter so jaded with killing that the only prize he yearns for is human prey. The pursuit that follows is a cliffhanger, until the victim escapes – a shaken but wiser man. Adapted from *The Most Dangerous Game* by Richard Connell.
Encyc. Brit. 30 min Color 1972

1307 Ice Storm. A librarian turned detective must pit her wits against an unknown killer. As assistant to the owner of a priceless book collection, she finds herself alone in her employer's mansion during a storm. Three visitors come to buy rare books. One is an imposter who will kill to get a share of the collection. By using her research skills, she unmasks the killer – just in time. Dramatization based on the mystery by Jerome Barry. Introduced by Orson Welles. Producer: Alan Gibson.
Encyc. Brit. 25 min Color 1975

1308 I'm a Fool. The title represents the final lines of Sherwood Anderson's story about a young man's discovery of romance on the Ohio racetrack circuit in the early 1900's. To impress a young lady, he leads her to believe he's a horse breeder instead of a stable hand. When it comes time to exchange addresses, his deception costs him any chance of ever seeing her again. Featured actor is Ron ("Happy Days") Howard. Director: Noel Black.
Perspective 38 min Color 1977

1309 The Ingenious Reporter. A brash American reporter for a Paris scandal sheet devises a way to improve circulation. Learning of a murder in which neither the victim nor the killer has been identified, he decides to pose as the suspect, get arrested, and slip out after his paper exploits the promotional possibilities. But the victim is identified as the reporter's sweetheart, and no one will believe his story. After the reporter's tragic end, his editor receives a visitor – and a surprising jolt! Dramatization based on the mystery by Pontsevrez.
Encyc. Brit. 25 min Color 1975

1310 The Inspiration of Mr. Budd. A meek barber meets adventure when a fierce-looking, red-haired man demands his hair be dyed. A newspaper account of a savage murder confirms the barber's suspicions. Nervous, yet feeling obliged to turn the suspect in, he dyes the hair brown, but with a slow-working chemical that gradually turns it green. The barber's cunning simplifies later police identification and, in a surprise ending, earns him a fortune. Dramatization based on the mystery of Dorothy L. Sayers. Introduction by Orson Welles.
Encyc. Brit. 25 min Color 1975

1311 In the Region of Ice. A young nun-teacher is intrigued by a brilliant but erratic student in her college literature class. Later in their

platonic relationship, when he is deeply troubled at events within his home life, he comes to her for money to run away. Whether she provides it is open to interpretation, as is the question: Did she hasten or delay his death shortly after? Author: Joyce Carol Oates. Produced by Peter Werner and Andre Guttfreund.
Phoenix 38 min B&W 1976

1312 Isaac Singer's Nightmare & Mrs. Pupko's Beard. Pupko, a Yiddish writer married to a woman with a beard, invests in the stock market and becomes rich. Pupko wants Isaac Singer to write about him, but Singer refuses because Pupko bribes critics. Pupko becomes ill and Mrs. Pupko arrives for a confrontation with Singer. Singer moves in and out of his own short story in a film that is both scripted and spontaneous. Shot mostly in his New York apartment, it captures the author in light moments. Directed by still-photographer Bruce Davidson. Based on "The Beard" by Isaac Bashevis Singer.
New Yorker 30 min Color 1972

1313 The Island. This mystery by L.P. Hartley stars British actor John Hunt as a young World War I army officer. Setting out on his affair with the beautiful and wealthy Mrs. Santander, he arrives at her desert-island mansion ... only to become the victim of a shocking and unsuspected trap. Directed by Robert Fuest.
Learning Corp. 30 min Color 1977

1314 Jack London's To Build a Fire. This interpretation of London's classic story dramatizes man's confrontation with nature at its most dangerous: coldness that seems to chill the very center of the body. Produced by Robert Stitzel.
BFA Educ. Media 14 min Color 1975

1315 James Thurber's The Night the Ghost Got In. Young James Thurber was bathing late one night and thought he heard a noise. He told his brother, who told his mother, who misunderstood. Before it was over, doors were broken, the police arrived and shots were fired. The hilarious chain of events may lead viewers to ponder the vagaries of human communication. This story is an episode from Thurber's autobiography *My Life and Hard Times*. A Robert Stitzel TBF Production.
BFA Educ. Media 15½ min Color 1976

1316 Jolly Corner. Arthur Barron directed and adapted this Henry James tale about an American who fled from the Civil War and, 35 years later, returned to New York whose commercialism attracts and repels him. Features the acting of Fritz Weaver and Salome Jens. Executive Producer: Robert Geller. Funded by the National Endowment for the Humanities.
Perspective 42 min Color 1977

1317 The Juggler of Notre Dame. This adaptation of the Anatole France story is about a good-hearted but poor little juggler. Using puppet-animation, the film tells the classic story of how the penniless performer gave a gift — his juggling skills — to the Holy Family. Producer: Thomas Craven.
Pyramid 30 min Color 1972

1318 The Juggler of Our Lady. This is a cartoon version of the Anatole France story about the poor monk whose only Christmas gift to the Virgin Mary is his love and his art of juggling. Produced by Terrytoons, a division of CBS Films.
Carousel 9 min Color 1961

1319 Just Lather, That's All. This short story by Hernando Tellez is about a Latin American army captain who casually stops in for a shave. As the only customer there, he speaks freely about his seeking, torturing and killing of revolutionaries ... dangerous information to share with this particular barber. This dramatization can stimulate discussion on issues such as revenge and justice. Directed by John Sebert.
Learning Corp. 21 min Color 1974

1320 The Lady, or the Tiger? This 1882 classic by Frank Stockton has been re-set in the space age, preserving the suspense of the original, but adding helicopters, sports cars, penthouses, and other contemporary touches. From the *Short Story Showcase* series.
Encyc. Brit. 16 min Color 1970

1321 The Lady or the Tiger? Dramatization of Frank Stockton's unresolved tale of two doors — one offering freedom and a lady, the other a tiger and certain death. Produced as a short subject by Metro-Goldwyn-Mayer.
Films Inc. 10 min B&W 1942

1322 La Grande Breteche. This tale of revenge is set in France during the Napoleonic wars. On a visit to his wife's bedroom, a count finds signs of a visitor. Suspecting a lover hiding in the closet, he tricks his wife into swearing the closet is empty. Pretending to believe her, he proceeds to have the closet sealed up behind a brick wall ... while his wife looks on in horror. Dramatization based on the short story by Balzac. Introduction by Orson Welles.
Encyc. Brit. 24 min Color 1975

1323 La Peau De Chagrin. This animation is taken from Balzac's fantasy in which a gambler makes a pact with the devil for a magic skin that will fulfill his every desire. Ironically, after his last wish is granted, the skin grows smaller and smaller until it's blown away like a flimsy scrap of leather. Codirected by Vlado Kristi and Ivo Urbanic. A Contemporary

Films release.
McGraw-Hill 10 min Color 1971

1324 The Last Leaf. This excerpt from the Hollywood feature film, *O. Henry's Full House*, dramatizes the story of a painter's sacrifice to keep a young invalid alive. Introduced by John Steinbeck. Directed by Jean Negulesco. Selected by the National Council of Teachers of English. Originally distributed by Teaching Film Custodians.
Indiana U. 20 min B&W 1952

1325 The Legend of Sleepy Hollow. Bing Crosby narrates and sings in this animated version of Washington Irving's classic. In it, Ichabod Crane, as the new teacher in a Hudson River village, charms the local ladies. But a slighted suitor resents his intrusions and, with a wild tale about a Headless Horseman, rids himself of his rival.
Disney 20 min Color 1949

1326 The Legend of Sleepy Hollow. This early American folktale by Washington Irving comes to life with the animated figure of Ichabod Crane. Provides insights into superstitions that haunted the drowsy Dutch town, while retaining the original language of Irving. Narrator: actor John Carradine. Animation by Stephen Bosustow.
Pyramid 13 min Color 1972

1327 The Lightning-Rod Man. This version of Herman Melville's short story consists of a debate between a lightning-rod salesman and a country gentleman. They symbolize through their words and actions the forces of fear against those of faith. Background music by Johann Sebastian Bach. Producer: John DeChancie.
Pyramid 16 min Color 1975

1328 The Little Story. In this animated fantasy, a little orphan gets his Christmas wish and is literally flattened by goodies raining down from the sky. Based on a short story by Ambrose Bierce. Directed by Jacques Colombat. Produced by Films Paul Grimault (France).
Films, Inc. 6 min Color 1969

1329 The Lost Phoebe. Unable to accept the fact of his wife's death, an old man lives in a world of memories. Neighbors and friends are sympathetic, but their efforts to help are rejected. Continually searching for his dead Phoebe, the old man's inability to face reality finally results in his own death. Adapted from Theodore Dreiser's short story. Produced by the American Film Institute. Screenplay and direction by Mel Damski.
Perspective 30 min Color 1977

1330 The Lottery. This is Shirley Jackson's realistic fiction about the warped sense of justice in a contemporary American town. It is designed

to stimulate discussion about society and individual rights. The violent finale may be objectionable; it would be wise to preview. Film-maker: Larry Yust. From the *Short Story Showcase* series.
Encyc. Brit. 18 min Color 1970

1331 The Maid of Thilouse. Honoré de Balzac's story of an elderly baron who seeks the hand of a young peasant but in the end settles for her mother instead. Enacted by Monty Wooley and a professional cast. From the *On Stage* series produced by Dynamic Films.
Macmillan 15 min B&W 1954

1332 The Man and the Snake. Loosely based on Ambrose Bierce's tale of psychological horror. This is a story of the conflict in a man's mind, the unsettling struggle between the common sense of day and the subtle abduction of the mind by the eerie effects of nightfall. Produced by Elizabeth McKay.
Pyramid 26 min Color 1975

1333 The Mannikin. This story of the supernatural by Robert Bloch (author of *Psycho*) is the basis for this picture about a woman singer who is tormented by oddly recurring back pains. Relief comes only when she revisits her former home and resumes the bizarre rituals conducted there. It becomes gradually clear she is possessed by a demon that is seeking to control her body. Starring are Ronee Blakley and Keir (*2001*) Dullea. Directed by Don Thompson.
Learning Corp. 28 min Color 1977

1334 The Man Without a Country. This is a dramatization of Edward Everett Hale's short story of U.S. Naval lieutenant Philip Nolan who was punished for denouncing America by being forbidden ever to return to it. Released by Bing Crosby Productions.
McGraw-Hill 25 min B&W 1955

1335 Martin the Cobbler. This is the Russian Folktale, "Where Love Is, God Is," by Leo Tolstoy. It's about a shoemaker who discovers new meaning in life by meditating on old truths. Especially suitable for holiday seasons such as Christmas, Thanksgiving, and Easter. Introduced and narrated by Tolstoy's daughter, Alexandra. Clay animation by Will Vinton.
Billy Budd 27½ min Color 1976

1336 The Masque of the Red Death. This is a nonverbal version of Poe's masterpiece of irony and terror. Its hand-painted animation, sound-effects, and music impart the story of the Count whose wealth was unable to keep the plague from his castle. Film-artists Pavao Stalter and Vladimir Jutrisa hand-painted each frame of this Zagreb (Yugoslavia) production.
McGraw-Hill 10 min Color 1970

1337 May Night. A Ukrainian legend, this operetta combines the fantastic and the real. Peasant girls, their work over, gather in the orchard of Panko, the bee-keeper, to hear him tell a story. Directed by Alexander Rou. Based on the story, *The Drowned Maiden*, by Gogol. Russian dialogue with English subtitles.
Macmillan 58 min B&W 1952

1338 A Message to Garcia. This film is from the *Calvacade of America* series, originally produced for early television programming. It dramatizes the Elbert Hubbard inspirational essay that reads like a short story of the heroic mission that enabled American troops to land in Cuba without casualties during the Spanish-American War. Previously distributed by Teaching Film Custodians.
Indiana U. 20 min B&W 1955

1339 The Metamorphosis of Mr. Samsa. Sand animation on glass reinterprets Franz Kafka's *The Metamorphosis*. Unusual sound effects and artwork combine nonverbally to suggest a typically Kafkaesque world of alienation and guilt. Produced by Caroline Leaf. Awarded the Critics' Prize at the International Animated Film Festival in Annecy, France.
Nat. Film Board 9¾ min Color 1977

1340 A Miserable Merry Christmas. Based on a chapter from *The Autobiography of Lincoln Steffens*, this film raises the question about the spirit and values of Christmas. One year, young Steffens wanted a pony. His sister's stocking was bulging with gifts on Christmas morning, but his was empty. Everyone was miserable. Hours later the pony arrived. As an adult, he was asked whether that Christmas had been the best or worst in his life. He wrote, "I think it was both. It covered the whole distance from broken-hearted misery to bursting happiness—too fast." A production of WNET-TV (New York).
Encyc. Brit. 15 min Color 1973

1341 Mr. Frenhofer and the Minotaur. This surrealist interpretation of Balzac's story, *The Unknown Masterpiece*, is also an oblique and prophetic discourse on modern art. Commentary is delivered in the style of a James Joyce interior monologue.
Grove Press 21 min B&W

1342 Mr. Magoo's Christmas Carol (Complete). That lovable cartoon grouch, Magoo, becomes Scrooge in this production of the Charles Dickens story. The voice of Jim Backus adds a humorous touch to the script. This UPA animation is also available in a 28-minute version (below).
Mar/Chuck Film 52 min Color 1975

1343 Mr. Magoo's Christmas Carol (Abbrev.). This is the 28-minute

version of the full-length edition, featuring the cartoon character as Scrooge. Voice: Jim Backus. Produced by UPA. Also available in the complete 52-minute edition (above).
Mar/Churck Film 28 min Color 1975

1344 Mrs. Amworth. Glynis Johns plays the title role of E.F. Benson's tale of the occult in which a mysterious epidemic attacks a quiet English village. One of the townspeople, a former physiology professor, diagnoses the malady as the work of a vampire. Suspicious of a glamorous new resident, the charming Mrs. Amworth, he takes the necessary (if unconventional) steps to destroy the sinister presence among them. Production directed by Alvin Rakoff.
Learning Corp. 29 min Color 1977

1345 The Mockingbird. In this adaptation of the Ambrose Bierce story, a private in the Union Army, while standing night guard, sees a figure, and shoots. Next day, troubled by the experience, he seeks out the corpse, only to learn that the victim is his twin brother in Confederate uniform. In shock, the soldier deserts. No narration or dialogue. Produced by Robert Enrico.
Macmillan 39 min B&W 1967

1346 The Monkey's Paw. In this classic horror story, an old couple have lost their beloved son. The mother will do anything to get him back. But when the father hears the knock at the door, there's a surprise in store. Adapted from the story by W.W. Jacobs. Produced by Martha Moran.
BFA Educ. Media. 19 min Color 1978

1347 A Mother's Tale. "Mama ... where are they going?", a calf's voice asks as cattle move along a hillside. Then the herd is in the valley, going to slaughter. Thus opens this live-action adaptation of James Agee's allegory in which the protagonists are a family of cows. The storyline poses the question of resistance to truth, focusing on the risks of individuality versus the pressure to conform. As such, it also represents the tensions between generations. Though no animals were injured in the making of this film, packing house scenes may be unpleasant to some viewers. Off-screen **voices:** Maureen Stapleton and Orson Welles. Film-maker: Rex Victor Goff.
Learning Corp. 18 min Color 1976

1348 Mousie Baby. The personal side of a strike in a big city advertising agency during the Depression. Betty, a pretty secretary from a Midwest town, imagines herself in love with her boss and dreams of being his wife. When the strike is finally broken, the **boss** threatens each worker with the prospect of being fired. He arrogantly tries to seduce Betty, revealing the true nature of their relationship. Showing new courage and a sense of

self worth, she walks out on her boss and her job. Based on a short story by Tess Slesinger. Produced and directed by Anne Shanks.
Phoenix 25 min Color 1978

1349 The Murderer. This is Ray Bradbury's comic short story of Albert Brock, an individual in a futuristic society immersed in communications devices that relentlessly demand his attention. Fed up with this world of bodiless voices, he decides to liberate society by simply "turning them off." The resulting havoc brings down the forces of "justice." Produced and directed by Andrew Silver.
Phoenix 28 min Color 1976

1350 The Music School. In a visit to his daughter's music school, a contemporary writer searches out the meaning of life. His existence lacks the balance and order of hers, in spite of his efforts to draw vital parallels from religion, technology, and social structures. Author: John Updike. Adapted and directed by John Korty. Produced by Robert Geller with funding by the National Endowment for the Humanities.
Perspective 30 min Color 1977

1351 My Dear Uncle Sherlock. A boy solves a neighborhood mystery, thanks to his training by an amateur sleuth uncle. From the ABC *Weekend Special* series. Adapted from the short story by Hugh Pentecost.
ABC Learning 24 min Color 1978

1352 My Financial Career. An example of the humorous essay, Stephen Leacock's tale of the reluctant depositor is animated in a style that complements the narrative. Students of English will see how a writer is able to take a simple experience and, with the tools of wit and exaggeration, build it into a story. Producer: National Film Board of Canada.
Sterling Educ. 7 min Color 1961

1353 My Old Man. Ernest Hemingway's short story about a butler and his conflict between accepting reality and preserving illusions. The film was produced in Paris, using racetrack scenes as background. From the EBE *Humanities* series.
Encyc. Brit. 27 min Color 1971

1354 The Necklace. Staged in the period of French author Guy de Maupassant (1850-1893), the story involves a young woman born into poverty. In an era when social class was of utmost importance, she had no possibility of overcoming the barriers of humble birth and marriage. Circumstances offer her an opportunity to break out of her oppressed state but consequences present a crushing irony. Produced by Mark Baer and Mark O'Kane.
Film Fair 23½ min Color 1979

1355 The New York Hat. This is the Anita Loos story of a young woman from a small town, a gift of a new hat, and the gossip it created. Old time silent actors include Mary Pickford, Lionel Barrymore, Mack Sennet, Lillian and Dorthy Gish – all directed by D.W. Griffith. Originally released by Biograph Studios as a silent movie production.
Film Images 9 min B&W 1912

1356 Next Door. An eight-year-old boy, left home alone one night, over-hears a lovers' quarrel. Though he doesn't actually see the antagonists, he can hear them clearly. Becoming upset over the argument, he tries to bring about peace between the pair of voices, but his interference results in a typical Kurt Vonnegut climax. Producer: Andrew Silver.
Phoenix 30 min Color 1975

1357 Nine and a Girl. This is a dramatization of Maxim Gorky's classic short story, set in turn-of-the-century Russia. It presents a *Lady or the Tiger* situation concerning the behavior of a young woman admired by nine bakers who make a bet about her morality. The conclusion is open-ended. Adult material: best to preview. Film-maker: Mike Weiskopf.
Viewfinders 24 min B&W 1974

1358 The Nose. This is Gogol's classic Russian short story produced in pin-board animation by Alexander Alexeiff. A Contemporary Films release. Formerly available from McGraw-Hill.
Cecile Starr 11 min B&W 1963

1359 An Occurrence at Owl Creek Bridge. This classic nonverbal production is based on Ambrose Bierce's story. It recreates the atmosphere of our Civil War in which a Confederate soldier is being hanged as a spy. At the climax of his apparent execution, does he miraculously escape? Or is his race for freedom the final fantasy of a mind that's facing death? Film-maker: Robert Enrico (France). Winner of many international film festival awards.
McGraw-Hill 27 min BW 1962

1360 One of the Missing. Filmed "on location," this is the Civil War story of a sniper who finds himself pinned down after an explosion, with his own rifle pointed between his eyes. The slightest movement will set the hair-triggered weapon off. As he tries to free himself, his life flashes before him, reminding him of the evil he has done. Choked with fear of a hopeless situation, he performs his final act of cowardice ... the ironically shocking last scene. Based on Ambrose Bierce.
Educ. Communications 52 min Color 1976

1361 The Open Window. An adaption of Saki's classic Japanese ghost story with subtle humor and ironic twist. The characters in this live-action

production are a self-possessed young lady, a nervous visitor, and ghosts from the bogs beyond the open window. Produced by Richard Patterson with financial help from the American Film Institute.
Pyramid 12 min Color 1972

1362 The Pardoner's Tale. Chaucer's short story from *The Canterbury Tales* is about three men who are brought to their death by their greed and distrust of their fellow man. From the *On Stage* series with actor Monty Wooley. Produced by Dynamic Films.
Macmillan 15 min B&W 1954

1363 Parker Adderson, Philosopher. This story, by Ambrose Bierce, is a study of man's understanding of death. A Union spy is caught behind Confederate lines, and, when brought before the commanding general, glibly projects death as painless spiritual transition. The general, more experienced, thinks otherwise. The difference in their reasoning forms the unraveling of the personal drama. Directed by Per O. Loseth.
Film Images 20 min Color 1970

1364 Parker Adderson, Philosopher. This version of the Ambrose Bierce short story reflects the author's personal involvement in the Civil War in which he fought and was wounded. Produced by Robert Geller, funded by the National Endowment for the Humanities, and directed by Arthur Barron.
Perspective 39 min Color 1977

1365 The Perfect Tribute. Dramatization of Mary Shipman Andrews' story of Lincoln's trip to Gettysburg, and his disappointment at the reception given his speech. His later conversation with a wounded Confederate soldier, who repeats the Address, revives Lincoln's spirits. Produced by Metro-Goldwyn-Mayer.
Films Inc. 19 min B&W 1935

1366 The Pit and the Pendulum. Three-dimensional characters, made out of plasticene, perform this version of Poe's classic tale. Although this production bears only a loose similarity to the original story, it manages to retain the theme of evil vs. evil, while satirizing some of the poet's more grotesque imagery.
Canadian Film 10 min Color 1975

1367 The Portable Phonograph. This "doomsday" science fiction centers around the last earthly possessions of four men, sharing but still competing right to the end. It incorporates the music of Claude Debussy's "Nocturne" both for content and for mood. From the story by Walter Van Tilburg Clark. Produced by John Barnes.
Encyc. Brit. 24 min Color 1977

1368 The Queen of Spades. This is Alexander Pushkin's story of a struggling clerk whose eagerness for success at gambling forces a supernatural secret out of an elderly countess. After her death, she proves his undoing. From the *On Stage* series with actor Monty Wooley. Produced by Dynamic Films.
Macmillan 15 min B&W 1957

1369 The Ransom of Red Chief. A couple of shabby and somewhat inept con men figure that kidnapping the banker's son in a sleepy Alabama town will be easy money. But the boy throws himself into the adventure, becoming "Red Chief, terror of the plains." Driven to distraction by the boy's antics, they cut short the kidnapping and, in a final twist, find the tables are turned. Based on the O. Henry short story. Directed by Tony Bill.
Learning Corp. 27 min Color 1978

1370 The Red Kite. From a collection of short stories by Hugh Hood. The setting for this one is Montreal, and the story is about a kite a man buys for his daughter. This mildly impulsive act leads to encounters with strangers that cause him to wonder about the purpose and meaning of life. Produced for the National Film Board of Canada by Morton Parker.
Wombat 17 min Color 1966

1371 Rescue Party. Viewers join a spaceship of alien races diverted to Earth to rescue its inhabitants, thought doomed by the imminent explosion of the sun. The rescue party finds Earth abandoned and its populace emigrating in a huge but primitive space fleet. The aliens decide to contact Earth's émigrés, while audiences ponder how and why the rescuers may later regret their decision. Story by Arthur C. Clarke, screenplay writer of *2001: A Space Odyssey*. A Bernard Wilets Production.
BFA Educ. Media. 20½ min Color 1978

1372 The Return. This adaptation relates to two different short stories: "The Middle Toe of the Right Foot" by Ambrose Bierce and "Nobody's House" by A.M. Burrage. As interwoven by film-maker Elizabeth McKay, it takes place in turn-of-the-century England. The suspense builds up around rumors of the appearance of a woman's ghost that leads an interested party, one evening, to a boarded up mansion. There, armed with a gun, he shuts himself up in the wedding chamber, and waits ... and waits ... and waits.
Pyramid 30 min Color 1975

1373 Revenge. A jealous husband goes to buy a revolver to use against his wife's lover. But, as the gun salesman waxes eloquent over the killing force of the weapon, the husband realizes that a prison sentence would only free his wife for more flirtations. Embarrassed at his change of mind,

he makes a token purchase instead. Adapted from a story by Chekhov.
Macmillan   26 min   B&W

1374 Right Thumb, Left Thumb. When little Victor has to go to the store for the first time, his mother ties a string around his right thumb, with instructions to follow in the direction of the thumb with the string. His experiences along the way include the importance of following directions, being able to distinguish right from left, and accepting responsibility. Based on a story by Osmond Molarsky. Produced by Moreland-Latchford, Ltd., Canada.
Paramount   9 min   Color   1972

1375 Rip Van Winkle. New techniques in clay animation give a three-dimensional look to the characters of Washington Irving's Catskill cast. Rip is here portrayed as a free spirit who'd rather tell stories than plow fields. Added to the original tale is a dreamy trip through space and a continuous thread of song and music. Produced by Will Vinton. Narrator: Will Geer.
Billy Budd   27 min   Color   1978

1376 Rip Van Winkle with Mr. Magoo. This is Washington Irving's story with Mr. Magoo as the ne'er-do-well who sleeps for 20 years, during which America changes from a colony to an independent republic. Awakening at last, he is startled to see his beard white, his wife gone, his children grown, and many other changes. Cartoon animation by UPA.
Macmillan   26 min   Color   1964

1377 Rite of Love and Death (Yukoku). Based on one of Yukio Mishima's short stories, *Patriotism*, this picture is about an incident of the pre-Fascist period. A young officer in the elite guard is ordered by the Emperor to execute his peers after an attempted coup. Faced with the conflict of loyalties to Emperor and to comrades in arms, the officer maintains honor in the only way possible for him: hara-kiri. His wife, after watching his agonies, follows suit. Mishima himself played the part of the lieutenant, wrote the script, and directed the production.
Grove Press   21 min   B&W

1378 The Rocking-Horse Winner. This production of D.H. Lawrence's psychological tale stars British actor Kenneth More as the uncle and confidant of a boy whose family problems lead him to develop the strange ability to predict racetrack results. Directed by Peter Medak. Music by Paul Lewis. Design by Disley (*Man For All Seasons*) Jones.
Learning Corp.   30 min   Color   1977

1379 Ronnie's Tune. Ronnie, a teenage suicide, is seen only in flashback and through the eyes of Julie, his 11-year-old cousin. Her happy memories of Ronnie help the family accept its grief. Based on a story by

Suzette Winter. Directed and photographed by Gene Feldman.
Wombat 18 min Color 1978

1380 The Sacrifice. Based on O. Henry's short story, *The Gift of the Magi*, this silent film is about the newlyweds who give up their favorite possessions to buy each other a present. Directed by D.W. (*Birth of a Nation*) Griffith.
Pyramid 10 min B&W 1908

1381 The Scout. A cavalry scout, in an unspecified war, chances upon an enemy soldier in a woods. Though undetected by his prey, the scout passes up an easy kill. Later, the scout is himself killed by a sniper—the very man he has spared. Based on Jack London's short story, *War*. Produced by Goldinger, Bender, and Hoeper.
Wombat 10 min Color 1976

1382 The Secret Sharer. A dramatization of Joseph Conrad's short story of conscience and inner conflict. In a companion 11-minute film, scholar Charles Van Doren reviews the story and raises questions for group discussion. Teacher's guide is available. From the *Short Story Showcase* series.
Encyc. Brit. 30 min Color 1972

1383 The Shadow. No, it's not the old-time radio character. This is a costumed dramatization of Hans Christian Andersen's adult-level classic. Set in early 19th-century Europe, the story is about a moral philosopher whose shadow assumes human form and, as such, tries to dominate the scholar. Its sardonic conclusion provides material for discussion of the concepts of wisdom and happiness. Produced by Leonard S. Berman.
LSB Productions 27 min Color 1976

1384 The Signalman. This is Dicken's tale of the vision of a lonely railroad signalman that foretells disaster and his own death. Monty Wooley, in the lead role, is supported by a cast of professional actors. One of 13 films from the *On Stage* series, produced by Dynamic Films.
Macmillan 15 min B&W 1968

1385 Silent Snow, Secret Snow. Based on Conrad Aiken's poetic short story about a boy who gradually withdraws into his own private world of fantasy. As a fiction artist's description of schizophrenia, the story is an example of personal perception. Photographed by Gene Kearney. Music by George Kleinsinger. Directed by Martin Scorsese.
Macmillan 19 min B&W 1964

1386 Silver Blaze. This mystery by Arthur Conan Doyle involves the theft of a race horse, Silver Blaze, and the unsolved murder of its trainer.

Christopher Plummer stars as Sherlock Holmes, with Thorley Walters as the faithful Dr. Watson. Filmed in the English countryside. Direction by John Davies.
Learning Corp.   31 min   Color   1977

1387 Soldier's Home. This is Ernest Hemingway's story about a veteran who returns to America after World War I, and struggles with a sense of alienation from his family and friends. Executive producer: Robert Geller. Funded by the National Endowment for the Humanities. Director: Robert Young.
Perspective   41½ min   Color   1977

1388 Swan Song. This short story by Anton Chekhov is a vignette of an old actor on a deserted stage, drunkenly reviewing the high and low points of his career and his life. Featured in this 1886 stage adaptation are Richard Kiley as the Actor and Michael Dunn as the Prompter. Released by Cinerep Productions (Houston, Texas).
Carousel   25 min   Color   1970

1389 The Tell-Tale Heart. Edgar Allan Poe's story of the apprentice who killed his master and then was driven to confession by what he thought was the sound of the dead man's beating heart. James Mason is the storyteller-narrator. Produced by Metro-Goldwyn-Mayer. Originally distributed by Teaching Film Custodians.
Films Inc.   20 min   B&W   1953

1390 The Tell-Tale Heart. Through animation of Edgar Allan Poe's tale, this film follows the labyrinth of a tortured mind. The storytelling ability of Poe, his gift for suspense, his knowledge of psychology – all are revealed in this story. James Mason is the narrative voice of the killer. Produced by Stephen Bosustow for United Productions of America.
Learning Corp.   7 min   Color   1962

1391   The Tell-Tale Heart. This dramatization of Edgar Allan Poe's study in psychological suspense features Alex Cord as a manservant and Sam Jaffe as his master. A discussion guide is available. Directed by Steve Carter for the American Film Institute.
Time-Life   26 min   B&W   1973

1392 A Terribly Strange Bed. A young man-about-town patronizes a gambling house for excitement. He wins big but he also drinks too much. A kindly stranger suggests the gambler stay for the night rather than risk being robbed ... even puts him to bed. The kindly concern is a ruse; the bed is an ingenious death trap. Although the young hero escapes, he learns a sobering lesson. Introduced by Orson Welles. Dramatization based on the mystery by Wilkie Collins.
Encyc. Brit.   24 min   Color   1974

1393 The Terribly Strange Bed. This is the Wilkie Collins suspense yarn with a moral. It's about a visitor at an inn who wins money at gambling, and then routs a pair of murderous scoundrels. Features the character-actor Monty (*The Man Who Came to Dinner*) Wooley. From the *On Stage* series, produced by Dynamic Films.
Macmillan 15 min B&W 1954

1394 Thank You, M'am. This enactment is about an encounter between an old black woman and the 10-year-old boy who tries to snatch her purse, only to be disciplined and befriended. Based on a short story by poet Langston Hughes. Directed by Andrew Sugerman.
Phoenix 12 min Color 1976

1395 Three Miraculous Soldiers. What happens when a young woman is forced to see the humanity of both sides in a war? This immersion into Stephen Crane's Civil War story shows how irony emerges from her encounter with both Confederate and Union soldiers. The surprise ending can engage viewers in moral questions related to those raised in *The Red Badge of Courage*, but the focus upon a young woman's viewpoint provides an added dimension. Produced by Bernard Selling.
BFA Educ. Media 17½ min Color 1977

1396 A Time Out of War. Describes a Civil War episode in which two opposing soldiers declare a temporary truce of their own, and relate to each other as human beings. Based on the Robert W. Chambers short story, *Pickets*. Produced by Denis and Terry Sanders. Previously distributed by Churchill Films.
Pyramid 22 min B&W 1954

1397 The Trap of Solid Gold. This is the story of a young executive caught in the trap of living beyond his income. The pressure of this trap finally forces him to find a solution that compromises his plans and goals. His dilemma raises questions of ethics and values within American society. Cast includes Cliff Robertson, Dina Merrill, and Dustin Hoffman. From a story by John D. MacDonald. Directed By Paul Bogart for the American Broadcasting Company.
Int. Film Bureau 51 min B&W 1967

1398 Two Daughters. Adaptation of a much neglected story by August Strindberg. After the death of her daughter, a woman returns to the apartment they had shared. There she is overwhelmed by the memories of her strained relations with her own mother. She wanders aimlessly about Stockholm. Later, when her thoughts are jarred by the raucous behavior of drunkards, she realizes she's still surrounded by life. Swedish soundtrack, with English subtitles. Produced by the University of California (Berkeley).
Extension Media 22 min Color 1976

1399 The Ugly Little Boy. This picture is the first story ever transposed to the screen by science-fiction writer Isaac Asimov. Its plot pits technology against morality in a futuristic world. Kate Reid portrays a nurse in charge of a child who's been retrieved from the Neanderthal age by scientists (led by actor Barry Morse) who ignore the human factor in their experiments. Codirected by Barry Morse and Don Thompson.
Learning Corp. 26 min Color 1977

1400 A Unicorn in the Garden. Based on James Thurber's contemporary fable, this animated story reminds us that other people do not necessarily see things as we do. A man sees a unicorn; his bossy wife sees nothing. What are we to make of people who see, or hear, or think things the rest of us do not? Useful for stimulating discussions of attitudes, behavior, and humor in literature. Produced by William Hurtz. Released by United Productions of America.
Learning Corp. 7 min Color 1969

1401 The Upturned Face. In an unidentified war, a young officer is killed, and two comrades must endure the grief of burying him. Hardest task of all is to shovel soil on his "upturned face." This story was the last one ever written by Stephen Crane who, at the time, was slowly dying of tuberculosis. Filmed by Changeling Productions.
Pyramid 10 min Color 1972

1402 Valentine's Second Chance. Adapted from an O. Henry classic, this is the story of 10-year-old Joe Willie and how he helps to reform the legendary safecracker Jimmy Valentine. From the ABC *Weekend Special* series.
ABC Learning 24 min Color 1978

1403 Volodya. Volodya is a 17-year-old boy who is burdened by the trauma of his father's suicide over his mother's extravagance. Now in love with a flighty newlywed, he is first led on, then finally rejected. Humiliated and frustrated — like his father before him — he, too, takes his own life. Based on the story by Chekhov.
Macmillan 25 min B&W

1404 What Price Education? This variation of Alphonse Daudet's *The Last Lesson* conveys the importance of a good education. As a teacher reads the story, we see a boy attending his last day of school just before the Germans take over his town during the Franco-Prussian War of 1870; at this moment, he realizes he has wasted his time and made poor use of his chance to learn.
Prentice-Hall 14 min Color

1405 What's in a Story? An example of literary form and content, the film compares the fable *The Milkmaid and Her Pail* and James Thurber's *A*

Unicorn in the Garden. The animated portion of *Unicorn* is incorporated into the film through the courtesy of Columbia Pictures, UPA, and the Thurber estate.
BFA Educ. Media. 14 min Color 1963

1406 The White Heron. It is 1896 and Sylvy is a shy, solitary girl who spends her time in the Maine forest, playing with the birds, the plants, and her cow. Her encounter with a hunter who is looking for a white heron to add to his collection brings her to a difficult decision of whether to help him, and is further complicated by her growing awareness of the young man and her own emerging womanhood. Based on the short story by Sarah Orne Jewett.
Learning Corp. 26 min Color 178

1407 A Work of Art. The gift of a nude statuette from a grateful patient is an embarrassing problem for a provincial doctor. He passes it on, with amusing results, to equally conventional friends. This Chekhov story not only illuminates the manners and morals of old Russia, but offers an example of Moscow Art Theatre repertory acting. Directed and written for the screen by M. Kovalyov. Russian dialogue with English subtitles.
Macmillan 10 min B&W 1960

1408 The Yellow Wallpaper. This film, set in the 1890's and based on the rediscovered literary masterpiece by Charlotte Perkins Gilman, is the story of a woman's mental breakdown. Elizabeth, an aspiring writer, is suffering an undefined illness and is taken to the country by her doctor/husband for the complete "rest cure" against her better judgment. This cure includes a planned schedule for each day, total rest, isolation—in short, a lack of the activity, and work that Elizabeth craves. Without stimulation in her world, Elizabeth's mind creates another world, the world of the wallpaper in which she envisions a woman trapped and unable to escape.
Women/Movies 14 min Color

1409 The Young Man and Death. In a confining flat, a young man paces in obvious perturbation. A black-clad ballerina enters and engages in a series of movements that identify her as Death. Alternately seductive and forbidding, she pursues and is pursued until he grovels at her feet. Turning her back, she fastens a heavy rope to a beam, then leaves him to hang himself. Based on a story by Jean Cocteau. Music by J.S. Bach. Danced by Rudolph Nureyev and Zizi Jeanmaire. Directed and choreographed by Roland Petit. Photography by Jean Dadal. Produced in France. Nonverbal.
Macmillan 16 min Color 1975

1410 Zero Hour. Ray Bradbury's classic centers on a girl named Mink, her friends, and a game called "Invasion." Mink's mother, initially unconcerned and amused, learns that "the invasion" is to come from outer space. "Zero Hour" comes. Terrified, both parents barricade themselves in the attic. The doorlock melts, and we hear Mink's childlike but now demonic voice whispering, "peekaboo!" A Bernard Wilets Production. *BFA Educ. Media* 19½ min Color 1978

Producer/Distributor Directory

ABC Learning
ABC Wide World of Learning
1330 Avenue of the Americas
New York, N.Y. 10019

ACI *see* **Paramount**

AIMS
AIMS Instructional Service
626 Justin Avenue
Glendale, Calif. 91201

American Educ.
American Educational Films
132 Lasky Drive
Beverly Hills, Calif. 90212

American Personnel
American Personnel & Guidance
   Assn.
1607 New Hampshire Ave. NW
Washington, D.C. 20009

Barr Films
Barr Films, Inc.
P.O. Box 7-C
1029 N. Allen Street
Pasadena, Calif. 91104

Beacon Films
Beacon Films
P.O. Box 575
Norwood, Mass. 02062

Benchmark
Benchmark Films, Inc.
145 Scarborough Road
Briarcliff Manor, N.Y. 10510

BFA Educ. Media
BFA Educational Media
2211 Michigan Avenue
Santa Monica, Calif. 90406

Billy Budd
Billy Budd Films, Inc.
235 East 57th Street
New York, N.Y. 10022

BNA Films
BNA Films, Inc.
9401 Decoverley Hall Rd.
Rockville, MD. 20850

Bosustow
Stephen Bosustow
   Productions
P.O. Box 2127
Santa Monica, Calif. 90406

Brigham Young
Brigham Young University
Motion Picture Studio
Provo, Utah, 84602

Bullfrog Films
Bullfrog Films
Oley, Pa. 19547

Cally Curtis
The Cally Curtis Company
1111 N. Las Palmas Avenue
Hollywood, Calif. 90038

Canadian Film
Canadian Filmmakers
Distribution Centre
144 Front St. West
Toronto, Ontario
Canada M5J 1G2

Carousel
Carousel Films, Inc.
1501 Broadway
New York, N.Y. 10036

Centron
Centron Educational Films
1612 West Ninth Street
Lawrence, Kansas 66044

Cine-Men
Cine-Men Productions
3931 Canterbury Road
Baltimore, Md. 21218

Conn. Films
Connecticut Films
6 Cobble Hill Road
Westport, Conn. 06880

Coronet
Coronet Instructional Media
65 East South Water Street
Chicago, Ill. 60601

Counselor
Counselor Films, Inc.
1740 Cherry Street
Philadelphia, Pa. 19103

Counterpoint
Counterpoint Films
14622 Lanark Street
Panorama City, Calif. 91402

Creative Film
Creative Film Society
7237 Canby Avenue
Reseda, Calif. 91335

CRM see **McGraw-Hill**

Dana
Dana Productions
Division of Saparoff Films
6249 Babcock Avenue
North Hollywood, Calif. 91606

Davenport
Tom Davenport Films
Pearlstone
Delaplane, Va. 22025

Daybreak Prod.
Daybreak Productions
1042 North Cole Avenue
Hollywood, Calif. 90038

Didactic
Didactic Systems, Inc.
P.O. Box 457
Cranford, N.J. 07016

Disney
(Walt) Disney Education
    Company
500 South Buena Vista Street
Burbank, Calif. 91521

Distribution 16
Distribution Sixteen
Division of Italtoons Corp.
111 Eighth Avenue
New York, N.Y. 10011

Doc. Assoc.
Document Associates
880 Third Avenue
New York, N.Y. 10022

Doc/Learn.
Documentaries for Learning
58 Fernwood Road
Boston, Mass. 02115

Educ. Communications
Educational Communications,
    Inc.
7330 Rampart
Houston, Texas 77081

Encyc. Brit.
Encyclopaedia Britannica
Educational Corporation
425 N. Michigan Avenue
Chicago, Ill. 60611

Extension Media
Extension Media Center
University of California
Berkeley, Calif. 94720

Fenwick
Fenwick Productions
134 Steele Road
West Hartford, Conn. 06119

Film Fair
Film Fair Communications
10900 Ventura Blvd.
Studio City, Calif. 91604

Film Forum
Film Forum
P.O. Box 2308M
Mission Viejo, Calif. 92675

Film Images
Film Images/Radim
1034 Lake Street
Oak Park, Ill. 60301

Films/Human.
Films for the Humanities
P.O. Box 378
Princeton, N.J. 08540

Films Inc.
Films Incorporated
1144 Wilmette Avenue
Wilmette, Ill. 60091

Film Wright
Film Wright Productions
4530 Eighteenth Street
San Francisco, Calif. 94114

Friend Prod.
(Jack) Friend Productions
P.O. Box 36
Chicago, Ill. 60690

G.G. Communic.
G.G. Communications
820 Statler Office Bldg.
Boston, Mass. 02116

Grove Press
Grove Press

Film Division
196 West Houston St.
New York, N.Y. 10014

Haida
Haida Films
69 Banstock Drive
Willowdale, Ontario
Canada M2K 247

Handel Film
Handel Film Corporation
8730 Sunset Boulevard
Los Angeles, Calif. 90069

Harper & Row
Harper & Row Media
2350 Virginia Avenue
Hagerstown, Md. 21740

Hartley
Hartley Productions
Cat Rock Road
Cos Cob, Conn. 06807

Indiana Univ.
Indiana University
A-V Film Sales
Bloomington, Ind. 47401

Institutional Cine
Institutional Cinema
10 First Street
Saugerties, N.Y. 12477

Int. Film Bur.
International Film Bureau
332 South Michigan Avenue
Chicago, Ill. 60604

Int. Film Found.
International Film Foundation
Suite 916,
475 Fifth Avenue
New York, NY 10017

Int. Rehab. Film
International Rehabilitation Film
   Review Library
20 West 40th Street
New York, N.Y. 10018

IQ Films
IQ Films, Inc.
689 Fifth Avenue
New York, N.Y. 10022

Janus
Janus Films
745 Fifth Avenue
New York, N.Y. 10022

Journal
Journal Films, Inc.
930 North Pitner Avenue
Evanston, Ill. 60602

Joyce Media
Joyce Media Productions
P.O. Box 4440
Northridge, Calif. 91328

Kit Parker
Kit Parker Films
P.O. Box 227
Carmel Valley, Calif. 93924

Learning Corp.
Learning Corporation of America
1350 Avenue of the Americas
New York, N.Y. 10019

Lilyan Productions
Lilyan Productions, Inc.
524 Ridge Road
Watchung, N.J. 07060

LSB Prod.
LSB Productions

1310 Monaco Drive
Pacific Palisades, Calif. 90272

McGraw-Hill
McGraw-Hill Films
110 Fifteenth Street
Del Mar, Calif. 92014

Macmillan
Macmillan Films, Inc.
34 MacQuesten Pkwy. South
Mt. Vernon, N.Y. 10550

Malibu
Malibu Films
P.O. Box 428
Malibu, Calif. 90265

Mar/Chuck
Mar/Chuck Film Industries
P.O. Box 61
Mt. Prospect, Ill. 60056

Mariner
Mariner Productions
C/O Raul daSilva
1400 East Avenue
Rochester, NY 14610

Martin Assoc.
(Burt) Martin Associates
P.O. Box 6337
Burbank, Calif. 91510

Mass Media
Mass Media Ministries
2116 North Charles Street
Baltimore, Md. 21218

Media Guild
The Media Guild
118 South Acacia
P.O. Box 881
Solana Beach, Calif. 92075

MCI Films
MCI Films
Greenwood Press
51 Riverside Avenue
Westport, Conn. 06880

Media Plus
Media Plus
Suite 11-D
60 Riverside Drive
New York, N.Y. 10024

Miller-Brody
Miller-Brody Productions
342 Madison Avenue
New York, N.Y. 10017

MTI Teleprograms
Motorola Teleprograms, Inc.
4825 North Scott Street
Schiller Park, Ill. 60176

Nat. Educ. Film
National Educational Film and
    Video Center
Route 2
Finksburg, Md. 21048

Nat. Film Bd.
National Film Board of Canada
16th Floor
1251 Avenue of the Americas
New York, N.Y. 10020

New Line
New Line Cinema
853 Broadway
New York, N.Y. 10003

New Yorker
New Yorker Films
43 West 61st Street
New York, N.Y. 10023

North American
North American Films
P.O. Box 919
Tarzana, Calif. 91356

Olympus
Olympus Publishing Co.
1670 East 13th Street South
Salt Lake City, Utah 84105

Open Circle
Open Circle Cinema
P.O. Box 315
Franklin Lakes, N.J. 07417

Paramount
Paramount Communications
5451 Marathon Street
Hollywood, Calif. 90038

Perennial
Perennial Education, Inc.
477 Roger Williams
Highland Park, Ill. 60035

Perspective
Perspective Films, Inc.
369 West Erie Street
Chicago, Ill. 60610

Phoenix
Phoenix Films, Inc.
470 Park Avenue South
New York, N.Y. 10016

Pictura
Pictura Film Distribution
111 Eighth Avenue
New York, N.Y. 10011

Pied Piper
Pied Piper Productions
P.O. Box 320
Verdugo City, Calif. 91046

Polymorph
Polymorph Films, Inc.
118 South Street
Boston, Mass. 02111

Prentice-Hall
Prentice-Hall, Inc.
50 White Plains Road
Tarrytown, N.Y. 10591

Prod. Unlimited
Productions Unlimited, Inc.
1301 Avenue of the Americas
New York, N.Y. 10019

Psych. Films
Psychological Films, Inc.
1215 East Chapman Avenue
Orange, Calif. 92666

Pyramid
Pyramid Film and Video
P.O. Box 1048
Santa Monica, Calif. 90406

Raymond Ltd.
(Bruce) Raymond Ltd.
207 Queens Quay West
Toronto, Ontario
Canada M5J IA7

RH Media
RH Media Productions
P.O. Box 40
Wimberley, Texas 78676

Roland
The (Anthony) Roland Collection
477 Roger Williams
Highland Park, Ill. 60035

Roundtable
Roundtable Films
113 N. San Vicente Blvd.
Beverly Hills, Calif. 90311

Salenger
Salenger Educational Media
1635 Twelfth Street
Santa Monica, Calif. 90404

Salzburg
Salzburg Enterprises
98 Cuttermill Road
Great Neck, N.Y. 11021

Sandler
Sandler Institutional Films

1001 N. Poinsettia Place
Hollywood, Calif. 90046

Screenscope
Screenscope, Inc.
1022 Wilson Boulevard
Arlington, Va. 22209

Sherman
(Al) Sherman Films of Scotland
P.O. Box 6, Cathedral Station
New York, N.Y. 10025

Skye Pictures
Skye Pictures, Inc.
2225 Floyd Avenue
Richmond, Va. 23220

Stanton
Stanton Films
7934 Santa Monica Blvd.
Los Angeles, Calif. 90046

Starr
(Cecile) Starr Films
50 West 96th Street
New York, N.Y. 10025

Sterling Educ.
Sterling Educational Films
241 East 34th Street
New York, N.Y. 10016

Studio Films
Studio Films
224 Willow Avenue
Corte Madera, Calif, 94925

Texture
Texture Films
1600 Broadway
New York, N.Y. 10019

Time-Life
Time-Life Video
1271 Avenue of the Americas
New York, N.Y. 10020

Tri-Continental
Tri-Continental Film Center
333 Sixth Avenue
New York, N.Y. 10014 *and*
   P.O. Box 4430
   Berkeley, Calif. 94704

Twyman
Twyman Films
329 Salem Avenue
Dayton, Ohio 45401

Universal Educ.
Universal Education and Visual
   Arts
100 Universal City Plaza
Universal City, Calif. 91608

Univ. of Rochester
University of Rochester
Dance Film Archives
Rochester, N.Y. 14620

Van Nostrand
Van Nostrand-Reinhold
Film Library
450 West 33rd Street
New York, N.Y. 10001

Viewfinders
Viewfinders, Inc.
P.O. Box 1665
Evanston, Ill. 60204

Vision Quest
Vision Quest, Inc.
P.O. Box 206
Lawrenceville, N.J. 08648

Warner Bros.
Warner Bros.
Non-Theatrical Division
4000 Warner Boulevard
Burbank, Calif. 91522

Weston Woods
Weston Woods Studios
Weston, Conn. 06880

Wombat
Wombat Productions, Inc.
Little Lake, Glendale Road
P.O. Box 70
Ossining, N.Y. 10562

Women/Movies
Women Make Movies, Inc.
257 West 19th Street
New York, N.Y. 10011

Xerox
Xerox Films
245 Long Hill Road
Middletown, Conn. 06457

Authors-on-Film Index

This index is writer-oriented. If you're looking for material by *or about* a specific author, here is the place to start. The numbers refer to film entries within the body of the book.

Film titles are not always the same as the original writings. When they are not, you can trace their literary sources by consulting the Original Title Index (which follows this one).

Naturally enough, biographical films often contain references to or quotations from an author's repertoire. For that reason, the *Biography* chapter may provide unexpected leads to literature. By the way, the decision to classify a film under *Biography* hinged mainly on the producer's idea of the content.

Anonymous items aren't included here. Most of them are in the sections on *The Bible* and *Fables & Folktales* while a few are under *Nonfiction*. Joint authors are identified individually. For example, *Born to Win* is credited both to James and to Jongeward. Maiden names, when known, are given here in addition to marital names.

251

Original Title Index

This index uses the original literary title of a work as its starting point and leads from there to the film or films related to it in any way. For example, the item herein, *Old Man and the Sea*, directs you to entry number 84, a Hemingway biographical film incorporating key scenes from that novel.

The special strength of this index is its capacity to help you uncover lesser works that are part of a larger body of information. The main intent of the index obviously is to help you to trace material about a piece of literature regardless of how the film version is titled. (*Strangest Voyage* is an excellent film but its title only suggests Coleridge's *Ancient Mariner*.)

Altogether there are 1012 items here. This figure does not include the intentional duplication of some works; for easy reference, for example, Plato's "The Apology" is listed both as *Apology* and as *Plato's Apology*, and *Daedalus and Icarus* are repeated as *Icarus and Daedalus*. Haiku, though a form and not a title, is found as an entry here for convenience's sake, as are Mother Goose Rhymes. Our criterion: will it help you find the film you want?

For simplicity's sake, all initial articles *The, A* or *An* have been omitted.